MW00812364

# Inventing Authority

# Inventing Authority

## The Use of the Church Fathers in Reformation Debates over the Eucharist

*Esther Chung-Kim*

BAYLOR UNIVERSITY PRESS

Scripture quotations are from the New Revised Standard Version Bible, © 1989, Division of Christian Education of the National Council of the Churches of Christ in the United States of America. Used by permission. All rights reserved.


Cover Design by Cynthia Dunne, Blue Farm Graphics




Library of Congress Cataloging-in-Publication Data

Chung-Kim, Esther, 1973-
Inventing authority : the use of the Church Fathers in Reformation debates over the eucharist / Esther Chung-Kim.
p. cm.
Includes bibliographical references and index.
ISBN 978-1-60258-213-2 (hardback : alk. paper)
1. Lord's Supper--History of doctrines--16th century.. 2. Religious disputations--History--16th century. 3. Fathers of the church. I. Title.
BV823.C48 2011
234'.16309409031--dc22
2010020206




Printed in the United States of America on acid-free paper with a minimum of 30% pcw recycled content.

*To my husband, Steven*

"Although the fathers did not hold to a bad opinion, they were not able to say sufficiently clearly what they wanted to say."

"Although the more learned fathers teach us something, nevertheless one must judge them according to the Word of God."

—Philip Melanchthon, *Commentary on Romans*, 1540

# Contents

# Acknowledgments

In preparing this book for publication, I have benefited from various mentors, colleagues, and friends who provided scholarly and moral support along the way. Without them, this project would not have come to fruition.

I wish to acknowledge with gratitude those who helped clarify and strengthen the argument in the process of going from a doctoral dissertation to a published manuscript. I am particularly grateful to David C. Steinmetz, my advisor at Duke University, whose scholarship and passion for learning continue to stimulate and inspire my own work. I also want to thank the other members of my committee, Elizabeth Clark, Thomas Robisheaux, Ronald Witt, and Warren Smith, for their guidance and helpful feedback. I have also learned a great deal from Irena Backus at the University of Geneva, who encouraged this project in its nascent stages (and later read parts of the manuscript), and John Thompson at Fuller Seminary, who became a valuable conversation partner and offered pivotal guidance in the practical logistics of publishing.

With great appreciation for sharing his expertise to make this book a better product, I want to thank Carey Newman, director of Baylor University Press, for exuding genuine enthusiasm for the project from the beginning and for his motivational feedback at our meeting in Dallas-Fort Worth Airport. I also want to thank my reviewers for their specific insights and attention to detail that have enabled me to improve the overall project. I would also like to recognize the distinctive contributions of several research assistants, Matthew Garnett, Chris Zeichmann, Elizabeth

Cossio, and especially Kirsten Gerdes, in assisting with proofreading and editing tasks.

Several institutions provided financial and other assistance. I am grateful for the Graduate Summer Fellowship through Duke University and the John Wesley Fellowship through A Foundation for Theological Education. The Institut d'histoire de la Réformation in Geneva, Switzerland, awarded me a summer fellowship, during which time I began uncovering the sources for my latter chapters. The Pre-Tenure Faculty Summer Fellowship through the Wabash Center for Teaching and Learning afforded me protected time to complete my last round of revisions. While Duke University Libraries, especially that of the Divinity School and Special Collections, provided substantial services, the libraries at Princeton Theological Seminary, the University of Geneva, and the University of Tübingen were also instrumental. Thanks to Equinox Publishing for allowing the reprint of a revised version of the article titled "Use of the Fathers in the Eucharistic Debates between John Calvin and Joachim Westphal," which originally appeared in *Reformation* 14 (December 2009).

Since research and writing are a shared journey, I am appreciative of the assistance of my friends and colleagues in the faculty at Claremont and in the Steinmetz cohort, especially G. Sujin Pak, who helped me to see the big picture. They knowingly or unknowingly made the enterprise of writing this book more enjoyable. I must also thank my parents, who encouraged me along this academic path and held an unwavering faith that I would arrive at this point.

Finally, I am deeply grateful to Steven, my husband and best friend, who urged me to prioritize this book and cheerfully tolerated my absence at family activities, as well as to my sons, Nathan and Eli, who illustrated their own works on the back pages of my manuscript drafts in order to show me that all my efforts were not in vain.

# Reformation of the Ancient Tradition
## *Interpreting the Fathers in the Eucharistic Debates*

Any notion of the Protestant Reformation as a religiously homogeneous, anti-establishment, anti-tradition movement is too simplistic. While the Protestant reformers' conception of *sola scriptura* established the Bible as the primary standard authorizing Christian theology and practice, they did not conceive of rejecting wholesale the history of the church's tradition. In fact, many reformers considered the early church fathers secondary authorities to Scripture as well as important teachers of biblical interpretation. Both Roman Catholics and Protestants found themselves needing to use authorities in the context of formal argumentation as a means of proving theological truth.[1] Although the reformers cited the ancient Christian writers initially against the scholastic writers of the late medieval and early modern Catholic Church, the fathers quickly became tools of criticism within Protestant circles. The debates among Protestants demonstrated their willingness to wrestle with ancient writings, not to eradicate tradition but to reinterpret it in such a way as to claim it as their inheritance.

Because the concentration of patristic references was highest in polemical writings, an examination of reformers' use of the church fathers ought to take into account those places where references appear most frequently. In the midst of polemical debates when the weight of consensus was lacking, reformers recalled the patristic sources to serve as subsidiary authorities under Scripture. These ancient Christian writers were initially considered helpful authorities because they (especially Augustine) were seen as reliable interpreters of Scripture. As exemplary scriptural exegetes, they were the means of demonstrating the correct understanding of Scripture and therefore correct theology. References to the fathers became a way to substantiate one's own reading of Scripture or to reject an opponent's interpretation.

One notable place in which the fathers figured heavily was the controversy over the Lord's Supper, not simply between Catholics and Protestants, but also among the Protestants themselves. Reformers were not willing to give up the ancient authorities easily because, as challengers to the standard orthodoxy, they needed to reinterpret the church's past and construct a "new" ancient tradition. What was at stake in the Reformation conflicts over the Eucharist was not a binary distinction between what is Catholic versus what is Protestant, but a definition of Christian orthodoxy that divided Protestant nations, towns, and families. In continental Europe, Protestant groups, particularly Lutherans and Calvinists (Reformed), developed alongside one another, sometimes in cooperation or coexistence and at other times in conflict.

This book examines three sixteenth-century Lutheran and Reformed debates over the Lord's Supper and the use of the fathers in these controversies. On the one hand, references to the ancient fathers are nothing new, since the medieval church had based its tradition on their works for centuries, and many Protestant reformers had first learned of the church fathers while they were still Catholics. On the other hand, the desire for change precipitated a reevaluation of the present. Against the backdrop of Renaissance humanist training, which prized antiquity, looking back to the time of the early church fathers (when Scripture alone was not conclusive) gave reformers a starting place to rewrite, or at least reinterpret, history and to present a tradition that supported new theological views.

## Recent Scholarship

Scholars have generally recognized the work of humanists in providing increased accessibility to early Christian sources and fueling interest in them. Yet what kind of value did the ancient fathers hold for the Protestant reformers and why were the fathers most often recalled in the midst of polemical debates? While the interest in patristic sources was not new, some ancient Christian writers were being recalled in a new way—to provide ancestral roots to an emerging Protestant tradition. Medieval thinkers had also cited the church fathers, and many Protestant reformers were first exposed to the fathers through medieval sources, such as canon law or Peter Lombard's *Sentences*. Gordon Rupp points out that, although the authority of Scripture is primary for the reformers, the appeal to the "old Fathers" is of genuine importance and "the typical scholarly work of the 16th century is peppered with classical allusions and garnished with patristic quotations."[2] For years scholars have discussed the significance of the fathers for the Reformation, and many recent studies have focused on a specific reformer's use of the fathers. A few books in this field have also tried to capture an array of scholarly perspectives on the issue by compiling various writers in anthologies or collections of essays. These works offer a menu of topics related to the use of the fathers during the Reformation. One such collection, edited by Leif Grane, Alfred Schindler, and Markus Wriedt, is *Auctoritas Patrum: Zur Rezeption der Kirchenväter im 15. und 16. Jahrhundert* (1993); it was followed by a companion volume, *Auctoritas Patrum II: Neue Beiträge zur Rezeption der Kirchenväter im 15. und 16. Jahrhundert* (1998). The essays in the *Auctoritas Patrum* series are usually focused on a particular reformer, one church father, or the examination of one event, such as the 1518–1519 Leipzig Disputation. While these essays are presented in a roughly chronological order, they only provide cursory vignettes of the reformers' use of the fathers, without making any connections between them, although Leif Grane's essay on the church fathers in the first years of the Reformation (1516–1520) shows an effort at synthesis for the early period of the Reformation.

Another work, *The Reception of the Church Fathers in the West* (1997), edited by Irena Backus, contains the work of a variety of authors and covers the role of the church fathers from the eighth-century Carolingian Renaissance to the early eighteenth century, although the essays are not necessarily related in theme or method and are of varying depth. Resulting from conference contributions, *Die Patristik in der Bibelexegese des 16. Jahrhunderts* (1999), edited by David Steinmetz, focuses on the sixteenth-century interest in the biblical exegesis of the fathers. The most recent volume edited by Günter Frank, Thomas Leinkauf, and Markus Wriedt, titled *Die Patristik in der Frühen Neuzeit: Die Relektüre der Kirchenväter in den Wissenschaften des 15. bis 18. Jahrhunderts* (2006) offers a range of contributions in German, English, French, and Italian based on an international conference in 2003 and demonstrates the need for further analysis and synthesis of the Reformation usage of the patristic tradition. Some recent works have offered a synthesis of the patristic scholarship among specific Protestant reformers such as Luther, Melanchthon, Calvin, Bucer, and Zwingli. This study approaches the use of the fathers during the Reformation through a comparative analysis of how several key Lutheran and Reformed thinkers used the fathers in their debates over the Eucharist. Looking at the patristic tradition in this way provides a broader perspective because the eucharistic controversies spanned most of the sixteenth century and progressively elicited an increasing number of church fathers

in the ongoing debates. On the one hand, addressing the patristic scholarship of the Reformation on a broad spectrum would be impossible for any
one study to undertake. On the other hand, this book focuses on the use
of the fathers in the context of the eucharistic controversies as a window
to understanding patterns and strategies for citing the fathers in sixteenth
century polemics, an arena where the fathers surfaced most often.

Of the recent monographs published relating to this topic, three of
the most helpful have been Anthony Lane's *Calvin, Student of the Church
Fathers* (neatly summarized into eleven theses), Irena Backus' *Historical
Method and Confessional Identity in the Era of the Reformation*, and Nicholas
Thompson's work on the *Eucharistic Sacrifice and Patristic Tradition in the
Theology of Martin Bucer*. Lane's work is a good example of an isolated study
on a single reformer's use of the fathers.[3] Lane recognizes that Calvin's ref-
erences to the fathers occur most frequently in his polemical writings and
cover Calvin's debate with Albert Pighius on free will and providence.
Backus carefully examines the Reformation methods of employing historical sources. Thompson explains the notions of eucharistic sacrifice in the
Reformation and points out that both Catholic and Protestant thinkers
who looked back to fathers such as Augustine, Jerome, Chrysostom, and
Basil were involved in the polemics over the ownership of these ancient
authorities.[4] As Steinmetz, Kolb, and Lane have noted, the reformers' use
of the fathers does not presuppose a modern scholar's access to volumes
of ancient Christian writers.[5] Therefore the historical questions surrounding sixteenth-century patristic usage are not so much focused on whether
the reformers correctly portray the early church fathers based on all the
writings that are now accessible to the modern scholar, but instead focus
on how the reformers interpret the early church fathers—and more
broadly, how they receive, understand, and transmit tradition.

At the beginning of the sixteenth century, a great interest in early
Christianity was bound to be present among German biblical humanists.
With their background in classical culture, the writings of the fathers
were considered to be "good literature." The fact that the fathers were
close in time to the Holy Scriptures carried weight. For both reasons,
the church fathers came to be instruments in the criticism of "sophistry
and speculation."[6] In the early part of the sixteenth century, reformers
turned to the fathers in order to counterbalance scholastic doctors. The
resurgent patristic interest was part of a criticism of tradition with
the intention to serve the reform of the church and the renewal of studies.[7] The enthusiasm for the fathers, especially at the beginning of the
Reformation, contributed to the sense that these ancient sources were
treasures to be rediscovered. The advent of the printing press assisted in

the production of an increased quantity of complete editions of patristic texts, as well as patristic anthologies.[8] For example, Jacques Le Fèvre published the writings of John of Damascus, Athenagoras, Hermas as well as a text of the Clementine Homilies, while the German humanist Beatus Rhenanus offered translations of Gregory of Nyssa, Basil, and the *editio princeps* of Tertullian (1521). Meanwhile, Erasmus was associated with editions of Jerome (1516), Cyprian (1520), Arnobius (1522), Hilary (1523), Irenaeus (Lat. 1526), Ambrose (1527), Augustine (1528), Chrysostom (Lat. 1530–1531), Basil (Gk. 1532), and Origen (1536).[9] By the middle of the century this unprecedented availability of patristic material gave a new edge to the appeal to primitive Christianity.[10] Like many reformers in the earliest years of the Reformation, Philip Melanchthon (1497–1560) understood that the church fathers were of a higher order than the scholastic doctors, and that to praise them was the same as listening to Erasmus, Reuchlin, and Luther.[11] In other words, sixteenth-century reformers posited the church fathers as "better" human authorities than the late medieval scholars and claimed this ancient authority to challenge the existing religious powers.[12]

From the earliest debates with the Roman Catholic thinkers, Protestant reformers determined whether a church father was "theologically sound" or "mistaken and misled," like their opponents. Philip Melanchthon in his letter to Oecolampadius expressed doubt about some of John Eck's quotations of Jerome and Cyprian.[13] Melanchthon simply states that the better informed fathers were on Luther's side, while Eck could only adduce those who were misusing the biblical texts. Since humanist scholars had taken up the work of translating the fathers with new fervor, Catholics and Protestants alike scrambled to claim the inheritance of the rediscovered ancient sources. Regardless of Catholic or Protestant views, it was a sign of the times that anyone who sought change in the church would look back to its history to reevaluate its beliefs and practices. For example, in a letter of December 6, 1518, to Zwingli in Zürich, Rhenanus expresses annoyance with priests who burdened the people with superfluous ceremonies. He claims that Zwingli and his supporters, however, were the exceptions who, in contrast to the majority, advanced the purest philosophy of Christ directly from the sources, drawn from Augustine, Ambrose, Cyprian, and Jerome.[14] Zwingli in his own letter states that to be a good theologian means to study the Scripture, Origen, Cyprian, Jerome, and the like.[15] When divisions among Protestant groups arose, their appeals to the early church fathers continued as Lutheran and Reformed writers strove to identify themselves with the reputation of the "good" fathers.

In 1539 Calvin argued in his *Reply to Sadoleto* that the Reformation
was a movement in line with the ancient church. To envision Calvin's
use of the fathers, one must suspend the modern notion of the scholarly
exercise of reading tomes of the church fathers as sources of direct citation. While Calvin very well may have engaged in this scholarly effort,
especially in his later writings, he also relied on other intermediaries as a
means of accessing the fathers, including the ones he may never have read
firsthand. It is generally accepted that Calvin's references to and citations
of the church fathers not only emerged from direct readings but were also
filtered through other authors such as Luther, Erasmus, and Bucer, and
sometimes even through his opponents, such as Pighius and Westphal. At
times, Calvin had the writings of the church fathers, most often Augustine, in front of him, and on other occasions, he quoted from memory as
he wrote.[16] In some cases, there is no evidence that Calvin directly read
the original sources. In addition to quotations from memory of an earlier
reading, there is the possibility of an anthology in which Calvin may have
kept a log of quotations as Bucer and Melanchthon did,[17] but no evidence
of such a collection has yet been found. Clearly Calvin's use of the fathers
extended beyond his explicit references to them, as he incorporated many
of their views into his own system of belief. In his own day, Calvin initially received invitations to religious colloquies because of his knowledge
of the fathers.[18] He utilized patristic scholarship increasingly, as he had
access to editions of the church fathers in his gradually expanding library
and he claimed the church fathers as a source of religious authority in the
controversial subject of the Lord's Supper.

## Debates over the Eucharist

Debates over the Eucharist were not simply about the technical details
of performing the sacrament of the altar, but included a complex inter-
play between received tradition and theology, Renaissance philosophy
and philology, pastoral care and liturgy, and the social, political, and eco-
nomic culture of the late medieval and early modern period. In addition to issues of Scripture and tradition, sacramental theology addressed
Trinitarian and christological dogmas of the early church councils, patristic works against ancient "heretics," and the medieval appropriation of
the church fathers.[19] In contentions over the Lord's Supper, appeals to the
fathers emerged in the words of reformers ranging from a doctor of
theology such as Martin Luther to laypersons such as the English martyr
John Lambert.[20] The early Protestants criticized the late medieval views
of the Eucharist as a sacrifice offered by the priest to God, the doctrine
of transubstantiation and the doctrine of concomitance, which justified

the withholding of the consecrated wine from laypeople.[21] Luther argued that the Eucharist was not a sacrifice, but rather a testament of something that God does. He also rejected the Aristotelian concept of transubstantiation and insisted that both of the elements ought to be distributed to lay believers following Christ's institution.

In 1521 Wittenberg theologians considered how their new theological insights would change church practices, specifically the Mass. In the absence of Luther (who was hiding at the Wartburg Castle and would return in March 1522), Andreas Bodenstein von Karlstadt initiated a Protestant "evangelical" form of worship on December 25, 1521. Dressed in everyday clothes rather than the proper ceremonial vestments, Karlstadt presented the eucharistic liturgy in the vernacular, omitting any notions of sacrifice, and served Communion under both species, meaning both the bread and the consecrated wine were given to the laity, instead of just the bread. Subsequent disagreements between Luther and Karlstadt led to Karlstadt's leaving Wittenberg and temporarily rejecting an academic career in 1523. Meanwhile, the Zürich reformer Ulrich Zwingli moved toward abolishing the mass and instituting a reformed Communion service. Influenced by Cornelius Hoen, Zwingli argued for a spiritual understanding of the Lord's Supper, according to which Christ was present in spirit, not in the elements but among the congregation. From 1524 to 1525, Zwingli and Johannes Oecolampadius published writings that challenged Luther's view of the Eucharist, prompting a string of responses from Luther. In 1529 Landgrave Philip of Hesse arranged the Marburg Colloquy in hopes of achieving a political alliance among Protestants against the Catholic powers of Emperor Charles V. In order to achieve such an alliance, a common united front, based on a theological consensus among Protestant groups, was sought. Apparently, agreement was reached on fourteen of the fifteen articles under discussion, but participants in the colloquy failed to reach an agreement on issues relating to the Eucharist. The Lutheran and Reformed sides set the stage for the recurring controversy over the Eucharist. Because both sides appealed to the early church fathers in their argumentation, the issue of ancient authorities would continue to arise in subsequent eucharistic debates.

Against the backdrop of the humanist-scholastic duels of the late fifteenth and the beginning of the sixteenth century, the number of references to patristic writers is not surprising. Luther and early Protestants appealed to the early church fathers as exemplars of an alternative tradition to what they perceived as the maladies of the late medieval church. Therefore one would expect the church fathers to be marshaled mostly against the Roman Catholics; yet the appeals to the ancient fathers increased dramatically in the polemics among Protestants. In the end, the divisive controversy over the Lord's Supper prevented agreement over the formation of a Protestant political alliance. Eventually the theological decisions made at the Marburg Colloquy resulted in not only religious, but also political divisions. By examining the use of the fathers at Marburg, we can see the role that references to the church fathers had in argumentation over biblical interpretation. For example, Luther claimed that the Swiss thinkers had Augustine and Fulgentius but that the rest of the fathers belonged to the Lutherans. Later reformers continued the practice of dividing up the fathers as had been done at the Colloquy of Marburg. In the second eucharistic controversy of the 1550s, this time between Calvin and the Gnesio-Lutherans, the practice of dividing up the pool of fathers between the two sides of the debate was abandoned and was replaced by the practice of vying over the same father(s). While reformers initially cited the fathers against scholastic writers, the fathers soon became tools of criticism against other Protestant reformers as well.

This book traces the development of Lutheran and Reformed polemics over the Eucharist and the use of the fathers as a source of authority in these debates. Despite the interest in the role of the fathers in the sixteenth century, few have ventured to examine the use of the fathers over the span of the sixteenth century, through three generations of reformers. The scope of this study is confined to an examination of the recurring controversy over the Eucharist, and traces the development of the use of the fathers in this one key polemical issue, beginning with the role of the fathers at the Marburg Colloquy, essentially the first Protestant eucharistic controversy.[22] The story of this conflict does not end with Marburg but continues in the Lutheran–Reformed debates of the 1550s, exemplified in Calvin's debates with Joachim Westphal and, later, Tilemann Hesshusen. When Calvin died, his successor in Geneva, Theodore Beza, defended the Reformed use of the fathers against Jacob Andreae, champion of Lutheran orthodoxy at the Colloquy of Montbéliard in 1586.

## Authorizing Interpretations in a Competitive Arena

When approaching the problem of authority, it is helpful to look at what sources the reformers appealed to—whether Scripture, reason, early church fathers, medieval tradition, or contemporary thinkers—when they made theological or religious assertions.[23] In the polemical argumentation over the Eucharist, the use of the fathers fell within the scope of the broader question concerning authority, namely the establishment of doctrine and practice in the name of "orthodoxy." The fact that the critical issue at the Council of Trent was the nature and source of authority concerning

Scripture and tradition is an indication that determining who had legitimate authority was the critical question of the age. The eucharistic debate of the 1520s, which led to the Marburg Colloquy, is a perfect example of how theological pluralism was accompanied by a total intolerance of other points of view.[24] The eucharistic debates demonstrated a diversity of theological views (as subsequent chapters will illustrate) that embodied what one thought not only about Scripture and tradition but also about incarnation, Christology, soteriology, eschatology, pneumatology, and ecclesiology. The northern Lutherans and the southern Zwinglians could agree on various points of theology and could conceive of a political Protestant league, but they could not agree on the theological meaning of "is" in the words "this is my body." Initially, the fathers were a necessary component of a Protestant strategy for historical validation against the established church. Eventually, the fathers became necessary for validating particular Protestant traditions as the Reformed and Lutheran sides of the conflict employed the fathers against each other. Thompson named this kind of appropriation, "magisterial," since it appealed to the authority and succession of the church's teaching ministry alongside the Scripture, but under the authority of the Word and the Spirit.[25] On one level, the church fathers were tools for the purpose of persuasion; on another level, they were seen as building blocks to an emerging Protestant tradition whose foundation was based on the authority of Scripture.

In the midst of interrelated political and religious processes, the ongoing theological divisions over doctrines, such as the Lord's Supper led to the development of distinct theological identities, even though the confessional situation between the 1550s and the 1580s was extremely fluid. Even in Münster, with its memory of Anabaptist millenarian revolution, Lutherans and Catholics coexisted peacefully until the 1580s. In the period from the 1580s to the outbreak of the Thirty Years' War, rapid confessionalization seemed to occur on all three fronts,[26] although to varying degrees. The debates over the Eucharist between Lutheran and Reformed leaders in the second half of the sixteenth century contributed to the confessionalizing tendencies in western Europe, where individuals, communities, and states began to adopt religious confessional identities along at least three confessional lines: Roman Catholic, Lutheran, and Calvinist/Reformed.[27] Since the Colloquy of Montbéliard (chap. 7) occurred in this period, the entrenchment of the confessional identities affected in the debates between Beza and Andreae, in which both men delineated a greater number of disagreements than before and refused to acknowledge each other as Christian brethren.

In expounding their views, reformers appealed to Scripture and the church fathers. The extent to which they appealed to the writings of the fathers depended on the extent to which they could utilize the ancient writings to support their own views or dismiss those of their opponents. As a result, when Lutheran and Reformed writers disagreed on a point, they not only divided up the fathers by naming only those considered supportive of their views, but they also addressed those sayings of the fathers that seemed to contradict their views. In the work of reclaiming the church fathers, the reformers had to address the ancient writings that could be seen as liabilities.

The reformers' typical attitude toward the fathers can be summarized in an excerpt from Wolfgang Musculus (1497–1563), a reformer in the cities of Augsburg and Bern. Musculus explained several reasons for reading the fathers, namely (1) to understand the meaning of difficult passages in the Bible; (2) to recognize the teachings of the ancient heretics; and (3) to establish godly living.[28] The reformers' use of the fathers applied to these three purposes in varying degrees. In polemical argumentation the first two purposes emerge more frequently than the third. Despite his immense respect for the fathers, Musculus reasons that "the fathers' opinions have *weight* because of their erudite scholarship and because of the sanctity of their lives, but their views do not have *authority* per se."[29] Such a view reflects the general perspective of the Protestant reformers, for whom the fathers were neither infallible nor final authorities; they were given the weight of authority as long as they were considered helpful in explicating the meaning of Scripture. Beyond exhibiting literary erudition, the reformers turned to the church fathers to reinterpret the history of the church. By reinterpreting the church fathers, they were creating a "new" ancient tradition, one that would give Protestant doctrine a past.

The primary reason for escalating conflicts between confessions claiming to represent true Christianity was the problem of authority. Although both Lutheran and Reformed thinkers in the sixteenth century believed that there was an authoritative source of religious truth and even agreed that it was the Word of God, they disagreed in their interpretations, and thereby exacerbated the unsolved problem of authority.[30] In making a sharp distinction between divine and human words and by locating the primary authority in the Scriptures, Luther denied the teaching authority of the church[31] and consistently reminded his opponents that Scripture stood above the church fathers. Oecolampadius, meanwhile, found support in the early church fathers for creating a greater distance from the late medieval views of the Eucharist. For him, the fathers were part of a struggle to uphold a newly developing doctrine of the Eucharist. Zwingli and Oecolampadius marshaled the authority of the early church to stand against the authority of the late medieval Catholics and Luther. The claims for authority in the exegetical debates of the Reformation resulted in the intense "hermeneutical crisis," when representatives from all sides of the debate appealed to the same biblical text.[32] In the Lutheran–Reformed debates over the Lord's Supper, this hermeneutical crisis extended beyond biblical texts, with reformers on both sides appealing to the same church fathers.

Despite the reformers' continuity with their medieval predecessors in citing the fathers for support, the Protestant reformers challenged existing authorities, first by holding up the principle of *sola scriptura*, and secondly by illustrating fallibility in the church fathers. In this sense, Lutheran and Calvinist reformers differed from many of their medieval predecessors in their unreserved willingness to criticize and even dismiss the writings of the church fathers as a form of rejecting the late medieval structure of religious authority. By recognizing the church fathers as human authorities, the reformers could reserve the right to challenge or correct them if necessary. Among Protestants, the fathers were used to provide an alternate tradition against that of the Roman Catholics, as well as to authorize the making of Protestant traditions. As a result, Reformed and Lutheran thinkers appealed more and more to the fathers in their argumentation. Nevertheless, the increased number of explicit references to the fathers does not mean a greater incorporation of ancient teachings. In some cases, quotations from the fathers are explained in depth, while at other times the names of the fathers are simply listed without much exposition. By the late sixteenth century, as Lutheran and Reformed views of the Eucharist solidified, the association with ancient writers was more important than the actual views of those writers. The deployment of the fathers served as the ground for the Lutheran–Reformed battle over the interpretation of Scripture, considered the primary authority, and consequently over their authority to determine doctrinal "orthodoxy." Many reformers tried to show that they were putting forth doctrine with the consent of the ancients.

Because of Rome's appeal to tradition and its claim to be, by antiquity and continuity, the only true church, any alternative voice had to wrestle with the source of papal authority. The church depended on the authority of tradition, and a part of that tradition was the early church fathers. Because the early reformers were former Catholics, it is not surprising that they would claim the tradition of the church fathers in order to reconstitute Christian authority. Protestants drew upon the support of "their" fathers to create a new interpretation of the ancient tradition

and to uphold their understanding of Scripture, which became, in place
of the church, the newly appointed supreme authority. As the Reformation developed, Protestants saw the debates not simply as Roman Catholic versus Protestant opinions, but as a search for the true meaning of
Scripture. Among the crucial questions asked was "Who decides?"—that
is, "Wherein lies the authority to decide what Scripture means?" Debates
over the Eucharist demonstrated the reformers' hermeneutical crisis and
their struggle to determine the correct way to understand the church
fathers. While the reformers occasionally notified their readers what specific passages of the fathers they were citing, the purpose of the book is
not to measure the Protestant reformers' accuracy of patristic use or to
compare their citations to modern textual discoveries, but to demonstrate
how they used and interpreted patristic sources to create a particular
tradition. In the struggle to develop a Protestant religious authority for
deciding the meaning of Scripture, they reinterpreted the ancient tradition in which the fathers could be the building blocks for a Lutheran or
Reformed view. In effect, by reappropriating the fathers for themselves,
the reformers created a "new" ancient tradition, one to which they would
be the heirs.

## Overview of Chapters

This book reveals, on the one hand, the ways in which Lutheran and
Reformed thinkers aligned their views with those of the church fathers,
and, on the other hand, how they worked to align the fathers' views with
their own. The repetition of some of the same ancient citations and
explanations through three generations of Protestant reformers reflects
a "traditional" Protestant usage of the fathers. Chapter 1 sets the stage
by looking at the Marburg Colloquy as a paradigm for the use of the
fathers in debates over the Lord's Supper. It is important to illustrate
how the colloquy serves as a paradigm for later reformers, especially the
Lutherans. Because this book is not a study solely on the Marburg Colloquy, it will be sufficient to discuss how the reformers involved—namely
Luther, Melanchthon, Oecolampadius, and Zwingli—claimed the fathers
in this debate. Although a study of each reformer's use of the fathers
merits an entire project, it is beyond the scope and objective of this work.
The next chapter provides a point of comparison and sets the context for
the debate over the Eucharist by presenting Calvin's use of the fathers
concerning the Lord's Supper in his theological work, his *Institutes*, and
his New Testament commentaries. This chapter also lays out Calvin's use
of the fathers in different genres and compares it with Melanchthon's
use of the fathers. Chapters 3 and 4 assess the use of the fathers in the

1550s debates between Calvin and Joachim Westphal, while chapter 5 takes up the subsequent exchange between Calvin and Tilemann Hesshusen. Finally, chapter 6 examines the use of the fathers by Theodore Beza and Jacob Andreae at the Colloquy of Montbéliard in 1586. The course of this book starts at the beginning of the Protestant Reformation in the 1520s, moves to the middle of the sixteenth century, and then continues on to an examination of the use of the fathers during the period of rapid confessionalization in the second half of the sixteenth century.

*Chapter 1*

# Colloquy of Marburg (1529)
## *The Fathers as Allies or Liabilities*

The purpose of this chapter is to analyze how patristic references supported
or challenged views in early Reformation debates over the Lord's Supper
even while Scripture was repeatedly hailed as the primary authority. From
the early writings of Martin Luther, Protestant reformers sought to define
their views on the Eucharist. Revisions in sacramental theology and ritual
practices sparked heated debates between those who clamored for change
and those who resisted it.

   In particular, the reformers communicated a new sacramental understanding of the Lord's Supper and composed the first series of polemical
treatises criticizing late medieval rituals, such as the practice of withholding the cup from the laity, and the church's views on transubstantiation
and Christ's repeated sacrifice. In *The Babylonian Captivity of the Church*
(1520), Martin Luther criticized the scholastic thinkers by claiming that
the church fathers never spoke of transubstantiation. While the reformers
would have been aware of the diversity within the late medieval church,
they often criticized these writers collectively, referring to them generally
as scholastics. In his earliest writings, Luther appealed to Augustine and
Cyprian for support, repudiated Origen, and portrayed Gregory as mis-
appropriated by the late medieval Catholics, such as Johannes Eck.[1] As
disagreements over the Eucharist arose among the Protestant reformers,
however, Luther began to criticize other Protestant reformers who initially
saw themselves as followers of his theology.

   Convinced that to be right about the sacraments was to be right about
salvation, various reformers were divided over theological views of the

Eucharist and the implications of these views for Christology. The Protestant reformers disagreed on how to understand the Eucharist as they argued over how the passages of the Bible ought to be understood. In essence, they argued over the authority to determine the "correct" meaning, even though they did not call it a struggle for authority. When they did not agree on the meaning of Scripture, the reformers appealed to various secondary authorities, such as early creeds and the church fathers.

### Pathway Leading to the Colloquy of Marburg

The differences in eucharistic doctrine arose early in Wittenberg. While Luther was in hiding at the Wartburg Castle, a series of events led Melanchthon to urge Luther's return to Wittenberg. The introduction of changes to the ritual of the Lord's Supper, such as offering both elements of Communion to the laity, simplifying liturgy in the vernacular, and eliminating both the vestments and the elevation of the host, caused a stir. Although such reforms were initially endorsed by a group of Wittenberg reformers, it was Andreas Bodenstein von Karlstadt (1480–1541) and Gabriel Zwilling who received most of the blame for the city's unrest. Since the Elector of Saxony Frederick III (also known as Frederick the Wise) suspected Karlstadt and Zwilling in past scandals, Luther himself requested that Karlstadt be more moderate or keep silent. The conflict over the Wittenberg Ordinance demonstrated the tension between Luther and Andreas Karlstadt.[2] Although Wittenberg representatives such as Philip Melanchthon, John Eisermann, Justus Jonas, and Nicholas Amsdorf had supported the ordinance, they were unwilling to defy the Elector, who refused to accept the ordinance. Karlstadt later complained that others had advocated a similar position but that he had been left "with his head in the noose while the others drew back."[3] Karlstadt initially supported Luther's program for reform, but in Luther's absence pushed for quicker changes in the worship service, such as relinquishing vestments (administering the sacraments in common clothes), using the vernacular German instead of Latin in the liturgy, and giving the cup to the laity. When Luther returned to Wittenberg in March 1522, he sought to distinguish himself from Karlstadt's reputation as an instigator of public disturbance and civil unrest. Luther identified Karlstadt and the Zwickau prophets as false prophets because they stubbornly resisted his fraternal admonitions.[4] Eventually Luther supported Karlstadt's banishment from Saxony.

While Luther's initial writings on the Eucharist ignited the attacks on Roman Catholic sacramental theology, Luther became increasingly entangled in the debates with other Protestant reformers. Although most of the reformers considered themselves as joining in a movement begun by

Luther, they did not necessarily accept everything taught by their leader. In 1519, after the Leipzig debate, Johannes Oecolampadius (1482–1531) was one of the first to declare publicly that he was a follower of Luther;[5] however, he was also one of Luther's major contenders in the debates over the Lord's Supper. In the 1520s, Luther and his close supporters, such as Johannes Bugenhagen (1485–1558) and Johannes Brenz (1499–1570), pressed Luther's understanding of real presence as a mark of faithfulness to Luther against other reformers, such as Zwingli and Oecolampadius, who defended a symbolic view of the Lord's Supper.

In the autumn of 1524, Luther wrote to several correspondents that Ulrich Zwingli and Leo Jud of Zürich were following Karlstadt's teachings on the Lord's Supper. His contentions with Karlstadt therefore tainted his view of Zwingli. In early 1525 Luther informed another correspondent that Karlstadt had converted unfortunate persons, such as Oecolampadius, Konrad Pellican, and Otto Brunfels, to his cause.[6] So, from the outset of his controversy with Zwingli and Oecolampadius, Luther categorized them as followers of Karlstadt when they denied that Christ's body and blood were physically present in the bread and cup of the Eucharist. Even though Luther was aware of Oecolampadius' and Pellican's rejection of Karlstadt's proofs, Luther considered them to be in agreement with Karlstadt.[7]

Luther's association of these reformers with Karlstadt in their views of the Lord's Supper was bound to exacerbate the conflict,[8] since Luther attributed the same spirit to these new opponents that he had previously attributed to Karlstadt, Müntzer, and the Zwickau prophets. In his *Letter to the Christians at Strasbourg in Opposition to the Fanatic Spirit*, written in January 1525, Luther wrote, "Oecolampadius and Pellican write that they agree with Karlstadt's opinions . . . Behold Satan's portents! . . . [T]hey have found the author and a leader of this doctrine."[9] Because Luther presumed that his opponents were putting forth Karlstadt's view, he reiterated his rebuke of Karlstadt for destroying Christian freedom: "the pope does it through commandments, Doctor Karlstadt through prohibitions."[10] In *Against the Heavenly Prophets in the Matter of Images and Sacraments*, Luther attacked any dogmatic decision about the tradition of elevating the host, "for Christ does not forbid elevation, but leaves it to free choice,"[11] although he had earlier criticized the tradition of elevation.

Although Zwingli had emphasized his agreement with Luther's teachings on the Lord's Supper, he diverged from Luther's view by 1524, when he appealed to Cornelius Hoen's symbolic interpretation of the words of institution, which Luther had rejected. The development of Zwingli's symbolic understanding of the eucharistic presence surfaced in his letter to

Matthew Alber of Reutlingen in November 1524, when he insisted that
the words "this is my body" means "this signifies my body." In this letter
Zwingli implicitly attacks Luther's position by making reference to Tertullian and Augustine and stressing the importance of faith.[12] Zwingli's effort
to differentiate himself from Alber's Lutheran view reflects his awareness
of the similarities between Luther's view of the Eucharist and the view held
by the Catholic thinkers in Zürich.[13] In March 1525, Zwingli's *Commentary
on True and False Religion* further explained his view of the Eucharist when
he argued that the bread and wine were both a sign and seal of Christ's
presence and blessings. In this interpretation, the bread is a symbol representative of the whole presence of Christ. He based his arguments on
his interpretation of John 6 and selections from Tertullian, Augustine,
Ambrose, Chrysostom, Theophylact, Hilary, Jerome, and Origen.[14] Later
Zwingli will argue that the words of institution were an example of metonymy, a figure of speech in which a part symbolizes the whole.

    Soon afterwards in the summer of 1525, Oecolampadius wrote a trea-
tise in a dual attempt to dispute the opinion of the Catholics in Basel and
to win over his former Heidelberg pupils and friends, who were working
as pastors and preachers between Heilbronn and Schwäbisch Hall. It is
important to note that in his *On the Genuine Interpretation of the Lord's
Words* (*De genuina verborum domini expositione*), Oecolampadius cited extensive portions of the church fathers to defend his view that the bread is
a figure of Christ's body and to criticize Luther's stance on the Lord's
Supper. Although he dedicated this treatise to the "beloved brethren in
Schwabia" with the intent to convince them of his position, these pastors
instead subscribed to the Lutheran views expressed by Johannes Brenz. In
October 1525 Brenz published his response to Oecolampadius in the *Syngramma Suevicum* (Swabian syngraph), which included the contribution of
fourteen "Swabian preachers" between Heilbronn and Schwäbisch Hall
who stood mostly against Oecolampadius' view. In addition, Brenz questioned Oecolampadius' use of the church fathers as a way to criticize his
interpretation.[15]

    As southwestern Germany became the principal battlefield between
Wittenberg and Zürich in the Reformation,[16] Wittenberg reformers tried
to resist the spread of Swiss doctrine of the Lord's Supper into south-
western Germany. In 1526 John Agricola (1494–1566) translated Brenz'
*Syngramma Suevicum* into German and Luther contributed a preface. Until
1526 Luther avoided a direct confrontation about the Lord's Supper
with Zwingli, but decided he needed to warn the Reutlingen congregation to resist the views of Karlstadt and Zwingli. According to Luther,
the source of the Swiss error was a false rationalism and a disdain for the

sacrament.[17] Despite several points of agreement among the early reformers, the increasingly apparent divergence between Luther and Zwingli prompted various theologians (among them Karlstadt, Oecolampadius, Bucer, Schwenckfeld, Billican, Bugenhagen, and Brenz, to name a few) to offer alternative explanations concerning this central sacrament of the church. It became apparent that Wittenberg and Zürich were competing for the spiritual, as well as the political, allegiance of south German cities such as Basel, Strasbourg, Augsburg, Nördlingen, Biberach, Memmingen, Ulm, Isny, Kempten, Lindau, and Constance.[18]

For the Frankfurt spring book fair in 1527, Zwingli wrote his *Friendly Exposition of the Eucharist Affair, to Martin Luther* (*Amica Exegesis*), in which he spoke of his early indebtedness to Augustine and his tractates on John. The influence of Augustine on Zwingli's writings is evident both in his extended quotations from many of Augustine's works and in his numerous uses of Augustine's exposition of John 6.[19] Zwingli also challenged the classification of Luther's view as normative for all those who considered themselves "evangelical" or followers of the gospel. In doing so, he sparked a series of polemical exchanges with Luther. In the period between late 1524 and 1527, more than two dozen published writings had directly or indirectly attacked Luther's view of the Lord's Supper. Meanwhile, Luther affirmed his stance on real presence in his comprehensive treatise titled *That These Words of Christ, "This is My Body," Still Stand Firm Against the Fanatics*. Zwingli's rejoinder, titled *And Martin Luther with His Latest Book Has by No Means Proved or Established His Own and the Pope's View*, and Oecolampadius' *That Dr. Martin Luther's Misunderstanding of the Everlasting Words, "This is My Body," is Untenable. The Second Reasonable Answer of John Oecolampadius* appeared in June 1527. Zwingli's tract gives Luther credit for his work in the interpretation of Scripture, but also qualifies the extent of Luther's authority in interpreting it. Zwingli points out Luther's errors so that Luther may from now on restrain himself "about [his] great fame among Christians as if [he] alone had accomplished everything,"[20] and further accuses Luther of abusing his authority, saying, "You always put forward first a long abusive section so that a simple person will be induced by your authority or name in which he has much faith, to hate your opponents, and . . . will rage and scream with you."[21] Just as Luther lumped Zwingli with Karlstadt, so did Zwingli lump Luther together with the papists.[22]

In March 1528 Luther summed up his position with an announcement that he had sufficiently refuted the sacramentarian argument in his two earlier treatises and that the present treatise, *Confession on Christ's Supper*, would be his last with the purpose of strengthening the weak in conscience. While Luther associated his opponents with Satan, other reformers associated their opponents with ancient heretics. In this treatise as well as his earlier works, Luther linked his opponents with a devilish spirit. In the autumn of 1528, both Zwingli and Oecolampadius answered this treatise in a carefully coordinated reply called *Concerning Dr. Martin Luther's Book Entitled "Confession": Two Answers by John Oecolampadius and Ulrich Zwingli.* Oecolampadius' and Zwingli's tactic was to resort to the church fathers, which other Lutherans, such as Melanchthon, were also doing. Meanwhile, Luther reiterated his rejection of views presented by Karlstadt, Zwingli, the Zwickau prophets, or any other "fanatics," whom he saw as threats to the social order. As he had announced earlier, Luther did not respond. Because the reformers remained divided over the Lord's Supper, controversy over the Eucharist became the religious hindrance to any political unity among the reformers.

The imperial estates at the Second Diet of Speyer in 1529 decided that it was time to uphold the Edict of Worms and stamp out the Lutheran movements. The evangelical estates, by contrast, protested such stringent measures, designed to halt the spread of Protestantism. Philip of Hesse, together with five other princes and fourteen cities, formally signed the protest and appeal. The protest itself resulted in calling those who were at variance with the established Catholic Church "Protestants."[23] Yet Philip of Hesse wanted more than just a protest against domination of the majority; he wanted tangible protection for the minority.[24] The landgrave believed that the time was ripe for making a pan-Protestant political alliance including the Swiss. In hopes of achieving Protestant unity, he called for a religious colloquy. He first approached Melanchthon, who was present at the diet, about arranging a colloquy between Luther and Zwingli. At the same time, he also wrote to Zwingli, suggesting that the Zürich reformer prepare to meet with Luther and Melanchthon to discuss their religious differences. Although pessimistic about any agreement, Luther reluctantly agreed, explaining that he did not want his opponents to boast that they were more well-disposed to peace and unity than he was.[25] Meanwhile, another group of Protestant rulers preferred to pursue alliances among Germans (whether Lutheran or Catholic) who were already in a general confessional agreement. Both Philip of Hesse and this latter group, often called the confessional party, used Luther's writings to rationalize their positions and tried to enlist the personal support of the reformers. In a letter to Melanchthon (June 11, 1530), Philip wrote that he did not understand why the Saxons were unwilling to accept the uplanders (northern Germans and the Swiss) as brothers since, as he saw it, the two sides were essentially in agreement on the basic premises of

Protestantism.[26] His goal for the Colloquy of Marburg was thus to arrive at a common confession endorsed by the major reformers of his time. In contrast, the confessional party and its leaders wanted to see Christians in Germany bridge their differences (without the pope), and feared that any toleration of Zwinglians would endanger hopes for reuniting Catholics and Lutherans. Melanchthon, for example, opposed any pan-Protestant alliance because he believed it would undermine the chances for a successful Lutheran-Catholic dialogue.[27] Just as Philip of Hesse called the Marburg Colloquy to overcome some of the opposition of the confessional party, the confessional party in turn tried to sabotage the dialogue before it even began by commissioning the Wittenberg theologians to devise, prior to the colloquy, a common confession that would exclude other Protestants, and by specifically instructing the Wittenberg theologians not to make an agreement with the Zwinglians.[28]

## Context of the Colloquy of Marburg, October 1529

The Colloquy of Marburg provides a logical starting point and a useful framework for understanding the use of the fathers in the sixteenth-century debates over the Eucharist. The contents of the Colloquy of Marburg are recorded in seven reports containing many overlapping materials, as well as the Marburg Articles formulated by Luther. Since the colloquy was not officially recorded, a reconstruction of the colloquy is based on the reports made afterwards by (1) Caspar Hedio of Strasbourg (in Latin), considered the most reliable source; (2) an anonymous reporter (in Latin), presumed to be one of Luther's close friends; (3) Rudolph Collin (in Latin), Zwingli's colleague and travel companion, content to furnish a similar account to Hedio's; (4) Osiander, in the form of a letter (in German) to the city council of Nürnberg; (5) Brenz' letter (mostly in Latin, with a short portion in German) to the people of Reutlingen; (6) another anonymous reporter (in Latin) of the *Rhapsodies on the Marburg Colloquy*; and (7) Heinrich Utinger's *Summary Report Concerning the Marburg Colloquy* (in German).[29] Of these seven reports, all except Utinger's *Summary*, which is of questionable origin, include references to the fathers. In Walther Köhler's valuable reconstruction of the Marburg Colloquy, Luther, Oecolampadius, and Zwingli dominate the conversation.[30] In the various accounts of the colloquy, Melanchthon's voice is mentioned less often than the others. Meanwhile, Köhler's reconstruction of a dialogue between Zwingli and Melanchthon shows that the main church father named and discussed is Augustine.

The reason for the Marburg Colloquy was to discuss differences in beliefs among Protestants, in hopes of achieving a theological consensus that would serve as a basis for a Protestant political alliance. The principal reformers involved in the preceding years of dispute came together in their first and only face-to-face meeting at the Colloquy of Marburg in order to deal with religious differences over interpretations of the Eucharist in light of the pressing threat to the Protestant churches. Although participants in the colloquy agreed on some things (presumably fourteen of the fifteen articles), they were deadlocked on issues relating to the Eucharist.[31] In their debate, the major reformers (Luther, Melanchthon, Zwingli, and Oecolampadius) discussed the early church fathers' opinions and authority. Oecolampadius in particular based his arguments on patristic evidence, appealing mostly to Augustine. His appeal prompted further debates and discussions on the use of the church fathers and clarified the function of the church fathers in the arguments. With their endeavors to interpret Scripture and explain their own positions, the reformers expanded their study of the fathers and claimed the support of the ancient tradition to stand in the *consensus ecclesiae*.[32] The fact that the fathers are consistently mentioned in the polemical argumentation over the Eucharist reveals their importance in shaping arguments, making claims, gaining authority, and increasing justification of each side's perspective.

Initially Luther, like the scholastics, did not expect to choose between loyalty to Scripture and loyalty to the fathers because he presupposed that the fathers had always taught the Scriptures correctly.[33] Yet over the course of the 1520s, reformers such as Zwingli and Oecolampadius appealed to the fathers in their writings on the Eucharist, which differed from and questioned Luther's interpretation. Because they often cited Augustine to validate their positions and to challenge Luther's view, Luther was forced to make choices. In the development of the eucharistic controversies of the 1520s, he clung to the words of Scripture, even when it meant parting ways with the father of Latin theology. At the Marburg Colloquy, while Luther conceded Augustine and Fulgentius to Oecolampadius, he still found it desirable to claim the rest of the fathers for his own position. Meanwhile, in Melanchthon's debate with Zwingli, Melanchthon claimed that even if Augustine had said it was necessary for the body of Christ to be in one place, Augustine would not concede to contemporary figurative interpretations.[34] Melanchthon also noted, "The majority of opinions which are cited from Augustine seem to defend Zwingli, but almost all the others from the ancients clearly approve Luther's opinion."[35]

Expecting that Zwingli and Oecolampadius would bolster their views with the sayings of the ancient fathers, Luther on the first morning of the colloquy rightly recognized that their differences depended on their interpretation of the fathers; he then added that he did not accept all interpretations of the fathers.[36] In this case, the authority of the fathers was contingent on whether or not their interpretations were accepted. According to Luther, the fathers could be relegated to a lesser status as interpreters because the Word of God is the one true authority: "I do not want adherence to the words on my own authority, but on the authority and at the command of Christ."[37] Meanwhile, Oecolampadius argued that it is wrong to attribute too much importance to the elements, since Augustine had dealt with this issue in his treatise *On Christian Doctrine*,[38] when he stated that the elements are signs pointing to a greater reality. Zwingli's initial reference to the church fathers was to set them up as models of faith even in disagreement. Without any specific evidence, he used the church fathers in an indirect attack on Luther's attitude toward him: "The early fathers, even if they disagreed, nevertheless did not condemn one another in such a way."[39] Afterward he added, "For Augustine did not want the body of Christ to be eaten essentially and bodily."[40] Zwingli and Oecolampadius were confident in their views because they had the support of the church fathers and thought it might help them convince Luther. The fact that they thought they could convince Luther with the sayings of the church fathers reveals their assumption that the fathers were their allies.

## The Colloquy of Marburg

*Debate over Doctrine*

According to an anonymous report on the proceedings at Marburg, the colloquy began with Luther's asking Oecolampadius and Zwingli to explain the chief parts of Christian doctrine. Luther believed that, in addition to the Lord's Supper, they disagreed on many important points concerning the doctrine of the Trinity (he identified Oecolampadius and Zwingli with Arius against the correct teaching of Augustine or other orthodox fathers), the two natures of Christ (he charged them with the faulty Nestorian distinction), original sin, baptism, justification, the ministry of the word, and purgatory.[41] Later Lutherans would continue to emphasize numerous doctrinal differences, whereas the Reformed writers presumed the major theological difference to be the Lord's Supper. Oecolampadius replied that he was not aware of having taught anything in opposition to Luther's doctrine; to his mind, the colloquy was called to discuss opinions on the Eucharist. When they reached an impasse in their interpretation of Scripture, Zwingli and Oecolampadius argued that they themselves were not the authors of this doctrine, but that the oldest teachers of the church had taught it. Zwingli brought up a passage from

Augustine that states that whatever exists in a certain place is a body. Luther contended that, while it is indeed true that whatever is contained in a place is a body, the converse is not necessarily true. Zwingli's rebuttal was another passage from Augustine: "Take away space from bodies and you will have taken away the bodies."[42] When Luther appealed to God's omnipotence, Zwingli brought forth a passage from Fulgentius' book *On the Immensity of God*:

> Since one and the same Son of God, true God, born of God the Father has become true man for us from human seed . . . he has a true divine and a true human nature . . . He is one and the same person who is a man locally circumscribed according to his human origin and who is immeasurable God according to his divine origin.[43]

From this, Zwingli presented Fulgentius' arguments in support of his case, but Luther wanted to dismiss this portion of Fulgentius as irrelevant because, he argued, Fulgentius had not said these things about the Lord's Supper but against the Manicheans and other heretics who denied the humanity of Christ. In his response, Luther appealed to the context of church history to explain (away) a theological point: if the purpose of an ancient writing was something other than the Lord's Supper, then, for Luther, any theological points made in that writing could be dismissed as irrelevant. Yet Luther did not dismiss Fulgentius altogether, since he emphasized another passage from Fulgentius which testifies that the body and blood of the Lord are offered in the Supper.[44] By attempting to delineate a right way to use ancient authorities, Luther showed a readiness to limit and subordinate the voice of ancient authorities when they seemed irrelevant or did not support his case. Despite his attempt to set these "contextual" boundaries on the ancient writings, however, most Lutheran and Reformed thinkers (as we shall see in subsequent chapters) did not maintain such strict contextual limits.

According to Collin's report on the Marburg Colloquy, Luther conceded that the fathers would be partly on Oecolampadius' side if his interpretation of them were admitted. Since Luther did not admit Oecolampadius' interpretation of the fathers and moved to exclude them from the discussion, the implication is that, for Luther, the fathers could not override his own views, which had the support of Scripture. In other words, Luther would not accept the Reformed interpretation of the fathers and, even if their interpretation were accepted, the fathers were not the ultimate authority.[45]

*Debate over Scriptural Interpretation*

The next topic of the debate was the biblical interpretation of John 6. Zwingli cited Luther's postil concerning John 6:63 ("The flesh is of no avail") and introduced Melanchthon's remarks about the same passage—that eating in a bodily way is not established by the verse. Although Luther saw the passage in John 6 as unrelated to the Eucharist, Zwingli argued, "When the fathers said that the body of Christ feeds the soul, I understand this to mean the resurrection. [Luther's view] does not agree with Melanchthon's statement in which he admitted that the words only signify."[46] By stating this difference, Zwingli was trying to maneuver Melanchthon's position closer to his own understanding and farther from Luther's interpretation. Although Luther dismissed Zwingli's comment, it nevertheless foreshadowed a conflict that later arose among Lutherans:[47] according to Osiander's report, when Zwingli and Oecolampadius attempted to prove their interpretations by citing the sayings of the fathers instead of the Bible, Luther implored them to do so in an orderly way,[48] warning that they should not mingle the two sources, that is, Scripture and church fathers, but refrain from mentioning the fathers until the sacred and divine Scripture had been dealt with first. Zwingli and Oecolampadius agreed to this procedure.

Luther reiterated that the sacrament is established upon Christ's word and not upon the holiness of the minister, "as the Anabaptists and Donatists do."[49] In this line of reasoning, Luther continued, "Augustine says in opposition to the Donatists that ministry must not be entrusted solely to the virtuous because the basis of our belief is the word of God."[50] Here Luther cited Augustine for support against the contemporary Donatists, the Anabaptists. He further accused his counterparts of a Nestorian separation of the natures of Christ (since Christ's body has ascended to heaven it cannot be in the Eucharist), and referred to Cyril of Alexandria's *communicatio idiomatum* (the communication of natures) as an affirmation that, where Christ's divine nature is, so also is his human nature, which makes the finite capable of the infinite.[51] On the contentious point of how Christ is present in the Eucharist, Oecolampadius distinguished between the two natures of Christ and argued that Christ is present in heaven according to his divinity and humanity, and in the Supper according to his divinity. When he highlighted passages from Augustine's *On the Gospel of John*, where Augustine explains that the body of Christ in which he arose must be in one place, Luther responded with a dismissal of irrelevance:

To this passage from Augustine, I say as I did before about Fulgentius
that it has nothing to do with the Lord's Supper. In his letter to Januarius, Augustine in words something like this speaks about the Lord's
Supper, emphasizing that the body and blood of the Lord ought to
be received by disciples who had fasted. In another letter Augustine
establishes the rule that the readers of his books . . . should measure
everything by the standard of Scripture. Whatever did not agree with
Scripture was to be accommodated through interpretation if this could
be done adequately or if this proved impossible, it was to be completely
rejected.[52]

Luther established his standard for accepting the church fathers as those
views that must agree with Scripture. When Oecolampadius offered
another passage from Augustine to prove that a true body is locally circumscribed, Luther requested a new argument since his reply would be
the same. To this, Oecolampadius rightly concluded, "If you refuse to be
moved by those arguments, it would be in vain for us to bring forward a
thousand passages from the fathers."[53] Oecolampadius' comment unveils
Luther's attitude toward the authority of the fathers as fallible human
interpreters and potential liabilities.

In the debate with Luther, Oecolampadius also complained that
Luther had introduced a new meaning contrary to the teachings of the
church because he was not willing to admit a trope in the words of institution. While Luther was willing to interpret the Lord's Supper as a synecdoche, he rejected Oecolampadius' metonymy.[54] Luther defended his
view by saying,

Synecdoche [is a form of speech, like] sword–sheath; mug–beer. Thus
"This is my body" is an inclusive way of speaking . . . This figure of
speech is in general use and the text calls for it. A metaphor [or metonymy, on the other hand] abolishes the content altogether, as when you
understand "body" as "the figure of the body"; synecdoche does not do
this.[55]

In response, Zwingli reiterated what Oecolampadius had earlier quoted
from Augustine: "If Christ's body is on high, it must be in one place."[56]
To this, Luther retorted, "We shall find out to what extent you can boast
about the fathers."[57] Luther resisted the strength his opponents had found
in the fathers and rejected any technical argumentation about Christ's
finite body being in one place.

During the Sunday morning session of the colloquy, a full-fledged
debate over the fathers emerged. When Zwingli asked Luther to prove
that the body of Christ can be in many places, Luther quoted the words of

institution. Continuing to rely on the fathers, Zwingli reiterated the passage from Fulgentius that states that the body of Christ is in one place.[58] Luther dismissed Zwingli's claim as irrelevant and unrelated to the discussion on the location of Christ's body, and used that same passage to highlight Fulgentius' emphasis on the true body of Christ in opposition to the Manicheans. He then cited a different passage from Fulgentius, claiming that the former passage mentioned by Zwingli had nothing to do with the Supper. In addition to the claim of irrelevance, Luther posited a shortcoming of the fathers by saying that it is a deficiency for them to say something in one place and leave it unmentioned in another.[59] In response, Zwingli defended his quotation from Fulgentius and argued that in the phrase "it is offered," "it" means "remembrance of the sacrifice." For additional support, Zwingli said that "Augustine in a letter to Boniface interprets it as a metonymy [or analogy]."[60] At this point, Andreas Osiander (1498–1552) chimed in: "What if the fathers have erred in speaking of a sacrifice?"[61] The records do not show whether any discussion on the fallibility of the fathers took place; rather, at this point, Luther maintained that the fathers must be subordinate to Scripture and reiterated his general rule for the fathers: "When the fathers speak, they are to be accepted in accordance with the canon of Scripture. Whatever they appear to write contrary to Scripture must either be interpreted or be rejected. Augustine's opinion that '[the body] must be in one place' . . . is to be rejected or interpreted."[62] This statement reveals three points concerning Luther's view of the fathers: (1) the fathers must be judged in accordance with Scripture and are always secondary to Scripture; (2) the fathers themselves require interpretation and in some cases need to be rejected; and (3) the recurrence of the same ancient passages indicates a common source of patristic knowledge such as an anthology, a collection of sayings, or canon law, rather than a comprehensive examination of primary sources, although some primary sources were also consulted.

The debate over the fathers continued in the Sunday afternoon discussion. When Oecolampadius repeated that the body of Christ is not in the sacrament as in a place and asked how Christ can be there as a body, Luther pressed the issue: "At the beginning of discussion we took Scripture as our basis. Scripture is not against us. You add the fathers; they are not against us either. Among them you have two, Augustine and Fulgentius, on your side; the rest are against you."[63] When Luther conceded that the Reformed views had Augustine and Fulgentius, but "the remaining fathers are on our side," Oecolampadius asked him to bring up the fathers who were on the Reformed side. This wish was not granted. At the end of the debate, Oecolampadius announced his reason for quoting the fathers, namely to demonstrate the tradition and antiquity of his opinion.

In response, Luther announced that the historical context was pre-cisely the reason for the limited usefulness of the fathers. Because the church fathers wrote about the Eucharist in the context of ancient con-troversies, he argued, they emphasized certain concepts, such as sacrifice, sign, and representation, depending on the identity of their opponents.[64] Therefore, Luther claimed to "know of no teacher who could bring about agreement among us, since none is aware of our situation."[65] Luther was right in saying the fathers did not write with sixteenth-century questions in mind, yet this assessment did not hinder him or other Protestant reformers from relying on them. In the context of the sixteenth-century controversies over the Eucharist, the reformers reinterpreted the concepts of the church fathers to make them relevant to the latest debates over the Eucharist. Luther, for example, cited a passage from Augustine's *City of God* ("I have seen the Lord our God") to prove that people see Christ in the Eucharist because of the words "this is my body."[66] Meanwhile, Oeco-lampadius countered any view in support of the bodily presence of Christ with passages from Augustine's *On Christian Doctrine* and anti-Manichean treatises. At the same time, he also conceded that the sacrament is not a mere sign, but that the true body is there through faith.[67] To this, Luther replied, "Augustine was a young man when he wrote against the Mani-cheans and he had no reliable text." Luther thus restated his view of the fathers' authority when he said, "It's necessary to subordinate the teachers to Christ."[68]

At the Sunday morning and afternoon sessions, Zwingli and Oecola-mpadius brought forth passages from the fathers, namely Fulgentius and Augustine. These passages stated that a body had to be in a particular place and that the bread in the Lord's Supper was a sign of the body and blood of Christ. According to Osiander, the participants listened to Zwingli and Oecolampadius practically the whole day on this matter as they searched for, read, and translated the passages. After a day of discus-sion on the Scriptures, Zwingli and Oecolampadius were ready to defend their cause; Luther, however, denied that a figurative interpretation was the intention of the fathers.[69] Remaining adamant in the face of his oppo-nents' appeals, Luther answered,

> That St. Augustine calls the bread a sign of the body of Christ is noth-ing extraordinary, since we cannot know from this whether his opin-ion was that the body was present or not. We ourselves consider and call it a sign and nevertheless hold that the body is there. When he speaks about a body having to be in one place alone, he is writing about other things and does not refer to the Lord's Supper at all. But when

he speaks about the Lord's Supper, he calls it the body and blood of Christ just as we do.[70]

The disagreement, according to Luther, was no longer over whether the elements are signs but whether the body of Christ in his humanity is present at the table.

## Early Uses of the Fathers

Throughout the debates at the Marburg Colloquy, Luther understood that the fathers could be a liability. Because he simultaneously wanted to claim that he was following the early church fathers, he responded in two ways. First, he concentrated on the better sayings of the fathers by differentiating between them. He offered the closest thing to an answer for an earlier question about the fathers that supported the Lutheran side when he asked, "Even if I were certain that Augustine had in mind what you assert, why should we depend on Augustine here and not rather, on Cyprian, Cyril, Ambrose, Jerome and many others who have given our interpretation in the clearest possible way?"[71] Second, Luther claimed that he followed the fathers' approach to their own writings, and that he was, in fact, the one most faithfully following the example of the fathers, namely Augustine. Luther said,

> Even if all the fathers would agree with our interpretation, how could we arrive at the point where for the sake of the fathers we would abandon God's word and depend on them? Follow the example of St. Augustine himself! . . . Let us gladly do the dear fathers the honor of interpreting . . . so [long as] they remain in harmony with Holy Scripture. However where their writings do not agree with God's word, it is much better that we say they have erred than that for their sake we should abandon God's word.[72]

In other words, those who follow Augustine are following God's word. Luther construed faithfulness to Augustine, in many cases, as faithfulness to the Scriptures. Even when he rejected the sayings of the fathers, he advocated the ancient writers' goal of illuminating Scripture and claimed to follow the tradition of faithful biblical interpretation.

Lutheran pastor of Schwäbisch Hall Johannes Brenz, who earlier had responded to Oecolampadius' 1525 treatise, *De genuina verborum Domini* also prepared a report of the Marburg Colloquy for Hans Schradin, a pastor in Reutlingen. Brenz continued to claim that the fathers were on Luther's side and supplemented his report with a section from his new treatise, *The Foundation in Holy Scripture which was Treated somewhat in the Colloquy at Marburg in Dealing with the Sacrament.*[73] Brenz' supplement answered the appeals to the fathers that were initially posed by the Reformed side, partially to guard against the notion that the Lutherans were deviating from church tradition (to resist the perception that their new theologies were heretical) and partially to claim the authority for interpreting Scripture since other Protestant groups (such as the Reformed and Anabaptists) were also claiming Scripture as their sole guide. Although Luther cited some fathers in response to Zwingli and Oecolampadius, Brenz added to the repertoire of fathers for Luther's case. While Luther found confidence in his interpretation of the Word of God, other Lutherans, such as Philip Melanchthon and Johannes Brenz, wanted to fight for the fathers as well. After Erasmus chided Melanchthon's lack of knowledge of the church fathers (which Erasmus considered a prerequisite for scholarly biblical interpretation), Melanchthon made a concerted effort not only to demonstrate his erudition, but also to illustrate patristic support for Lutheran views. Meanwhile, in order to make a case about presence, Brenz recalled Jerome's argument that the sacrifice of martyrs reflects the sacrifice of Christ. He argued that "if according to the opinion of Jerome the martyrs are everywhere with Christ then Christ was able to be everywhere according to his humanity."[74] Brenz' additional reference to Jerome showed that, despite Luther's relegation of the fathers, he was not content to leave the fathers with Oecolampadius.

In *Rhapsodies on the Marburg Colloquy*, Luther argues that if Augustine or the other teachers want to interpret these signs, then they should follow Christ and interpret as he interprets. If they do so, Luther claims, we can depend on them and believe them; if not, we must let go of these teachers and believe Christ and not consider them to be right simply because they are teachers.[75] From the exchanges at the Colloquy, it is clear that Zwingli and Oecolampadius were of the opinion that God's word is profitable and good when pious and holy persons use it. Luther, in his presentation at Marburg, managed to portray the Reformed use of the fathers in terms of Augustine's debate against the Donatists. He and Zwingli cited different passages from Fulgentius as they debated over whose view had the early father's support: Zwingli brought up a passage to prove that Christ's body is in a certain place, while Luther produced another passage to show that the body of Christ is offered in the bread and the chalice to those who commune.[76] Overall, the sequence of argumentation between the Lutheran and Reformed sides of the debate followed a pattern such as this, as an examination of the various reports on the colloquy shows: (1) Zwingli read a passage from the fathers (specifically Augustine or Fulgentius); (2) Luther replied with a dismissal strategy of irrelevance and usually offered another quotation from the fathers more amenable to his stance; (3) Zwingli or Oecolampadius brought up another passage from the fathers or expanded on their interpretation of a quote; (4) Luther occasionally appealed to the authority of God's word to trump any interpretation of the fathers.

The Protestant reformers had a general respect for the fathers and summoned them particularly as a defensive strategy. At Marburg, Luther made it clear that he subordinated the fathers to Scripture—namely his own interpretation of Scripture. Oecolampadius and Zwingli agreed, in principle, with Luther to set Scripture as the primary authority. At the same time, they put forth several well-known ancient voices to describe and support their stance, which they believed was not a deviation from but a continuation of the ancient tradition. Whenever the fathers seemed unhelpful or mistaken, or could be marshaled in support of Oecolampadius' opinion, Luther employed three tactics to downplay the ancient voices. First, he could dismiss the ancient authorities by appealing to historical context and usually rendering the words of individual church fathers irrelevant. Second, he could either counterattack with another quote from the same father to contradict Oecolampadius' point or counter with a quote from a different and "better" father. Third, he could claim that he was following the spirit of a particular church father to provide the clearest biblical interpretation, regardless of the actual opinions of the fathers. To varying degrees, both sides considered it important to stand within the apostolic lineage, since they were resisting an established authority. Among the various opinions on the Eucharist, the fathers offered one option for claiming a reliable source for notions concerning the Eucharist, which had been the center of church worship for centuries.

## Aftermath of the Colloquy of Marburg

Unresolved points over the Lord's Supper at the Colloquy of Marburg prevented agreement between Wittenberg and Zürich—and consequently the formation of a Protestant political alliance. Gradually shifting political alliances forged areas of theological compromise, resulting in political cooperation within the Holy Roman Empire as well as the formation of distinct religious identities. When a political union of all Protestant communities failed to materialize (an idea that excluded the Anabaptists), the movement was split into a spectrum of allegiances ranging between Wittenberg and Zürich. Yet the German Reformed cities could not indefinitely remain estranged from the Lutheran churches. At the Augsburg *Reichstag* in 1530, the supposedly "Zwinglian" cities of Strasbourg, Constance, Lindau, and Memmingen produced the "Four Cities'

Confession," or *Confessio Tetrapolitana*, affirming that the true body and true blood of Christ, not mere bread and wine, were truly eaten and drunk. Meanwhile, other Lutherans, such as Brenz, continued to uphold the notion of "ubiquity," according to which Christ's resurrected body could be present everywhere in creation. What may surprise the modern reader about the Marburg Colloquy is not the notion of orchestrating a theological compromise, but that a doctrinal consensus was considered necessary to pursue a political union.

The Colloquy of Marburg demonstrated how Protestants early in the Reformation struggled to define the function of the church's ancient tradition in their debates over the Lord's Supper. Considering the church fathers as mostly faithful interpreters, the early reformers deemed the fathers valuable to biblical interpretation and therefore considered them as exegetical comrades. Even when the fathers seemed to be liabilities, they were somehow construed as positive examples, and the early Protestant reformers usually cited them as allies to bolster their own views and simultaneously challenge other doctrines.

## Chapter 2

# John Calvin's Use of the Fathers in the *Institutes* and New Testament Commentaries

While the Colloquy of Marburg failed to produce a common doctrine of the Eucharist, in the spring of 1536, Martin Luther, Philip Melanchthon, Johannes Bugenhagen and Martin Bucer (representing the south Germans) negotiated the Wittenberg Concord. This agreement stated that Christ's body and blood were truly and substantially present and received in the Eucharist, and it allowed the full political and later doctrinal unity between northern and southern Germany that had been elusive seven years before. Initially drafted by Melanchthon, the Wittenberg Concord contained appeals to the fathers so that the ancient tradition might serve as the basis for promoting a common Protestant doctrine of the Eucharist. Although Bucer tried to rally the Swiss reformers to support the Wittenberg Concord, by the time of Zürich synod in 1538 it was clear that any fragile agreement between Luther and the followers of Zwingli was falling apart.[1] Meanwhile, another reformer stationed in the free imperial city of Geneva joined the discussion on the Eucharist with his *Institutes* (1539) and the *Short Treatise on the Lord's Supper* (1540): John Calvin (1509–1564), who tried to uphold some of the emphases of both Luther and Zwingli in his own distinctive view of a real spiritual presence. He was critical of Luther's doctrine of ubiquity, which posited that Christ through unique divine will and power could be present everywhere. While Calvin thought the doctrine of ubiquity did not safeguard Christ's humanity, he was also critical of Zwingli's purely symbolic interpretation of the Eucharist. Calvin essentially argued that Christ's body and blood were truly present but that believers were lifted up spiritually to Christ; Christ was not dragged down to them.[2] In other words, Calvin saw the sacrament both as an instrument through which those partaking in Communion share in Christ's body and blood and as a means of grace in which believers are lifted up by the Holy Spirit in Communion with Christ's body and blood. By focusing on the subject of the Lord's Supper, this chapter traces the development and significance of Calvin's increasing use of the fathers throughout several editions of the *Institutes* and in three of his commentaries.

In 1536, the same year that William Farel urged Calvin to remain in Geneva for the work of reform, Calvin published the first edition of his *Institutes* (originally called the *Institution of the Christian Religion*), which he intended as a theological framework for reading Scripture. Calvin wrote several editions of this monumental work. Each edition was larger than the previous one, and Calvin's references to the church fathers also increased with each subsequent edition. While the 1559 edition of the *Institutes* was considered the "finished product" because of Calvin's own satisfaction with it, consideration of the earlier editions (namely those of 1536, 1539, and 1543) reveals a development in his use of the fathers. We will return to the 1559 edition of the *Institutes* in chapter 4, after discussing Calvin's disputes with Lutheran Joachim Westphal in the 1550s, since historical controversies with the Lutherans shaped Calvin's theology and, consequently, his use of the fathers in the 1559 version of his work. More specifically, Calvin's use of the fathers developed as he sought precedence and support in his debates with others. The alterations and expansion of the later editions of the *Institutes* indicate a growing need for doctrinal clarification in the midst of conflicting claims. The *Institutes* reveal what Calvin thought was important for his readers to know before turning to his New Testament commentaries. In his discussion of the Lord's Supper, Calvin discusses his view with references to Scripture and to the church fathers. Despite the recognition of Scripture as the source of theology, in the midst of competing interpretations, other authoritative voices became increasingly important. Calvin's explicit references to the fathers are present even in the earliest version of the *Institutes*. It is not surprising that the French reformer would look to the patristic traditions of the church since he would have been exposed to the church fathers through canon law during his legal training as well as through his humanist education. Many of the patristic citations in the 1536 *Institutes* were drawn from Lombard's *Sentences* and Gratian's *Decretum*, which were standard late medieval Catholic textbooks for canon law and theology.[3] In light of Calvin's increased access to the fathers in his later years and his increased involvement in theological debates, the number of references to the church fathers increases dramatically from the first to the last edition of the *Institutes*. For example, the 1539 *Institutes* has approximately 301 patristic citations, while the 1543 edition has 418 additional references and the 1559 *Institutes* has 866 citations, the most in any one of Calvin's works.[4]

## Calvin's *Institutes*

### 1536 Edition

In his *Institution of the Christian Religion*, Calvin refers to some of the church fathers as exemplary interpreters.[5] The fathers are introduced as qualified exegetes. The value of the fathers lies in their contributions to the clearest interpretation of Scripture. In the section concerning the sacraments, Augustine arises as a key witness because he calls a sacrament "a visible word" and says that the efficacy of the Word is brought to light in the sacrament not because it is spoken but because it is believed.[6] This saying of Augustine will come up again and be claimed by both sides. Calvin also cites Augustine to show that the sacraments of the Mosaic law foretold Christ, whereas Christian sacraments convey Christ.[7] In the section on the Lord's Supper, Calvin makes only a general reference to the ancient church. Although he demonstrates his knowledge of the fathers, explicit citations of their work are sparse. Calvin does mention the name of one ancient figure, Marcion, a second-century writer condemned for his heterodox views. Because Marcion questioned the humanity of Christ, Calvin faults him for not taking the humanity of Christ seriously. For Calvin, the qualifications of true corporeality require that the body be contained in a place with its own dimensions and its own shape. In order to uphold the "human-ness" of Christ, Calvin repudiates those who described Christ's earthly experience of being born of a woman, hanging on the cross, being laid in a tomb, and reigning in heaven after the resurrection, as a special temporary dispensation. Calvin compares this perspective with an ancient heterodox view in which Christ in heaven is portrayed as having only the appearance of a man. Although he does not explicitly mention the name of his source, he applies Tertullian's words, "What is this except Marcion resuscitated from hell? For who doubts that if Christ's body existed in this state, it would be a phantasm?"[8] With the help of this quotation, Calvin lists Marcion as a negative ancient example and writes, "And how much does this open the window for Marcion, if the body of Christ appears mortal and humble in one place and in another place is considered immortal and glorious?"[9] The reference to Marcion becomes a way to quash any opinion that denies the qualifications of true corporeality. Calvin's portrayal of the church as it struggles between orthodoxy and heresy is thus staged in terms of exemplary and erroneous ancient writers.

From the early years of the Reformation, references to the ancient fathers emerged as a way to critique the established church. Calvin's references to the ancient church often serve as historical evidence for pointing out how far the late medieval church has strayed from early church practice. When he defends the partaking of both the bread and the wine, for example, Calvin argues that there are extant church histories, namely books of ancient writers, that give evidence of the practice of Communion with both kinds of substances, not just with bread.[10] Calvin uses references to the ancient church to emphasize the distance between the theology and practices of the early church and that of his opponents. Like Luther's use of the fathers against the late medieval Catholic theologians, Calvin's citation of the ancient fathers has a polemical intent. Yet Calvin goes beyond Luther's use of the medieval fathers (namely Luther's seeking them for affirmation of his views), since he is eager to highlight the dissimilarities between the traditions of the church fathers and the late medieval Catholic Church rather than to emphasize the affinity between the early church and his own theology. While Luther also points out differences from the early church in order to refute some Catholic claims, Calvin in the early stages of his career chooses to emphasize the disjuncture between the early church tradition and the late medieval Catholic tradition.

Meanwhile, like Luther, Calvin draws heavily from passages in Scripture to explain and defend his views of the Lord's Supper. Although explicit references to the church fathers are missing, it would be inaccurate to say that Calvin did not apply his knowledge of the early church to his views of the Eucharist. His familiarity with the work of early theologians is most evident in his marginal notations. When he argues for the distribution of Communion in the form of both bread and wine to the laity, he briefly lists several ancient sources, including Eusebius, Cassiodorus, Chrysostom, Augustine, Jerome, Tertullian, and (Pseudo) Cyprian.[11] In the dedicatory epistle that accompanies the 1536 edition (addressed to the king of France), Calvin devotes a section to countering the accusation that the Evangelicals (those who claim to follow the gospel) have thrown out the church fathers. In the development of his theology, Calvin's working knowledge of the father expands through his contact with other reformers and his increasing access to the published editions of the fathers' works. During Calvin's lifetime, a great number of patristic texts, including church councils, became available in print, though the Greek fathers were usually published first in Latin translations. Calvin's interest in and use of the works of the fathers grow as he becomes more involved in doctrinal controversies with other Protestants. In subsequent editions of the *Institutes*, he does not diminish his arguments from Scripture; rather, he adds further support from the fathers, resulting in a more lengthy discussion of the Lord's Supper and an ever-expanding edition of the *Institutes*.

## 1539 Edition

Along with other significant changes, Calvin begins to enlist the church fathers for support and confirmation of his views in the 1539 edition of the *Institutes*. Specifically two ancient figures emerge as positive examples in his discussion on the Lord's Supper: Augustine, whom he appeals to three times, and Cyril of Alexandria. First, in emphasizing the importance of faith, Calvin writes, "Augustine whom they appeal to as their patron . . . indicates that eating itself is of faith and not of the mouth."[12] Calvin mentions Augustine's opinion to support the necessity of faith to constitute spiritual eating; it is a lack of faith, he argues, that barricades the unfaithful from spiritual eating. Calvin uses Augustine's words to set up a basis for rejecting the notion that there can be any kind of spiritual eating without faith. Second, Calvin refers to Augustine in a passing cursory remark. In his explanation of how the body of Christ is of a fleshly nature that exists in a certain location and in its own form, Calvin tells us how he is aligned with Augustine. In light of the question about whether a certain defined region of heaven is assigned to Christ, Calvin writes, "However I respond with Augustine that this is the most curious and superfluous question, nevertheless we only believe that he is in heaven."[13] In this case, there is no direct citation or even an explanation of Augustine's view. Third, toward the end of the chapter on the Lord's Supper, Calvin presents it as something that ignites charity, peace, and consensus among participants. He writes: "As we bear the care of our body, so we ought to care also for our brothers who are members of our body. For this reason Augustine so often calls this sacrament the bond of love."[14] Ironically, while Calvin cites Augustine for discussing charity and compassion concerning the sacrament of the Lord's Supper, the divisive debates over the Eucharist often frustrated many attempts to reach a consensus. Apart from Augustine, Calvin mentions Cyril of Alexandria for support. In this case, Calvin's appeal to Cyril's interpretation of the Eucharist elucidates the connection between partaking of the elements and participating in new life. By aligning himself with Cyril, Calvin recognizes a lineage of "correct" interpretation.

At the same time, Calvin also mentions ancient writers to denounce beliefs and practices that he opposes, such as the sacrificial understanding of the Eucharist. He writes: "If it is a question of approving a sham sacrifice such as the papists have contrived in the Mass, the ancient writers do not support such sacrilege at all."[15] Here Calvin employs the strategy of emphasizing dissimilarity. No specific names are offered because, in fact, many church fathers utilized sacrificial imagery to describe the Eucharist. Although Calvin returns to offer an explanation, his intention is to demonstrate the discontinuity between the sayings of the ancient writers and late medieval Catholic views.

At the same time Calvin does not see the church fathers as infallible. His willingness to criticize and "correct" the ancient writers is apparent from an early stage. He writes: "I observe that the ancient writers also misinterpreted this memorial in a way not consonant with the Lord's institution, because their Supper displayed some appearance of repeated or at least renewed sacrifice . . . Not content with the simple and genuine institution of Christ, they have turned aside too much to the shadows of the law."[16] Calvin portrays their mistakes as tendencies toward one extreme or another. While Calvin wants to uphold the fathers' piety, he judges that they have misunderstood the Eucharist in their descriptions of renewed sacrifice. Nevertheless, in the same year, in his *Reply to Sadoleto* (1539), Calvin argues that the Protestant churches are faithful adherents to the early church tradition.

## 1543 Edition

The 1543 edition of the *Institutes* includes 418 more references to the fathers than the previous 1539 edition.[17] A share of these additional references surfaces in the discussion over the Lord's Supper.[18] Calvin's quotations of the fathers reflect his use of the patristic editions produced by the Christian humanists of Basel and Paris.[19] Building on his references to Augustine from the 1539 *Institutes*, Calvin continues to cite Augustine. In his famous treatise *On Christian Doctrine* Augustine states that eating the flesh of Christ ought to be understood as a figure. Calvin returns to this point frequently because the Eucharist as a figure defies a literal corporeal presence. Yet when Augustine's words seem to express a corporeal meaning, such as when he writes that "three thousand men who were converted by Peter's preaching by believing drank Christ's blood,"[20] Calvin prefers to emphasize the importance of faith, lest Augustine's words be taken to support a carnal eating. Calvin argues that in many *other* passages "Augustine highly commends that benefit of faith for through it our souls are as much refreshed by partaking of Christ's flesh as bodies are by the bread they eat."[21]

For further support, Calvin backs up this understanding with a reference to Chrysostom, who "writes the same thing in another passage."[22] Yet Augustine and Chrysostom did not always mean the same thing. When Chrysostom says, "Christ makes us his body not by faith only but by the very thing itself," Calvin explains this statement by emphasizing a different point altogether. He says that Chrysostom means that such good as Christ's presence and the associated blessing are not obtained from any other source than faith, but that he only wishes to exclude the possibility that anyone, when he hears faith mentioned, should conceive of it as mere imagining.[23] Calvin feels a need to explain what Chrysostom meant, lest anyone should misunderstand him or want to misuse his writings. Calvin also cites Chrysostom in order to condemn the liturgical practice of communing only once a year. Complaining that this custom was thrust in by the devil's artifice, Calvin argues that prescribing one day a year renders people slothful the rest of the year. He writes,

> Indeed we see that already in Chrysostom's day this degrading abuse had crept in; but we can see at the same time how much it displeased him . . . [H]e exclaims: 'O custom, O presumption! In vain therefore, is a daily offering made; in vain we stand before the altar; there is no one who will partake along with us.' So far is Chrysostom from having approved this by lending it his authority![24]

Such statements are intended to strip away any semblance of ancient support for the late medieval tradition of infrequent Communion for the laity. If Calvin cannot procure the fathers' unequivocal support because they did not speak as he wanted, he at least tries to prevent his opponents from claiming the words of the ancient authorities.

Basing his work on the views of Augustine and Chrysostom, Calvin focuses on the duty of participation. His critique of the infrequent celebration of the Lord's Supper is based on Augustine's testimony that in the early church there was frequent Communion, such that "[s]ome partake daily . . . in some places no day passes when it is not offered, elsewhere, only on Saturday and Sunday; still elsewhere only on Sunday."[25] Such citations of Augustine are not necessarily meant to provide prescriptive guidelines for Genevan or other Reformed churches of the sixteenth century. Rather, descriptions from the ancient church are meant to provide a sharp contrast to the practices of the late medieval church in order to emphasize dissimilarity—a recurring theme. Calvin then looks to Chrysostom to provide the rebuke for the laxity he observes in current church practices of Communion. Calvin claims that it is the duty of holy persons to rebuke laxity in order to avoid complicity or the permission of indifference. Iden-tifying the unwillingness to correct as a lack of holiness, Calvin finds an example in Chrysostom's *Homilies on Ephesians* that criticizes the with-drawal from partaking:

> It is not said to him who dishonored the banquet, "Why did you recline at Table?" but "Why did you come in?" Whoever does not partake of the mysteries is wicked and shameless to be present there . . . So when you stand among those who prepare themselves with prayer to receive the most holy food, in the fact that you have not withdrawn, you have confessed that you are one of their number, but at the end you do not partake! Would it not be better for you not to have been present?[26]

Calvin then offers a list of the church fathers who support partaking of both elements. Calvin's strategy is to use the testimony of the fathers to legitimate his stance against the late medieval practice of withholding the cup from the laity. He begins by claiming extant church histories, books of ancient writers that give evidence of the partaking of both bread and wine. Next he offers a list of specific quotations from Tertullian, Ambrose, Jerome, Chrysostom, and Augustine:

> "The flesh," says Tertullian, "is fed with the body and blood of Christ that the soul may be nourished of God." "How," says Ambrose to Theo-dosius, "will you with such hands receive the sacred body of the Lord? How will you make bold to partake of the cup of his precious blood with your lips?" Jerome mentions, "the priests who perform the Eucharist and distribute the Lord's blood to the people." Chrysostom says: "Not as in the Old Law the Priest ate part, the people part, but one body and one cup are offered to all. Those things which pertain to the Eucharist are all common to priest and people." Augustine in numerous passages attests the same thing.[27]

In the following section, Calvin continues his list of church fathers. He writes, "Let all the Greek and Latin writers be read, and such evidence will be found in abundance."[28] This statement is not so much an attestation to the fact that Calvin has actually read all the Greek and Latin writers, but rather it demonstrates a rhetoric of trust that much evidence could be found among the ancient writers, although Calvin will only offer a sampling. He continues,

> Gregory, whom you can rightly call the last bishop of Rome, taught that the custom was kept in his time: "You learn what is the blood of the Lamb not by hearing but by drinking; his blood is poured into the

mouths of believers." . . . For so speaks Gelasius: "We have found that some, receiving only the portion of the sacred body, refrain from the cup. Doubtless, since they seem to be bound by some sort of superstition, they are either to receive the sacraments entire or to be entirely barred from them." For this mystery cannot be divided without great sacrilege. Men heeded those reasons of Cyprian which of course ought to move a Christian mind. "How," he says, "do we teach or call upon them to shed their blood in confession of Christ, if we deny Christ's blood to those about to fight? Or how do we make them fit for the cup of martyrdom, if we do not first in the church by the right of communion admit them to drink the cup of the Lord?"[29]

These two lists of fathers seem to be the closest thing we have to an existing anthology from Calvin, albeit brief and probably copied from memory from the works of other reformers.

Finally, Calvin refers to Augustine and Chrysostom one more time concerning the mass as a sacrifice. Building on the 1539 edition of his *Institutes*, in which he simply claimed that the ancient writers do not support a sacrifice executed in the Supper, Calvin writes, "Hebrews in the animal victims offered to God celebrated a prophecy of the future victim which Christ offered; Christians by the most holy offering and partaking of the body of Christ, celebrate the remembrance of a sacrifice already made . . . Consequently Augustine himself in many passages interprets it as nothing but a sacrifice of praise."[30] Calvin adds that Chrysostom also speaks in the same sense, but does not give any specific examples. In the subsequent 1559 edition of the *Institutes*, he will repeat these references to Augustine and Chrysostom to dismiss the mass as a sacrifice and add other citations from Augustine.[31] For Calvin, Christ's death on the cross was a unique sacrifice that occurred once in history as an unrepeatable act; therefore a commemoration of the sacrifice does not necessitate a reenactment of the sacrifice. He further argues that it is wrong to claim the honor of Christ's priesthood since, according to Augustine, "it would be the voice of Antichrist that a bishop is intercessor between God and man."[32] Here Calvin's use of Augustine has a subversive quality and ultimately undermines the authority given to the bishop in the church hierarchy. Even so, it would be wrong to assume that Calvin supported a radical equality or anarchy. Rather, by drawing on the early church fathers for his interpretive strategies, Calvin is not trying to obliterate church authority per se but to make room at the table for a new kind of authority (as well as a new church order), not as a bishop but as a reformer.

## Melanchthon's Use of the Fathers

Despite the contentious debates between Calvin and later Lutherans, an important source for the use of fathers (for both sides) was Melanchthon. In fact, both Reformed and Lutheran theologians appealed to Melanchthon for additional support. Since various scholars have already written on Melanchthon's use of the fathers,[33] I will simply offer a brief summary here.

Melanchthon considered the secondary authority of the fathers and councils as included in and not excluded by the appeal to the authority of Scriptures. In his use of the fathers, he accepted their authority only through the filter of Scripture. For example, in his letter to Oecolampadius in 1529, Melanchthon argued that although some statements of the ancients seem to favor Oecolampadius' view of Christ's presence in heaven, a judgment about heavenly things must be made in accordance with the word of God.[34] Consequently, Melanchthon considered some fathers better sources than others. His *On the Church and the Authority of God's Word* offers, in addition to enumerations of councils and synods, his opinion on a list of early church fathers, including Origen, Pseudo-Dionysius, Ambrose, Jerome, Tertullian, Basil, Gregory Nazianzus, Chrysostom, Cyprian, Hilary, Irenaeus, and Augustine (especially Luther's anti-Pelagian Augustine).[35] Melanchthon clearly modified the unquestioned value of the fathers, but it was his reverence for the ancient tradition (and his desire to prove his erudition) that caused him to seek out the fathers in the first place. While he set up a rule not to teach anything without precedent, he also sought to redeem those ancient fathers who, he felt, had thought correctly but had spoken badly. Melanchthon's appeal to antiquity was an effort to find confirmation of his own interpretations of the word of God. His use of the fathers, in turn, helped shape Calvin's estimation of specific fathers and prompted him to accept the ancient tradition as selectively valuable. Like Melanchthon, Calvin also provided theological reasons for favoring or rejecting ancient interpretations.

## Calvin's New Testament Commentaries

Calvin's desire for clarity and brevity in his comments on the Bible emerged as a response to methods used by other reformers.[36] In his own work on biblical exegesis, he opted for a method that would demonstrate what he termed "lucid brevity," as a *via media* between the two extremes of his contemporaries, Bucer and Melanchthon.[37] Just as Calvin found Melanchthon's "renaissance" method of arriving at definitive theological points (*loci*) inadequate because it omitted important points in the text, he saw Bucer's method of combining theological doctrine and straightforward commentary as leading to unnecessary verbosity and obscurity.[38] Calvin's solution consisted of a division of labor. He confined the *Institutes* to a discussion of many of the doctrinal issues, while in his commentaries he usually offered a verse-by-verse exposition of the text that explored its literary and historical aspects in addition to its theological import. Since he prepared the *Institutes* to discuss doctrinal questions arising from biblical text,[39] Calvin planned to keep his commentaries brief without many digressions. Because of his principle of "lucid brevity," his commentaries do not contain as many references to the fathers as the *Institutes* and his treatises. Even so, Calvin considered the patristic references in his commentaries vital to an understanding of the biblical text.

In his dedicatory preface to his *Romans Commentary* of 1540, Calvin describes the ancient commentators as those "whose godliness, learning, sanctity and age have secured them great authority so that we should not despise anything."[40] Despite his rhetoric of respect for the fathers, Calvin's deference does not denote wholehearted acceptance of all ancient teachings. In the preface to the proposed edition of Chrysostom's *Homilies*, written sometime between 1538 and 1540,[41] Calvin states that many of the fathers' commentaries were no longer extant or were not very helpful in biblical interpretation.[42] The divergent comments on the fathers in these two works of Calvin reveal an amalgam of competing forces—the rediscovery of the sources of Christian antiquity by reform-minded Catholics, the theological and religious revolution initiated by Luther, and the sometimes tense relationship between the patristic tradition and Scripture in the mind of a reformer.[43] Calvin's underlying view, a predominant one in his time, is that the church fathers are authoritative voices in the interpretation of Scripture. His willingness to criticize ancient commentators and even reject those interpretations that do not clarify the plain meaning of Scripture shows the limitations of the fathers' authority for him. Yet even criticism can actually mask real respect.[44] Calvin's approach to the fathers is one of reserved acceptance; he claims to accept the fathers, but in cases where he does not, it is for a good reason.

While Calvin recognizes the value of the early church fathers by demonstrating their support as an authority beyond Scripture,[45] he clearly establishes Scripture as the normative basis for all theological doctrine.[46] For example, in his polemics against Pighius, Calvin discounts a position supported by tradition when he declares that the fathers are often mistaken and that their assertions have been variously interpreted. The ancient doctors are thus a possible source of information, but are neither as necessary nor as obligatory as the Holy Scriptures. Compared to the Bible, they are on the same plane as nature or history: they need to be interpreted in the light of Scripture in order for their value to be assessed. Scripture thus remains the criterion of judgment for the fathers.

While Calvin appeals repeatedly to the teaching of the fathers, he simultaneously recognizes their human status and denies them any absolute authority. Calvin believes that his view is verified by private and public witness, where private witness signifies the internal testimony of the Spirit speaking to the reader and public witness represents the common consensus of the true church, which includes the church fathers. Yet when common consensus is lacking, Calvin seeks to clarify his biblical interpretation in the midst of competing opinions. In a letter to Simon Grynaeus, Calvin writes, "Since in this life we cannot hope to achieve a permanent agreement in our understanding of every passage of Scripture, however desirable that would be, we must be careful not to be carried away by the lust for something new . . . but to do what is necessary and to depart from the opinions of earlier exegetes only when it is beneficial to do so."[47] In the same letter, Calvin says that it is almost the only duty of the exegete to make truly understandable the meaning of the writer.[48] To do so, Calvin looks to the historical, geographical, and institutional circumstances that are determinative for the author.[49] For Calvin, it is necessary to build on the foundation of earlier exegetes, but his purpose is not simply to pass on everything as is. Rather, it is an effort to recreate a semi-idealized past and then draw from it connections to the contemporary context.

Calvin's use of the fathers is a masterly sixteenth-century attempt to relate Protestantism to historic Christianity, to trace many of its doctrines to the early church and to show how error had arisen.[50] In his commentaries, Calvin accepts the fathers as commentators whose views must be taken into account, yet he is also willing to debate with them.[51] Calvin sees the fathers as partners in conversation; their teaching is not binding on him, nor does it foreclose the range of his exegetical options. Rather, the commentaries often become the place where Calvin demonstrates his quarrels with them.[52] In the context of the diverse views on the Eucharist, he is not only interested in the historic early church but also returns to the fathers to recast them in light of the sixteenth-century Reformation context.

Calvin asserts that the traditions of the fathers must be examined to observe what they contain. "If we discover that they have no other tendency than to the pure worship of God," he writes, "we may embrace them, but if they draw us away from the pure and simple worship of God, we must reject them."[53] In other words, the value of the fathers' sayings depends on their ability to guide believers to the pure worship of God. Because his intent is to select what is useful for illuminating Scripture,

Calvin's use of a particular ancient father sometimes focuses only a phrase or partial view of that father.[54] Calvin writes his commentary on 1 Corinthians in 1546, then on the book of John (1552), and afterwards on the Synoptic Gospels (1555)[55] because he reasons that the Synoptic Gospels should be understood in the light of the teachings of the Epistles and the Fourth Gospel. In the work of interpreting these scriptural texts on the Lord's Supper, he utilizes the fathers as both positive and negative examples.

## 1 Corinthians 11

> *Indeed, there must be heresies among you, so that it will become clear who among you are genuine. When you come together, it is not really to eat the Lord's Supper. For when the time comes to eat, each of you goes ahead with your own supper and one goes hungry and another becomes drunk. What? Have you not houses to eat and to drink? Or do you despise the church of God and shame them that have not? What shall I say to you? Shall I praise you in this? I do not praise you. For I have received of the Lord that which also I delivered to you, That the Lord Jesus the same night in which he was betrayed took bread: And when he had given thanks he broke and said, Take, eat this is my body, which is broken for you; this do in remembrance of me.*

In the passages concerning the Lord's Supper in 1 Corinthians 11, Calvin begins with a general reference to the ancient fathers to delineate the difference between "schism" and "heresy." He claims, "It is well-known in what sense the ancients used those two terms, and what distinction they made between heretics and schismatics."[56] Based on the writings of the fathers, Calvin describes heresy as disagreements over doctrine and schism as alienation of affection when anyone withdraws from the church from envy, dislike of the pastors, or ill nature.[57] Calvin sees schism and heresy on a continuum, where one leads to the other:

> Schisms are secret grudges – when we do not see that agreement which ought to subsist among the pious – when inclinations at variance with each other are at work – when every one is mightily pleased with his or her own way and finds fault with everything that is done by others. Heresies are when the evil proceeds to such a pitch that open hostility is discovered and persons deliberately divide themselves into opposite parties.[58]

Yet even heresies serve a good purpose, Calvin argues. When the Apostle Paul says that "there must be heresies," he means that believers must encounter heretics so that the good may shine forth more conspicuously. Calvin attributes such trials to the providence of God so that the "hypocrites are detected."[59] Ironically, however, he says that believers must not enter into thorny disputes, then blames belligerent opponents for initiating controversy and breaking up the unity of the church. While the purpose of the Eucharist is not to create divisions among believers, doctrinal differences over the Eucharist are real indications of the diverse understandings of Christ, the church, and salvation.

Calvin looks to the fathers as resources or secondary aids to assist with biblical interpretation.[60] Although his admiration for the fathers outweighs his criticism of them, there is a greater tendency in his commentaries to include a critique of their works and an appeal to extenuating circumstances in order to excuse their language. In reference to specific fathers, Calvin mentions three: Chrysostom (twice), Tertullian, and Augustine. Despite Chrysostom's doctrine of the merit of good works, Calvin resonates with Chrysostom's concern to unfold the simple sense of Scripture for the common people and in theory adopts his principle, if not his conclusions. In his desire for lucid brevity, Calvin's appreciation of Chrysostom as an exegete is based on the Antiochene's refusal to engage in flights of fanciful exegesis.[61] Because of Chrysostom's rejection of allegorical interpretation, the references to him in Calvin's commentary on 1 Corinthians outnumber that of any other book in the New Testament.[62] Although Calvin's plans to translate Chrysostom's homilies did not come to fruition, the idea to do so seems to have been part of a larger plan to make the works of the church fathers available in the vernacular in order to help the faithful understand the Bible.[63] This intended project is significant because it shows Calvin's understanding of the potential usefulness of the fathers in biblical exegesis.

Calvin mentions Chrysostom for two reasons: (1) to correct potentially misleading comments and (2) to append additional criticisms to his own opponents. The first reason arises in the discussion of 1 Corinthians 11:19, when Calvin modifies Chrysostom's rendering of the particle "in order that" (ἵνα). Chrysostom understood the particle as setting off a result clause to denote the existence, but not the cause, of divisions and heresies.[64] Calvin, however, translates the particle as the introductory word in a purpose clause. For him, Paul's words "there must be factions among you ἵνα [in order that]" indicate that heresies and schisms do not happen by chance but by the *certa Dei providentia*, for the purpose of testing his people as gold in a furnace.[65] This emphasis stems from Calvin's rejection of Chrysostom's tendency to preach on human free will. Calvin's *Annotations of Chrysostom* illustrates that he cites Chrysostom's words to clarify potentially misleading comments by a selective use of Chrysostom's viewpoint. For example, Calvin underlines the following sentence in Chrysostom's Sixtieth Sermon *Ad populum Antiochenum*: "At that time the table was not of silver nor the cup of gold, the very cup out of which Christ gave his own blood to the disciples: nevertheless both those things were precious and awesome, because they were filled with spirit."[66] This sentence is meant to indicate that true meaning does not lie in the outer appearance of gold or silver adornments in a church. From Chrysostom's remark, Calvin finds room to criticize the late medieval emphasis on the act of the ritual. In her analysis of Calvin's use of Chrysostom, Irena Backus writes,

> Chrysostom, true to his principles, incites his hearers to perform concrete good works, which are directly inspired by an act of faith . . . At the same time he attempts to inculcate an austerity of life that would help Christians living in the world draw a little nearer to the ideal of the *vita angelica*. In other words, the passage when read in context advocates those very good works that Calvin warned his readers against in the unfinished preface. However, taken out of context, the passage does bear resemblance to a critique of Roman Catholic practices common in Calvin's time. Read with those critiques in mind, it could legitimately be taken as a warning issued by the fourth-century church against an excessively ornate celebration of the Mass. The austere model of church office was the one also adopted by the early church – that was the lesson Calvin chose to draw from Chrysostom's 60th Sermon *Ad populum Antiochenum*.[67]

In his analysis of 1 Corinthians 11:21, Calvin highlights Paul's admonition to the Corinthians that the mere coming together, or the act of gathering, does not constitute the eating of the Lord's Supper. Calvin sets up his next two references to specific church fathers with a warning about how greatly antiquity can influence a long-continued custom even when it is not sanctioned by a single declaration of the word of God.[68] In this case, Calvin is quick to establish the criteria of biblical support in order to debunk a church custom, even an ancient one, for even ancient things are subservient to the primacy of Scripture. Trying to ascertain the origin of abuse of eating (or overeating) at the Lord's Supper or the closely related fellowship meal, Calvin turns to Chrysostom and Tertullian: "Chrysostom is of the opinion that it originated in the love feasts and that while the rich had been accustomed to bring with them from their houses the means of feasting with the poor, they afterwards began to exclude the poor and to hoard their delicacies by themselves."[69] Calvin procures from

Chrysostom an example of wrongdoing on which he can build his case against contemporary abuses of the Lord's Supper. Even though they might not be the same problem, they can be categorized as corruptions of the Lord's Supper. The second reason for recalling Chrysostom's comments is to identify the possible origins of the abuse and to add further criticism to what he sees as permeations of that abuse. Yet Calvin does not expand on Chrysostom's moral teachings on this passage. Instead, Chrysostom's comments serve to verify the historical abuse of a traditional rite in antiquity and to locate the late medieval eucharistic ritual on a trajectory of corruption.

In his selective use of Chrysostom, Calvin highlights certain aspects while he omits other points that are central for Chrysostom. He uses Chrysostom in a punctiliar fashion to bring forth a single issue raised by Chrysostom, not necessarily to reflect Chrysostom's complete theological views.[70] When the Corinthians first gathered in an assembly, all people, rich and poor, came together. This assembly was followed by a banquet, and Paul was admonishing the conduct of the Corinthians at the banquet. The Corinthians' conduct bears no relation to the brotherly affection characteristic of the assembly; therefore, at the banquet, "it is not possible to eat the Lord's Supper," or "the supper that you eat there is certainly not the Lord's Supper."[71] According to Chrysostom, the supper that the Corinthians were eating lacked the very essence and distinctive mark of the Lord's Supper, namely commonality. By making the supper a private matter to the exclusion of the poor, they deprived the table of its essential rationale—that it must be "*koinos*," or communal.[72] Chrysostom explains that by the use of the word "Lord's," a community of the feast ought to be expressed.[73] And while he emphasizes overcoming division and exclusion, Calvin uses Chrysostom's words to show the distortion of "right practice." What Calvin finds useful in Chrysostom's words is the recognition of a degenerated practice that provides further arguments to relinquish the corrupted version of the Supper. Thus Chrysostom's words provide the basis for Calvin to build his rhetoric of judgment toward the "wrong" practice of the Lord's Supper. In addition to citing Chrysostom, Calvin also adds a simple reference from Tertullian to provide historical validation of combining fellowship meals (or love feasts) with Communion. Although Calvin allows that this custom may have been a gesture of fraternal affection and consisted of alms, it clearly fell apart over time and was not in accordance with the Lord's Supper. Calvin's rhetoric continues on the course of emphasizing the degeneration of a custom. By observing the sacrament in a wrong way, Calvin claims that it "leads us to profane the holy sacrament."[74] For Calvin, the heart of the problem lies in the fact that the Corinthians were mixing two events that should be kept distinct from each other. He reproves the abuse that had crept in among the Corinthians because they were mixing up profane banquets with the sacred and spiritual feast and did so with contempt for the poor.[75] For Calvin, Paul is arguing for the purity of the sacrament since he does not want the *sacrum mysterium* to be mixed up with ordinary feasts.[76]

In the subsequent set of verses (1 Corinthians 11:23-29), Calvin's interpretation shows that, since the abuse has been exposed, it is now necessary to show the proper method of rectifying it.[77] Although he mentions no specific father at this point, it is important to notice that Calvin continues his comments on the Lord's Supper on the premise of abuse, which he has already established in the previous verses through his use of Chrysostom. If we look at the citations of Chrysostom in the verses preceding Calvin's passage on the Lord's Supper (namely on verses 19 and 21), we see that Chrysostom serves as a springboard for Calvin's interpretation of the Corinthian pericope. Calvin uses Chrysostom's criticism of early abuses as a legitimating reason to correct the late medieval abuses of the eucharistic rite.

In his explication of the Lord's Supper, Calvin criticizes the late medieval Catholic theologians for deviating from Christ's first institution and corrupting it "in a thousand ways."[78] Yet by this point Calvin considers not only his differences with the Catholics, but also his debates with the Lutherans. He writes that the participation in the body of Christ as presented in the Supper does not require a local presence, nor the descent of Christ, nor infinite extension, because Christ is received by believers while he remains in heaven.[79] Upholding the use of metonymy (a figure of speech in which a word stands for something closely related, such as bread for Christ's body), Calvin explains that Christ (identified as *res*, the thing signified) is not applied to the sign simply as a representation of it, but rather as a symbol by which the reality is presented to believers.[80] While in other writings Calvin attributes this kind of language to Augustine, he is content to argue at this point that he regards it as beyond all controversy that the reality is here joined with the sign. Resisting the Lutherans' accusation that he does not believe in Christ's real presence in the Eucharist, Calvin writes, "[The fact] is that we do not less truly become participants in Christ's body with respect to spiritual efficacy."[81] Several verses later, Calvin cites Augustine in his discussion of unworthy eating and argues there are various degrees of unworthy participation, so that the Lord punishes some slightly and others more severely. He then makes the distinction between those who eat unworthily, as in the case of weak persons, and those who, without any repentance or faith, do not partake of anything but the sign. For Calvin, Augustine means the same thing when he says that "the wicked receive Christ merely in the sacrament, which he expresses more clearly elsewhere, when he says that the other Apostles ate the bread—the Lord; but Judas only the bread of the Lord."[82] The question of unworthy eating would continue to be a point of contention between the Lutheran and Reformed interpreters of 1 Corinthians.

## John 6

> *I am the living bread that came down from heaven. Whoever eats of this bread will live forever; and the bread that I will give for the life of the world is my flesh. The Jews then disputed among themselves, saying, "How can this man give us his flesh to eat?" So Jesus said to them, "Very truly, I tell you, unless you eat the flesh of the Son of Man and drink his blood, you have no life in you. Those who eat my flesh and drink my blood have eternal life and I will raise them up on the last day; for my flesh is true food and my blood is true drink. Those who eat my flesh and drink my blood abide in me and I in them . . . It is the Spirit that quickens; the flesh profits nothing. The words which I speak to you are spirit and life.*

Calvin considers the Fourth Gospel a key to understanding the other Gospels. His interpretation of John 6:51-56 and 63 includes a general reference to the ancient fathers as well as specific references to Augustine and Chrysostom. In his explanation, he rejects two interpretations of the eating of Christ's body and blood. On the one hand, he dismisses those who infer from Christ's use of the metaphor that the act of eating is a mental exercise of faith, as Calvin's own interpretation of Jesus' words does not permit a sense of "eating" or receiving Christ simply in the mind of the believer. On the other hand, Calvin also rejects an interpretation that identifies the objective person of Christ with the bread as if the bread encloses and contains the actual, physical matter of Christ. For Calvin, "eating Christ" is the effect, rather than the cause, of faith in Christ. Consequently, he denies that the outward symbol of Christ's flesh, the bread, contains within it any objective sense of Christ's flesh, even though he affirms that Christ's gift of life through his flesh is attached to the symbol.[83]

In his discussion of John 6:51, Calvin calls Christ the living bread in the context of the Lord's Supper. He argues that Christ's sacrifice, which was offered only once, is efficacious in the Eucharist. This reference to Christ's sacrifice and the Eucharist triggers a polemical remark against the Roman Mass.[84] Like other Protestant reformers, Calvin rejects the notion of the Eucharist as a repeated sacrifice. According to him, Christ claims for himself the office of sacrificing his flesh, so that priests ought not to take upon themselves in the mass what belongs exclusively to the one high priest.[85] Although many early church fathers linked this Johannine passage with the Eucharist, Calvin's exposition of verse 53 resists such a connection, just as Luther had done before. Calvin claims that the passage itself does not mention the sacrament explicitly; likewise, Luther dismisses the use of John 6 for eucharistic discussions because the events of the chapter take place before the institution of the Eucharist and the passage is spoken in a spiritual figure. Calvin argues that the ancients made a grave mistake in supposing that little children were deprived of eternal life if they were not given the Eucharist, and argues that Jesus' words do not refer to the Lord's Supper, but to the continual communication apart from the reception of the Lord's Supper.[86] From this, it seems that Calvin's dismissal of John 6 follows Luther's, but in fact he is willing to deviate from the early church fathers' practice of explaining this passage in light of their eucharistic theology. Despite the striking similarity of terminology in John 6 to that of other passages on the Lord's Supper, Calvin disagrees with the ancient fathers by claiming, "When [Christ] uses the word 'eat' He is exhorting us to faith."[87] Calvin does not want eternal life or salvation contingent on a ritual or an act, even if it is a holy act.

Calvin's continual references to eating the flesh of Christ, however, make it difficult to dismiss the connections with the Lord's Supper. What purpose could Calvin have for dismissing the passage in John as related to the Lord's Supper? On the one hand, Calvin resisted such a connection because it was not the "plain and literal" sense; on the other hand, it would have been just as easy for him to explain how John 6 related to the Eucharist, thereby concurring with the ancient fathers. Yet the sixteenth-century debates over the Lord's Supper haunted Calvin. In 1522, when his *Commentary on John* was written, he still had hopes for a common agreement on the Lord's Supper among the main Protestant reformers, including the Lutherans. Well aware that John 6 was a point of contention between Luther and Zwingli in their debates over the Lord's Supper, Calvin was eager to offer a position that would be amenable to both sides. Therefore, in his explanation of verse 53, he argued that this pericope did not relate to the Lord's Supper, but to the uninterrupted communication of *the flesh of Christ* that is obtained apart from the use of the Lord's Supper. Calvin referred to Augustine to validate his initial premise that "it would have been foolish and unreasonable to discourse about the Lord's Supper, before [Christ] had instituted it," and declared, "It is certain, then, that [Christ] now speaks of the perpetual and ordinary manner of eating the flesh of Christ, which is done by faith only."[88] For Calvin, this is the reason why the Evangelist John makes no mention of the Lord's Supper and also why Augustine, in explaining this chapter, does not touch on the Lord's Supper until he comes to his conclusion, where he shows that this mystery is symbolically represented whenever churches celebrate the Lord's Supper. For Calvin, Augustine confirms that the hunger of the soul needs to be fed with heavenly bread.[89] Although Calvin dismisses a direct correlation between the passage in John 6 and the Lord's Supper, he manages through the words of Augustine to sneak in his view of the spiritual eating of the heavenly bread, and simultaneously aligns himself with both Augustine and the Evangelist John. Therefore Calvin's references to Augustine serve to provide credibility for and a subtle reentry of Calvin's own view,[90] even while accepting the Lutheran premise that John 6 is unrelated to the Lord's Supper.

Despite his rejection of a sacramental meaning for this passage, one cannot deny that Calvin's exegesis of John 6 has eucharistic overtones. In fact, in explaining verse 55, Calvin says, "For when Christ expressly mentions food and drink, Christ declares that the life which he bestows is complete in every respect . . . provided that we eat his flesh and drink his blood. Thus also in the Lord's Supper, which corresponds to this doctrine, not satisfied with the symbol of *the bread*, he adds also *the cup*."[91] Finding it hard to resist the connections to the Eucharist, he explains that the doctrine that is taught in this passage is sealed in the Lord's Supper.[92] It is noteworthy that, immediately after his rejection of an eucharistic interpretation of the passage in John 6, Calvin writes, "At the same time, I confess that there is nothing said here that is not figured and actually presented to believers in the Lord's Supper."[93] By the time of the *Institutio* in 1559, Calvin explicitly relates John 6 with the Lord's Supper.

In his interpretation of the controversial verse 63, Calvin cites Chrysostom for correction and Augustine for support. He refers to Chrysostom only to demonstrate his dissatisfaction with Chrysostom's interpretation and to criticize him for attributing the phrase "the flesh profits nothing"[94] to the Jews' carnal hearing—that is, to a lack of understanding. He writes, "Chrysostom improperly, in my opinion, refers it to the Jews . . . but the words of Christ do not bear that meaning . . . Nor do I approve of the views of those who say, that the flesh of Christ profits, so far as he was crucified, but that, when it is eaten, it is of no advantage to us; for, on the contrary, we must eat it, that, having been crucified, it may profit."[95] Calvin's willingness to correct Chrysostom arises so that others may not be misinformed by such an interpretation. Calvin takes a more agreeable tone in his reference to Augustine:

> Augustine thinks that we ought to supply the word *only*, or *by itself*, as if it had been said, "The flesh alone, and by itself, profits not," because

it must be accompanied by the Spirit. This meaning accords well with the scope of the discourse, for Christ refers simply to the manner of eating. He does not, therefore, exclude every kind of usefulness, as if none could be obtained from his flesh; but he declares that, if it be separated from the Spirit, it will then be useless.[96]

In this case, Augustine serves as a guide for a better understanding of the Scriptures. Calvin takes the phrase "if it be separate from the Spirit, it will then be useless" to refer to Christ's flesh, eaten carnally without true faith.[97] He finds Augustine's words helpful for rejecting a purely "carnal eating." Throughout his explications of the Lord's Supper, he is at pains to stress the presence of both the substance of flesh and faith. Despite his general references to the ancients, which sometimes seem to portray the fathers as a monolithic group, Calvin clearly differentiates between them on points of biblical interpretation.

## Matthew 26

> *While they were eating, Jesus took a loaf of bread and after having blessed it he broke it, gave it to the disciples and said, "Take, eat: this is my body." Then he took the cup and after giving thanks he gave it to them, saying "Drink from it, all of you; for this is my blood of the covenant, which is poured out for many for the forgiveness of sins. . . ."*

In the *Harmony of the Gospels* Calvin collapses the synoptic gospel accounts and comments on Matthew 26:26-30, as well as Mark 14:22-26 and Luke 22:17-20. While some of Calvin's language is reminiscent of the church fathers, he only makes one general reference to the ancient doctors and one specific reference to Augustine. While the Johannine framework of the Last Supper places it before the beginning of Passover as an anticipation of the Passover, the synoptic version presents the Last Supper as a new version of the Passover meal, thereby replacing the old rite with a new one. Calvin favors the synoptic version and wants to make certain that the Lord's Supper is not seen as a continuation of the Passover meal, but rather as a new and more excellent supper.[98]

Calvin's commentary on this passage is interspersed with attacks against those whom he perceived to be his opponents, whether Roman Catholic, Spiritualist, or Gnesio-Lutheran. Against the Roman Catholics, Calvin argues that when Christ declares that the bread is his body, there is no change in the substance, but rather it is applied to a new purpose. Calvin believes that many have been "bewitched by the subtlety of the devil, [by the introduction of] the monster of transubstantiation."[99] Against the Spiritualists, he rejects Schwenckfeld's idea of celestial flesh and identifies Spiritualists as those who follow the Marcionite heresy. He reiterates that the word "consecrated" means that the bread becomes the symbol of Christ's flesh.[100] The bread, which provides nourishment of the body, is sanctified by Christ for a different use—that is, to be spiritual food. For Calvin, the conversion that occurs with the words of consecration is not from bread to body, but from bodily to spiritual nourishment. Calvin adds, "And this is the conversion which is spoken of by the ancient doctors of the Church."[101] Without any specific citations, he claims to express the common voice of the ancient church and to align himself with this voice. In addition to refuting Catholic theologians and Spiritualists, Calvin criticizes the Gnesio-Lutherans, whom he describes as "madmen" who reject the figure of Christ and improperly apply the word "body" to the bread, which is a sign of it.[102] In the same year as his *Commentary on the Synoptic Gospels*, Calvin publishes his first reply against the Lutheran Joachim Westphal. Therefore Calvin simultaneously addresses his eucharistic views in multiple genres besides his commentary, such as in his treatises criticizing Westphal and his followers.

Finally, in discussing the plain and literal sense of the Communion bread, Calvin mentions Augustine as a representative of the ancient church. By citing Augustine, he emphasizes that it is not an innovation to understand the bread as a symbol of Christ's body: "This principle of language has not been recently forged by us, but has been handed down by Augustine on the authority of the ancients and embraced by all, that the names of spiritual things are improperly ascribed to signs and that all the passages of Scripture in which the sacraments are mentioned, ought to be explained in this manner."[103] By portraying the source of his interpretation as Augustinian, Calvin strives to validate his interpretation as the "plain sense."

Although Calvin's commentary on the Synoptic Gospels includes only one reference to Augustine, his use of the fathers is not limited to explicit references. Even though Chrysostom is nowhere explicitly mentioned, a closer look at Calvin's gospel commentary shows how Chrysostom serves as a theological support to some points of Calvin's exegesis.[104] For example, in his explanation of Matthew 26:14, Calvin points out Judas's blindness to his own evil desires, and how he was hardened in wickedness, just as Chrysostom begins his exegesis of the verse with an exclamation about how great Judas' blindness was. Chrysostom observes that, even after partaking of the mysteries and being admitted to the most holy table, Judas does not change. From the start, Calvin echoes three themes from Chrysostom's introductory paragraph to the Matthew 26:26-28: the blindness of Judas; the lack of change on Judas' part, despite

Christ's admonition and inclusion in the Supper; and the intertextual evidence from Luke on the role of Satan. Calvin's selective use of Chrysostom's teachings also includes statements that Christ knew heretics would arise, forewarned his disciples of his impending passion and death, and assured them of his resurrection. One reason Calvin does not mention Chrysostom is that, although these interpretive conclusions have roots in Chrysostom's sermons, Calvin may have come across them through an intermediary source. Furthermore, many of these points were not contested in Calvin's day and enjoyed the consensus of many theologians.

## Conclusion

Against Catholic opponents, both Luther and Calvin claim Scripture as the source of their views and recognize sayings of the ancient fathers against doctrines and practices unsupported by Scripture. Most notably, they look to the fathers in order to emphasize: (1) support from the early church for their doctrinal stances and (2) dissonance of the early church tradition with late medieval Catholic practices. While Luther makes greater use of the first strategy by noting supportive ancients who confirm his interpretation, Calvin demonstrates a preference for the latter strategy of highlighting discontinuities, especially in his earliest writings. As the Lutherans and Calvinists engaged in further debates over the Eucharist, additional uses of the fathers become apparent.

In Calvin's commentaries concerning New Testament passages on the Lord's Supper, explicit references to the church fathers are not numerous. Although some scholars claim that Calvin "sees himself bound by and indebted to the exegetical tradition of the church, above all the early church, especially Augustine,"[105] Calvin is willing to transgress any boundary set by the church as long as it is according to the word of God, inspired by the Spirit, and beneficial to the church. His selective use of the ancient fathers demonstrates both his distinctive way of presenting their theological points as favorable to his interpretation and his readiness to offer "better" explanations of the fathers' works when they seem insufficient or incorrect. While Calvin mentions Tertullian once, he recalls Chrysostom and Augustine several times, and the cursory reference to Tertullian echoes what Calvin cites from Chrysostom. Recognizing the value of the fathers (although he is not bound by them), Calvin, like Luther before him, engages the ancient tradition as a means of reading and reevaluating them in light of Scripture, not in any sort of systematic assessment but as the opportunity arises. Unable to ignore some of the things he finds objectionable in the writings of the fathers, Calvin reveals his willingness, and occasionally his eagerness, to rectify what he deems to be misdirected interpretations.

In many cases, Calvin finds theological rapport with Augustine in support of his exegesis on the Lord's Supper. He usually names Augustine as a representative voice whose words reiterate his own view, even if he sometimes needs to resort to Augustine's "underlying intent" to reach a satisfactory interpretation. For historical confirmation and verification, Calvin recalls Chrysostom, and references to Chrysostom also serve as an opportunity to clarify a mistake or build an argument on a historical premise. Despite his praise for Chrysostom as the apex of Greek patristic achievement, Calvin also disagrees with him on several theological points. In such cases, Calvin brings up Chrysostom's sayings for critical reevaluation. For instance, in the *Preface to Chrysostom's Homily*, Calvin "apologizes" for Chrysostom's incomplete, imperfect interpretation, although he finds himself relating to Chrysostom's context of responding to the errors of the Arians.[106] Depicting himself in a "similar situation," Calvin finds in Chrysostom a source of rhetoric for responding to the "erroneous" views of the Lord's Supper for his own debates. More importantly, Calvin's respect for Chrysostom overrides his criticism because his own exegetical principles resonate with Chrysostom's method of expounding the clear and plain meaning of Scripture rather than the allegorical and mystical meaning. Whether he reads Augustine with an approving eye or Chrysostom with a critical eye, Calvin's references to the ancient fathers demonstrate the historical value of their texts in shaping his theological objectives.

Despite their efforts to define the Bible as the ultimate authority for Christian doctrine and practice, the reformers' call for all literate people to read the Bible for themselves threatened to diffuse the authority of Scripture too widely. Therefore there was increasing effort on all sides to define what the Bible was "truly" saying. Calvin joined wholeheartedly in this effort and employed the fathers to support his interpretative work in his *Institutes* and commentaries as well as his later treatises.

Calvin's initial tactic against the Catholic theologians was to point out their differences from the ancient fathers. He expanded this approach to associate his opponents with ancient figures accused of heresy. With the support of the early church, Calvin tried to invalidate what he considered to be misguided teachings and wrong interpretations of Scripture. For example, when he criticized the withholding of the cup from the laity, he listed a number of church fathers in his defense, including Tertullian, Ambrose, Jerome, Chrysostom, Augustine, Gregory, and Cyprian. These fathers served to underscore Calvin's polemic against contemporary Roman Catholic theologians.[107] And while Calvin did not accept the late medieval structure of authority, such as the supreme authority of the pope, or all the councils, he still accepted the teachings from the earliest councils and recognized the significance of identifying with a Christian tradition. When consensus was lacking, Calvin resorted to subsidiary authorities in the history of the church, ones that many of his contemporaries would recognize and respect. He sought the support of the "better" church fathers as a way of authorizing his views within a recognizable theological tradition. Yet Calvin understood their authority to be limited. For example, when he argued that the Lord's Supper could not exist apart from the Word, he asserted that true consecration involved the recitation of the promises and the declaration of the mystery, since silence was abuse and fault.[108] He concluded that silent consecration has no purpose, yet, when it was brought to his attention that those who practice it follow the example of the ancient church, Calvin claimed, "I admit the statement, but in so great a matter, one in which error entails great peril, nothing is safer than to follow the truth itself."[109] If the venerable fathers faltered in recognizing some aspects of truth, then it was up to new scholars, teachers, writers, and pastors in subsequent generations to recognize and relate those truths. Calvin was vying for a position among the new scholars, and in many areas he was successful.

## Chapter 3

# John Calvin and Joachim Westphal
## *First Phase of the Debate (1555–1556)*

By the mid-sixteenth century, John Calvin had established himself as the leading pastor of Geneva and one of the international leaders of the Reformed movement. When he initial made some efforts to unify the Lutheran and Reformed churches, he encountered further opposition to his teachings. Meanwhile, as the Lutheran pastor (and later superintendent) of St. Katherine's Church in Hamburg, Joachim Westphal (1510–1574) became one of the leading spokespersons for the Lutherans in the controversy over the Lord's Supper.[1] In the mid-1550s, John Calvin and Joachim Westphal engaged in a debate over their interpretations of the Lord's Supper. While they did not represent all Protestant views, they stood for two main streams of Protestant thought, namely Lutheran and Reformed, which would become established churches in the Holy Roman Empire. As they took up their pens to defend their views, they deployed the church fathers not only as tools for support but also as weapons of attack for demarcating those views which stood outside the bounds of their theological acceptance. When reformers in general reached competing interpretations of Scripture, they employed different strategies for understanding and defending the ancient church that would dismiss other views. While earlier reformers had showed some willingness to accept possible layers of meaning in Scripture, later reformers were much less willing to accept all interpretations as equally valid.

For Calvin and Westphal, their views of the Eucharist became a defining mark of their theological identities. And, as they strove to place themselves in the lineage of the church fathers, they presented their doctrines as having the consent of the ancients. They both drew from the scholastic model of explaining away apparent contradictions with the fathers, and, in doing so, forged a new Protestant scholasticism. They also drew from the humanist model of looking at ancient texts as a whole for rhetorical argument and intention, and thereby upheld the fathers' intention to illumine the Scripture. The fathers figured heavily in their debates over the Eucharist as both sides claimed the support of the ancient tradition to establish a precedent for their views. Among the Lutherans, Melanchthon included an excursus on the ecclesiastical fathers in the middle of his Romans commentary, while Reformed thinkers such as Heinrich Bullinger appealed to the ancient church by claiming that the true church cleaves to Christ while the false church persecutes those who believe in Christ.[2]

The increased production and accessibility of the writings of the church fathers and the efforts by various theologians to recall the fathers as a form of religious authority resulted in the rise of patristic scholarship among Protestants in the sixteenth century. Both Catholic and Protestant thinkers who looked back to authors such as Augustine, Jerome, Chrysostom, and Basil were involved in the polemics over the ownership of these ancient authorities.[3] The debates over the Eucharist were not simply disagreements over theological nuances of sacramental doctrine and practice but a struggle over the religious authority to decide theological acceptance.

In the context of the new Protestant scholasticism, reformers not only worked to illuminate Scripture, but they also found occasions to illustrate fallibility in the church fathers. In this sense, these new reformers differed from some of their medieval predecessors in their willingness to critique the works of the patristic writers and to provide correction based on Protestant theological views. By recognizing these ancient writers as human authorities, the reformers could reserve the right to challenge or rectify them if necessary and could distinguish between "better" and "mistaken" fathers. Implicit in the prerogative to criticize ancient authorities was the right for the reformers' views to be heard, since critique often invites corrective. The deployment of the fathers served as an important means of debating the interpretation of Scripture and enabled the reformers to draw from the wellsprings of antiquity in order to expound on their own views of the Eucharist. Even so, reformers did not give absolute weight to the fathers; rather, the value of the fathers lay in their ability to teach right Christian doctrine.[4] Often the writings of the church fathers required further interpretation, for the fathers did not write about the Eucharist with sixteenth-century questions in mind. Therefore the Protestant reformers' task was to teach the sayings of the church fathers as compatible with Lutheran or Reformed theology.

## Initiating the Calvin–Westphal Exchange

The catalyst for this mid-sixteenth-century controversy revolved around two developments. First, in May 1549 the Genevan and Swiss churches united around a common doctrine of the Eucharist,[5] in an agreement titled the *Consensus Tigurinus*. Despite Calvin's ecumenical intent for the *Consensus*,[6] Lutherans in the north had a different perception of this agreement. In its twenty-fourth article, the *Consensus Tigurinus* stated: "For we deem it no less absurd to place Christ under the bread or couple him with the bread, than to transubstantiate the bread into his body."[7] Westphal rightly understood this declaration as a rejection of Luther's explanation of Christ's presence in the Supper. While the Protestant reformers had rejected the notion of transubstantiation, they still could not agree on how to interpret Christ's words of institution "this is my body." Westphal was troubled by the publication of the *Consensus Tigurinus* in 1551 because he saw the Reformed churches as reaffirming the Zwinglian symbolic interpretation.

The second development occurred in the wake of large-scale Protestant emigrations from England in the mid-1550s. During the reign of Edward VI, many Protestant Dutch and French expatriates traveled to England, where their "evangelical" views found favorable reception. But when Edward died and his half-sister Mary, a Catholic, took the throne from 1553 to 1558, hundreds of leading Protestants left England. The migration of these "London exiles" produced English, Dutch, and French refugees who sought to settle in the cities of northern Europe. John Laski, a pastor for the refugee churches, published a series of sermons expressing his support for the *Consensus Tigurinus* in 1552. These sermons, which attacked Luther's eucharistic doctrine, spurred Westphal into action when he became increasingly alarmed by the apparent success of the leading Reformed churches in promoting a doctrine of the Eucharist that deviated from Luther's.[8] In the same year, Westphal wrote a treatise titled *Farrago of Confused and Divergent Opinions on the Lord's Supper Taken from the Books of the Sacramentarians* in order to guard against the "treachery, malice and deceit of heretics."[9] In the *Farrago* (a title that denotes a hodgepodge or confused mixture of views), Westphal designated Zwingli, John Laski, and Calvin as "sacramentarians" and schismatics whose opinions were marked by disagreement and discrepancy among themselves. The word "sacramentarian" was a derogatory term used by Luther and other Lutherans to refer to any reformer who could not accept Christ's body but only the *sacrament* of it. In criticizing these "sacramentarians," Westphal allotted the most space to Calvin.[10] In order to demonstrate the chaos that had arisen among Reformed thinkers because of their divergent interpretations, Westphal summarized in a chart over twenty different expositions of the words "this is my body." In the *Farrago*, he grounded his argument on the basis of the Corinthian experience in which schismatics were judged, while the perfect church was of the same mind.[11]

   Although Westphal devoted a large portion of his booklet to attacking Calvin, the *Consensus Tigurinus* was certainly not a full representation of Calvin's views on the Lord's Supper. Rather, the *Consensus* represented the extent to which Calvin was willing to stretch his eucharistic opinions in favor of peace among the churches of Switzerland. The *Consensus* resembled a theological patchwork that represented the concerns of all parties at least to the extent that all could agree to sign the document.[12] In the case of the *Consensus Tigurinus* of 1549, Calvin's references to the fathers were minimal because the agreement over the Eucharist between Zürich and Geneva carried authority by the nature of its collective consensus. Calvin believed that a majority constituted an authoritative voice and assumed that a good number of Lutherans would side with him on this issue. Initially, he dismissed Westphal's *Farrago* as a "light-weight book," and even wrote to Bullinger (April 29, 1554) that it was not worth their time to draft a response. Yet Calvin ended up writing not one, but three, responses. What prompted Calvin to draft his multiple rebuttals was not only the clarification of a theological point and the importance of rooting the Reformed tradition in the ancient tradition, but also the political situation of the London exiles.

   Although the content of the Calvin–Westphal exchange dealt with the interpretation of Scripture and the nuances of the two reformers' theological views, their debate carried social and political repercussions that were most readily felt by the London exiles migrating through continental Europe. Westphal's writings were not simply private responses to the *Consensus Tigurinus*; rather, they were public warnings intended to uphold Lutheran teaching and guard against other interpretations. His warning about Reformed views, for instance, also had political ramifications, as it caused many Lutheran princes to be suspicious of the Reformed refugees. A recurring point of contention was over the eucharistic rite, in part because of the situation of the refugees. As the London exiles moved from Scandinavia to the European continent, they were initially well received in Denmark. A sermon by one of the Lutheran court preachers, however, which the exiles interpreted as a veiled attack, soon soured the atmosphere. Consequently, the Danish king stated that he would grant permission for them to remain in Denmark only if they conformed to the Lutheran rites of the Eucharist.[13] Instead of conforming, the exiles decided to move southward into German-speaking territories. In Hamburg, they met one of their most bitter opponents: Joachim Westphal. Here, a dispute between Westphal and Marten Micronius, a minister appointed to the Dutch exile community, ended with the town council's ordering the refugees out of the city. Although the refugees were denied entrance into Hamburg, it is likely that some of the city's residents provided relief efforts to the London refugees, because the council later passed a regulation forbidding citizens to offer them food or shelter, on pain of fines. Westphal's effort to expel the religious refugees continued even after they left Hamburg and dispersed to different cities, such as Berlin, Wesel, and Frankfurt.

In Wesel, the exiles' *Confession* was submitted to Melanchthon for arbitration. Although he, in fact, argued against the foreigners' expulsion, the Council read to the presiding ministers only those portions of his letter that identified points of difference between the foreigners' doctrine and the Augsburg Confession. The exiles were given the choice of accepting the Augsburg Confession or leaving the town, and they chose the latter. Many of the exiles traveled to Berlin and Frankfurt, while others settled in towns where they expected to be received more favorably, such as Geneva and Zürich. While Calvin and Bullinger may have initially hesitated in writing a response to Westphal, news from Laski about the exiles' treatment on their northern peregrination convinced Calvin that a reply was necessary.[14] Calvin also felt compelled to answer because the Lutheran view of the Lord's Supper was gaining acceptance and was being enforced by rulers, even the King of Denmark.[15] In Frankfurt, the exiles were able to build a community for a while, but the Lutheran ministers, after some difficulty, succeeded in securing the closure of the exiles' church and the expulsion of the refugee communities. In the case of Frankfurt, Westphal had written a letter to the town council with an explicit demand for the exiles' expulsion.[16] The discouraging experience of the London exiles in Denmark and Germany not only illustrated the tense relationship between Lutheran and Reformed sides but also exacerbated it. It is in this context that Calvin and Westphal resorted to the fathers to uphold their views. Calvin's first response to Westphal was published in early 1555, and was followed by Westphal's answer later that same year. In 1556 Calvin wrote his second response and Westphal did not delay in responding. It becomes clear that the eucharistic controversy of the 1550s gave a decisive impulse to the development of rival confessions within Protestantism.[17]

## The First Exchange

### *Calvin's* Defensio Sanae et Orthodoxae Doctrinae

In 1555 Calvin drafted a response to Westphal's *Farrago* in *The Defense of the Sound and Orthodox Doctrine on the Sacraments, Their Nature, Power, Purpose, Use and Fruitfulness* (hereafter referred to under its Latin title, *Defensio*) in order to defend the *Consensus Tigurinus*.[18] When Calvin sent his draft to Zürich for review, the ministers there offered a chart of seven church fathers whose writings supported a symbolic or figurative understanding of the words of institution. Although the Zürich list included Tertullian, Jerome, Chrysostom, Theodoret, Ambrose, Augustine, and Fulgentius, Calvin's published version mentions only one of these authorities repeatedly: Augustine. Calvin claims that there is nothing deserving of censure in the *Consensus Tigurinus* when "we meant nothing more than what, with *universal consent*, Augustine (*Hom. in Joann.* 80) teaches, namely that the elements become sacraments only when the word is added, not because it is pronounced, but because it is believed."[19] Calvin upholds Augustine as one of the wise teachers who explains a view that has received widespread agreement, although he never elaborates on who is in this agreement. Noting the moral dimension of interpretation, Calvin describes the fathers (especially Augustine) as well-intentioned teachers because they meant to teach truth despite sometimes faltering. Such a statement upholds the value of the fathers while simultaneously subjecting them to scrutiny. Equipped with this perspective, Calvin's role is to distill the best teachings among them and demonstrate his alignment with the highest biblical truths.

Just as Luther and Oecolampadius did before him, Calvin expresses that he is not introducing something new but following a precedent that was forgotten, altered, or misconstrued. Therefore, one reason for him to cite the fathers was to guard against the charge of innovation and idiosyncrasy. Calvin cites Augustine's writings, with an appended explanation, three more times as the basis for his own eucharistic views. By doing so, he establishes the antiquity or tradition behind these views. By citing Augustine as a representative to support his own viewpoint, Calvin tries to convey that any attack on his views would be an attack on Augustine. Westphal, however, rejects this logic and instead portrays Augustine as supporting Lutheran views.

Another reason Calvin cites the fathers is to correct competing views. Because Westphal also cites Augustine for support, Calvin feels the need to provide clarification of Augustine's views. Recognizing that some of Augustine's writings could be construed to support Westphal, Calvin gives longer explanations of potentially liable statements, lest Westphal try to claim Augustine for himself. Calvin's explicit reference to the fathers, however, is limited to Augustine, whom Calvin sees as a champion of his cause.[20] In Calvin's first response to Westphal, his appeals to the fathers mostly highlight the best teachings, find precedents, and correct contemporaries. These ways of citing the fathers are repeatedly applied throughout the eucharistic debates.

## Westphal's Adversus cuiusdam sacramentarii falsam criminationem

After Calvin's *Defensio* appeared in January 1555, Westphal responded in July of that year with a booklet titled *A Just Defense against the False Accusations of a Certain Sacramentarian* (hereafter cited under its partial Latin title, *Adversus*).[21] As the fathers had been part of the discussions that took place between Luther and Oecolampadius, Westphal was fully aware that the fathers, particularly Augustine, would play a part in this debate as well.[22] Even before Calvin sent his *Defensio* to the printers, Westphal wrote a treatise compiling passages from Augustine that supported the Lutheran view, *A Collection of Quotes from the Holy Aurelius Augustine, Bishop of Hippo, on the Lord's Supper, Together with a Refutation Freeing from Corruption the Countless Loci of Augustine which the Adversaries Erroneously Cite in their Favor* (hereafter referred to as *Collectanea*).[23] This booklet included (1) quotations from Augustine's writings that were said to conform to the Lutheran formula; (2) passages that the adversaries employed to support their cause; and (3) the refutation of the objection that the nature of material bodies was opposed to ubiquity.[24] Calvin would address the *Collectanea* in his third treatise against Westphal.

In the same year, Westphal also published a study on Cyril of Alexandria in which he assembled his observations on the writings of Cyril that emphasized corporeal and natural participation, such as the statement "We both taste and eat this flesh [which] truly is food."[25] In his work on Cyril, Westphal also offered his own understanding of the authority of the fathers:

> True faith does not depend on human authority, nor rest on human approval, but solely on the word of God. Therefore I do not bring forth the opinions of the ancients, as if our faith concerning the presence of the body and blood of Christ in communion of the mystical supper would need the testimonies of humans. I do not make equal the writings of the fathers and of the canonical Holy Scripture since surely they do not want to bring so much to themselves. But because the sacramentarians provide the ancient doctors false testimony in this, I bring and

claim their sound testimony from corruption in order to testify exposing their opinions for us and against the sacramentarians.[26]

For Westphal, the main reason to discuss the fathers is to wrest them from the contamination of his opponents, since they are esteemed human authorities. In this endeavor, Westphal claims the fathers for the correction of a contemporary opponent by labeling his opponents as newer versions of former heretics, and therefore guilty by association.

Westphal's *Adversus* was published in Frankfurt, where the French and English exiles had found refuge. Although Calvin is not identified by name in this work, those who are aware of the controversy know that the "certain sacramentarian" referred to is Calvin. Reiterating his claim in the *Farrago* that the sacramentarians do not agree among themselves, Westphal reviews their diverse views and concludes that their only points of unity are that they do not admit the real presence of Christ's body in the Supper and that they leave nothing but empty symbols.[27] Although Calvin may have hoped for a consensus over some aspects of the Lord's Supper, Westphal does not conceive of a consensus with the Genevan or Swiss reformers. In the *Adversus*, Westphal describes the "certain sacramentarian" as "inferior with Marcion himself,"[28] and thereby connects Calvin to a second-century accused heretic who saw matter as evil and argued that the earthly body cannot serve as a dwelling place for the divine. Westphal then refers to the early figures of Athanasius and Arius and parallels them with Luther and the sacramentarians, respectively. He portrays Athanasius as upholding the orthodox faith concerning Christ's divinity against Arius, just as Luther prevails over many bitter enemies. Therefore Calvin belongs to the group of those who have resuscitated ancient heresies through the lens of earlier reformers such as Karlstadt and Zwingli.[29] Westphal identifies Calvin with Marcion and Arius and delineates his debate with Calvin along orthodox and heretical lines. By employing the names of early heretical or heterodox thinkers, Westphal simply groups what he interprets as ancient errors with the contemporary "errors" of the sacramentarians, such as Calvin.

Westphal, like Calvin, repeatedly mentions Augustine. In reference to the broader context of faith, however, he also brings up Gregory Nazianzus, who once declared in an oration before 150 bishops, "Soldiers of Christ are in other things meek but contentious for the sake of faith,"[30] a statement that Westphal uses to explain his own passionate response. Meanwhile, Westphal also argues that Calvin and his followers act foolishly because they look only at bare signs and not (as is preferred) to the promises that are joined to those signs.[31] This is an odd accusation since Calvin has already accused Westphal of the same thing. Even John Laski, in his September 1555 letter, complains bitterly that Westphal's attack on Calvin draws on Calvin's own words. Because of the *Consensus Tigurinus* between churches in Geneva and Zürich, Westphal directs his critique of Zwingli to Calvin, whom he understands as coming from the same mold. Although both Calvin and Zwingli located Christ's presence at the right hand of God, their views on the Lord's Supper are not identical, despite Westphal's understanding of them. The nature of this polemical debate indicates that both Calvin and Westphal saw one another as a threat and detriment to a biblical theology of the Eucharist. Their purpose was to get rid of false views rather than to understand the nuances of an opponent's content. Westphal's caricature of Calvin and his followers portrays them as unfaithful materialists who argue because they do not see Christ's body. In other words, they argue because they do not have the eyes of faith.

Both Westphal and Calvin cite as their preferred expression Augustine's saying that the elements become the sacrament when the word is added to it, which Luther also cited. Both claim this passage as the best expression for their own views. Thus it appears that Augustine's words could be a point of common ground after all, yet the immersion in a polemical argument clouds any sense of unity. By claiming to portray Augustine rightly for the sixteenth-century context, both Westphal and Calvin exercise the strategy of starting with what Augustine actually said as a reference point for elaborating their own stances. Although they both cite Augustine favorably, they do not come any closer to resolving their disagreement over the Eucharist. At times Westphal sets forth the principle that the fathers are not of primary importance in order to undercut Calvin's use of their works; if Calvin's brings up the support of the fathers, Westphal opts to downgrade their authority. Westphal also claims better access to the fathers and their support. If this latter rhetorical strategy becomes troublesome, he can always revert to the first strategy. Therefore Calvin is wrong on two counts—first because he places too much value on the fathers, and second because he misunderstands the fathers. Either way, Calvin gets it wrong.

## The Second Exchange

### *Calvin's* Secunda Defensio Piae et Orthodoxae de Sacramentis Fidei

In January 1556 Calvin's second reply to Westphal was published under the title *Second Defense of the Pious and Orthodox Faith concerning the Sacraments in Answer to the Calumnies of Joachim Westphal (Secunda).*[32] Calvin dedicated this treatise to the churches of Saxony and Lower Germany in hopes that they would agree with his assessment and stand against

Westphal. In his text, he rightly recognizes the issue at stake in the Eucharist controversy to be the interpretation of Scripture when he points out that Westphal deems as a sacramentarian anyone who expounds on the words of Christ in a way other than according to the letter. If this is the case, then Calvin can say,

> Augustine is brought into our ranks. He wrote, in the *Reply to Faustus*, that our Lord said, "This is my body," when he was giving a sign of his body. Seeing that he expounds the words of Christ figuratively, Augustine will no doubt be regarded as a sacramentarian. Will Westphal find two who differ more from each other than Augustine does from himself?[33]

According to Calvin, three issues sum up the crux of the controversy over the Eucharist. The first issue deals with whether a figure is meant by Christ's words. Because Calvin believed he had Augustine's support for the figurative significance of the words of Christ, he attributes the source of dissension to a moral issue rather than a theological one: a proud disdain in Westphal and other Gnesio-Lutherans.[34] Calvin emphasizes his willingness and even eagerness for a reconciliation of doctrines. Although the rhetoric of reconciliation arises in his *Second Defense* (hereafter referred to by the partial Latin title *Secunda*), it is difficult to take such an offer seriously. While it may convey Calvin's original intent for an ecumenical Protestant Communion, on the point of the Eucharist, both Lutheran and Reformed thinkers by this point were focused on clarifying (not minimizing) their differences.

The second issue deals with the mode of Communion and whether the body exists everywhere. The Lutherans had resolved the question of Christ's real presence with the doctrine of ubiquity. Calvin accuses Westphal of being too much of a literalist, for if the body of Christ is not actually placed before us, Westphal believes there is no real Communion. Calvin maintains, on the contrary, that no extent of space interferes with the "boundless energy" of the Spirit, which is able to give life from Christ's flesh. As Calvin sharpens his view, his clarification provides a new view of the Eucharist. Yet Westphal lumps Calvin's view with Zwingli's more symbolic emphasis, despite the fact that, by this time, Calvin is no longer speaking of a purely symbolic presence but rather a real spiritual presence.

The third issue deals with whether the substance of the bread is the body of Christ, with the related question of the eating of the unfaithful (*manducatio infidelium*). Westphal, as well as other Lutherans, argued that the bread is substantially the body. In other words, the unbelieving person can consume the body and blood of Jesus Christ, but to their judgment.

For Calvin the unbelieving person does not receive Christ's body and blood, but instead unbelief prevents the sacred ordinance of Christ from retaining its force and nature since Christ's body and blood is offered to all as spiritual food. Therefore, without faith, bread and wine remain earthly elements, preventing any spiritual benefit from reaching those who partake without faith.

As in the first *Defensio*, references to Augustine dominate in the *Secunda*. It is Calvin's turn to save Augustine from the clutches of Westphal. Arguing against the necessity of Christ's bodily presence in the Lord's Supper, Calvin locates the physical body of Christ in heaven. To describe the body of Christ in the Lord's Supper, he describes Christ's presence as the virtue of his Spirit, divine essence, divine energy, and the secret influence of his Spirit. For Calvin, it is not necessary that Christ descend bodily because he is present through the Holy Spirit. Westphal, by contrast, insists that Christ's presence in the Eucharist requires a bodily presence in the Supper.

Calvin tries to secure Augustine for his own view by correcting or reinterpreting an understanding of Augustine that appears to support the Lutheran position. It is in the efforts of this strategy that Calvin develops his mature eucharistic doctrine. He writes: "[W]hen Augustine teaches that by adding the word the element becomes a sacrament, the context clearly shows his meaning, that by the word the element becomes a sacrament, so that its virtue or effect may reach us."[35] For Calvin, Christ's virtue is Christ's power and presence, which provides the benefits of Christ in Holy Communion. He names other church fathers but quotes almost exclusively from Augustine. What is more, he turns the tables on Westphal when he employs Westphal's strategy of comparing an ancient heretical or heterodox figure to a contemporary opponent. In fact Calvin even uses the same heretic with whom Westphal has identified him: Marcion. Calvin aligns Marcion with Westphal and others who have caused the church to go awry, and then identifies himself with the good teachers who are faithful interpreters of God's word.[36]

At times, references to the fathers are not necessarily pertinent to the issue of the Eucharist. Rather, in some cases, Calvin draws on ancient polemical discourses to discredit Westphal. For example, while Westphal means for a reference to Gregory Nazianzus to be directed against Calvin, Calvin takes the quote in another direction and asserts, "[T]here is great truth in the words [Westphal] quotes from Nazianzus, that the soldiers of Christ, though meek in other things, must be pugnacious for the faith. But not only common experience, but this man's intemperance, shows

it to be equally true that the servants of the devil are more than pugnacious against the faith."[37] Each reformer recalls the polemical words of
the fathers for the sixteenth-century context. Therefore, both Calvin and
Westphal link moral intention to doctrinal differences, and Calvin specifically identifies malice as the reason for Westphal's disagreement.

Lastly in the *Secunda*, Calvin complains that Westphal wrongly
assumes that he is maintaining that there is nothing but bread and wine
in the Supper. Calvin wants to emphasize that the sacraments derive their
value from the word with which they are so closely connected. Criticizing
the intention behind Westphal's words, he writes, "Westphal's motive,
no doubt, was this. He did not think that his hostility to [the Reformed]
would seem fierce enough if he did not out of mere spite attack the
plainest truth, seize upon the minutest particles as materials for strife,
and infect honey itself with his bitter[ness]."[38] In the controversy over
the Lord's Supper, both Calvin and Westphal represent their views in
alignment with the ancient church, usually by selecting several key church
fathers as supportive voices. Being on the "right" side translates into
authority over the "'erroneous heretics." Therefore it is crucial for Calvin
not only to depict himself as a follower of Augustine but also to caricature
Westphal as a slanderer of Augustine. By holding Westphal responsible
for identifying Augustine as a sacramentarian, Calvin is able to endorse
Augustine for the Reformed side and to portray Westphal as rebuffing a
premier church father.

## Westphal's Confessio fidei

In the fall of 1556, Westphal's major counterattack came in *The Confes-
sion of Faith on the Sacrament of the Eucharist, in which the Ministers of the
Church of Saxony Defend the Presence of the Body and Blood of the Lord Jesus
Christ in the Supper by Solid Arguments of Sacred Scripture in Answer to the
Book Dedicated to them by John Calvin* (hereafter referred to by the partial
Latin title *Confessio*).[39] In this work, Westphal claims that he took Calvin's
advice and wrote to the ministers of his territory, asking them to judge
between his and Calvin's teaching, and to compose a confession on the
Lord's Supper. In writing the *Confessio*, Westphal was now publishing the
results by which he hoped to demonstrate the unity in the teachings of
the Saxon churches. The fact that the *Confessio* explicitly lists a conglom-
erate of Saxon churches verifies that these churches stood behind him.
Although Calvin's *Secunda* was ostensibly addressed and dedicated to all
the honest ministers of Christ in the Saxon churches in order to solicit
their support, Calvin had misjudged Westphal's clout and found himself
contending not with a single pastor from Hamburg but with a united
front of Saxon churches.[40]

Containing both general and specific references to the church fathers, the *Confessio* includes four of Westphal's letters as well as materials coming from the other churches, such as those at Magdeburg, Bremen, Hannover, Brunswick, and Wismar. As a conclusion to the collection, two of Luther's letters and one of Melanchthon's are added.[41] Using syllogistic argumentation, Westphal claims that Augustine supports the Lutheran view in thirty places, although he does not cite those thirty places. In the first section of the *Confessio*, Westphal describes Irenaeus, Tertullian, and Hilary as fathers who fought against heretics of their own time—Irenaeus in many places, Tertullian in his prescription against the heretics, and Hilary in *On the Trinity*.[42] Elsewhere in the document Westphal lists eight church fathers, whose names are followed by a short excerpt from each: Justin Martyr, Cyril, Hilary, Irenaeus, Cyprian, Theodoret, Ambrose, and Augustine. This list provides a quick reference to the key fathers who are cited as support for Westphal's view of corporeal presence. The writings of these fathers are not discussed at length since this is not Westphal's objective; rather, the excerpts of their works serve as proof texts for Westphal's view of corporeal real presence. Westphal sees spiritual eating as excluding the real presence and leaving out the true substance of Christ. Therefore he associates Calvin and his followers with the heretics, and the Lutherans with the fathers who battled the alleged heretics. In this case, the naming of these church fathers does not include a discussion of the fathers' views. For Westphal, the terms "corporeal" and "real" are interchangeable in the fathers' writings. Calvin, however, does not consider what is corporeal to be the same as what is real. In other words, while Calvin objects to a Lutheran rendering of corporeal presence, he does not deny that there is a real presence (of a spiritual kind) in the Lord's Supper.

## Conclusion

The Calvin–Westphal debate helped to create distinctive Lutheran and Reformed traditions. For example, many of Calvin's references to Augustine are followed by explanations that provide clarifications of the Reformed perspective. Westphal also refers to Augustine numerous times, but he also cites other fathers, such as Irenaeus, Tertullian, and Hilary, as fathers who fought against heretics of their own time. In their argumentation over the Lord's Supper, both Calvin and Westphal deploy the fathers through several reading strategies. First, they both cite the fathers as a springboard for elaboration. After quoting from one of the fathers, they explain how the quotation ought to be understood, which often leads to a second strategy of presenting the fathers as spokespersons of the contrasting sides of the Eucharist controversy. Third, they both refer to the fathers in order to provide correctives to their opponents. In one case, they may use the polemical language of the fathers even when the content of the original documents may be unrelated to the Eucharist. In another case, they counter each other's quotations of a particular ancient father with other passages from the same author or, occasionally, from a different father. Fourth, they moderate ancient passages that seem to empower each other's views by offering "better" alternative interpretations. Frequently they cite the fathers to show how they have been misunderstood. In addition to correcting misunderstandings, a fifth strategy is to name ancient heretics as ancestral associates of a contemporary opponent. Westphal employs this tactic from the beginning of his polemics; Calvin learns from his example and begins to employ this fifth strategy with his *Secunda*.

While Calvin does not hold the fathers' status as equal to Scripture, he does not want to dismiss their authority. For instance, when Augustine seems to voice support for a fleshly, corporeal Christ in the Eucharist, Calvin tries to explain the historical context in which such an explanation was necessary. In fact, once Calvin establishes an ancient saying as a faithful exposition of Scripture, his approach is to utilize those preapproved sayings as practically authoritative as Scripture. Meanwhile, Westphal clearly wants to relegate the fathers' sayings to the Bible. In his preface to *The Faith of Holy Cyril*, he explains that his faith concerning the presence of the body and blood of Christ does not need the testimonies of humans and emphasizes that he does not consider the writings of the fathers equal to the Holy Scriptures. Westphal's main reason for citing the fathers is to prevent them from empowering Calvin's cause. This intention may partly explain why Westphal shows a prominent interest in Augustine and devotes an entire work to compiling quotations from him. Ironically, at this stage, Calvin cites very few fathers even though he tries to leverage their authority against Westphal, while Westphal cites many more fathers even though he professes that the Scriptures alone give sufficient support for the Lutheran stance.

The polemical debates between Westphal and Calvin contributed to an irrevocable rupture between Lutheran and Reformed views of the Eucharist. The first eucharistic controversy at the Colloquy of Marburg in 1529 between Luther/Melanchthon and Oecolampadius/Zwingli set the stage for the second eucharistic controversy between Calvin and Westphal. For the strict Lutherans, such as Westphal, the earlier debate between Luther and Zwingli had set the terms of the current debate, for Westphal continually tried to lump Calvin together with Zwingli and repeatedly accused Calvin of espousing a spiritualistic interpretation. Since Luther, especially in his early Latin writings, had contributed to the formation of Calvin's doctrine, Calvin hoped (as Bucer had before him) to find some common ground with the Lutherans. As the debate with Westphal progressed, however, Calvin found himself drawing dividing lines just as starkly as Westphal did. Any voiced concerns for a Protestant ecumenical front based upon a consensus on the Eucharist became superficial before disappearing altogether. With the publication of Westphal's *Confessio*, it became clear that many of the Saxon churches stood behind Westphal in this debate. With Calvin's realization that he had underestimated Westphal's influence, any hopes he retained for a compatible sacramental doctrine between the churches of Germany and Switzerland were dashed. Furthermore, in the debates over the Eucharist, Calvin and Westphal presented different readings of the ancient tradition, which supported the formation of two different churches.

The Calvin–Westphal debates represent a transition in the use of the church fathers. Calvin and Westphal deployed an increasing number of ancient writers as their disagreement intensified. But the nature of this kind of appeal to the fathers meant that the fathers would be read in new ways. When the Protestant reformers initially sought support from the early church fathers, they quoted their writings. As the Lutheran–Reformed division became entrenched, with both sides claiming the support of the ancient tradition, the reformers not only cited but also appended lengthy interpretations of the fathers. Although this debate included all five strategies for recalling the fathers, the first phase of the Calvin–Westphal exchange (1555–1556) shows a progressive, though not strictly chronological, transition from deploying the fathers mainly as a defensive tactic against the accusation of novelty, to the new strategy of upholding the fathers as representatives of a reformer's view. The use of the fathers in the eucharistic debates between Calvin and Westphal solidified the development of a Protestant interpretation of the church's ancient tradition.

Lutheran and Reformed leaders claimed their interpretation of the Eucharist was supported by the church's ancient tradition and therefore was part of the true tradition of the church. This meant that Lutheran and Reformed interpretations could have religious legitimacy in the Holy Roman Empire. As in many cases, the conflict between Calvin and Westphal galvanized the like-minded and clarified boundaries and identities. The fathers were part of a strategy to determine who could decide orthodoxy among competing camps of Protestant reformers.[43] Calvin's letters, particularly to Laski and Bullinger, reveal how extensively this debate affected places, where Lutheran and Reformed people had to coexist in close proximity, and in particular the London exiles who had a difficult time finding a home.

In summary, the sixteenth-century use of the fathers reflected a departure from the medieval use of them as supreme authorities whose tradition was equal to Scripture. Protestant reformers declared the supremacy of Scripture and relegated the fathers to the status of human authorities. In the polemical debates over the Eucharist, Calvin and Westphal accepted this general view of the fathers. Nevertheless, they turned to the fathers as key secondary authorities to support their doctrinal views. They no longer claimed the supremacy of the ancient tradition but claimed the supremacy of their own interpretation of the ancient tradition. Both Calvin and Westphal were also engaged in reinterpreting the ancient fathers in order to show how their Protestant views had a precedent in the history of the church. Westphal and Calvin assessed the value of the early church fathers to support their interpretations of Scripture as they turned to the fathers often for affirmation, qualification, explanation, or modification. Lutheran and Reformed leaders could not simply discard the fathers; they needed the fathers in order to understand their own position within the Christian tradition.

## Chapter 4

# Calvin and Westphal, Continued
## *Second Phase of the Debate (1557–1558)*

For both Calvin and Westphal, citing the fathers was part of an attempt to authorize a new interpretation of the ancient tradition. In the work of reclaiming the tradition of the early church, references to the ancient fathers dramatically increased in the Lutheran–Reformed debates. The reformers argued over the fathers in order to make parts of the ancient tradition the very building blocks for a Lutheran or Reformed theological heritage. In other words, they had to go back into the past in order to go forward in creating a new church. While the content of the debate between Calvin and Westphal was theological, the consequences of these debates included sociopolitical conflicts. Like many of his contemporaries, Westphal wanted to employ the sword of the magistrate against his Reformed opponents.[1] With the well-being (or threat, depending on one's perspective) of the Reformed communities in German territories at stake, the debate between Calvin and Westphal continued until 1558. Soon after the debate ended, Calvin composed his final Latin edition of the 1559 *Institutes*, in which a good deal of new material, including a greater concentration of patristic references, focused on these issues.

### Calvin's *Ultima Admonitio*

Calvin directed his response *The Last Admonition of John Calvin to Joachim Westphal who if He heeds it not must henceforth be Treated in the Way which Paul Prescribed for Obstinate Heretics* (hereafter referred to by the partial Latin title *Admonitio*), toward Westphal and, in great part, the Magdeburgians who had provided many arguments for Westphal's *Confessio* against Calvin the year before.[2] By far the longest of his three responses, the *Admonitio*, which appeared on August 20, 1557, is a three-part answer, first to Westphal's brief *Epistola* (a precursor to the longer *Confessio*), next to Westphal's use of Augustine in his *Collectanea*, and finally to the *Confessio* of the Saxon churches. By tracing all of the explicit references in the *Admonitio* to early church figures, we can see how each side weighed the authority of the fathers and the efforts they made to incorporate the church fathers in the explanation of their views. As iron sharpens iron, it is in writing against Westphal that Calvin hones his views on the Eucharist. The full development of Calvin's notions of accommodation and instrumentality are offered in his writings against Lutheran opponents as well as in his New Testament commentaries and his *Institutes*.[3] More specifically, Calvin develops an explanation for the importance of substantial partaking, other than simply saying it is necessary for the life of the soul, over the course of his debate with the Lutherans.[4] In addition to the constant motif of nourishment in Calvin's eucharistic teaching, one of the developments in Calvin's eucharistic theology is that he becomes more insistent on the flesh of Christ as a reality in the Supper even as he strengthens his notion of eating as a metaphorical concept.[5]

For Calvin, references to the fathers serve three purposes. First, Calvin defends himself against the accusation of innovation. Since what is ancient carries more value than what is new, it is important for Calvin to prove that his view is an ancient one. In his *Admonitio*, Calvin argues that his purpose for citing the fathers is to remove the charge of novelty. Because the Lutherans cite the fathers against Calvin, he deems it necessary to produce passages from pious writers to show that the doctrine that he presents is consistent with what the ancients taught without controversy.[6] Second, while the church fathers undoubtedly had their share of conflicts, Calvin sets up an image of a common ancient doctrine, even when he knows it did not exist. By describing ancient doctrine as accepted without controversy, Calvin tries to indicate that his own doctrine, which ought to be identified with the ancients, should be received without resistance. Third, if a common doctrine of the Eucharist could be attributed to the ancient fathers, then Calvin can use one father as a representative of the entire early church.

## Against Westphal's Letter

In the first part of his answer, when responding to Westphal's brief *Epistola*, Calvin likens Westphal to Julian the Apostate. By comparing Westphal with a figure condemned by the ancient church, Calvin shows a shift in strategy from his first *Defensio*, a strategy adopted in the *Secunda* and amplified in the *Admonitio*. Mimicking Westphal's strategy, Calvin opts to highlight "bad" ancients as a form of name-calling instead of simply upholding "good" ancients whose correct views ought to be explained. According to Calvin, "Westphal vociferates a thousand times without measure or restraint, against the faithful servants of Christ."[7] Meanwhile, Calvin claims that he does not write to avenge a private injury but rather to prevent a good cause from being overwhelmed. His rhetoric in the *Admonitio* also includes a conciliatory tone in which he writes that he would not dismiss reconciliation if Westphal wished for it. Both Westphal and Calvin seem to uphold humility, modesty, and charity as Christian values, yet such values are the measuring stick that each uses against the other, as both are quick to accuse the other of stirring up strife. Upon closer inspection, Calvin's offer of peace is perfunctory, since he proceeds to explain that Westphal's conditions for peace demand too high a price. Calvin takes up Westphal's references to Ambrose and Gregory Nazianzus for recommendations of meekness and contests Westphal's interpretation by simply stating that he "has lost his memory and his senses."[8] Calvin fails to offer an alternative interpretation, however. By this point, the call for charity can barely be heard as both have resorted to zealous invective in order to discredit their opponent's errors.

One part of this controversy that ought to be mentioned is that both sides appealed to Melanchthon for support. Calvin had declared that the Augsburg Confession (as it was published in Regensburg) was not contrary to his doctrine. Since Melanchthon wrote two versions of the Confession, Calvin assented to the later version, written in 1540 and called it the *Variata*. Yet Lutherans such as Westphal preferred the earlier version called the *Invariata*, which followed a stricter Lutheran interpretation. Both Calvin and Westphal were claiming adherence to the Confession of Augsburg and referring to two different documents. Both were also claiming the author of the Augsburg Confession for their side. Calvin even hoped that Melanchthon would soon break his silence on this controversy and support the Reformed cause.

## Augustine's Sayings as Support

In the second part of his answer, in addressing Westphal's collection of Augustine's sayings, Calvin claims that although all the writings prove that Augustine supports his view, Westphal "obtrudes as an adversary, not hesitating to claim [Augustine] for himself with the same audacity with which he uniformly turns light into darkness."[9] Calvin argues that although Westphal professes to speak almost in the very words of Augustine, the two authors differ very much from one another, in both

words and meaning. Recalling Westphal's appeal to the local magistrate
to prohibit the settlement of Calvinist-Reformed refugees, Calvin contrasts Westphal's behavior with a description of Augustine's actions. By
comparing their behavior, Calvin hopes to convey that they share nothing
in common. He even tries to highlight a difference in character when he
notes that Augustine was always prepared to refute error before calling
in the aid of a magistrate, while Westphal "puts a black mark on any of
his colleagues that he chooses, and forthwith contends that they are to
be driven into exile."[10] This semi-hagiographical account of Augustine as
a fair, peace-loving pastor contrasts sharply with the historical Augustine
who called for physical coercion against the Donatists. Yet Calvin at this
moment is not concerned with the historical Augustine but with depicting Westphal as different from Augustine. As both sides claimed to have
the consent of many churches, the debate was not just over the details
of eucharistic doctrine but also over the authority to define Christian
doctrine. Because Westphal condemned Calvin for erroneous doctrine,
Calvin questions his authority to make such an accusation. Consequently
Calvin asks: Whose condemnation of whom ought to stand? Referring to
Westphal's location in Hamburg, he writes facetiously, "Is it because he
is near to the frozen ocean, and while he beholds its shore, considers it
the utmost limit of the globe, that he regards all other churches wherever
dispersed as non-entities?"[11] Despite the sarcastic tone of this remark, the
authority to define doctrine did depend to a large extent on location and
region. Denmark, Sweden, Norway, parts of Poland, and much of the
Holy Roman Empire, especially the northern and eastern lands, accepted
the views of Westphal, while Scotland, the Netherlands, the free imperial
city of Geneva, and pockets of communities in England, France, Hun-
gary, Transylvania, the Swiss cantons, and even within the Holy Roman
Empire resonated with Calvin's views.

Calvin devotes much of this section of the *Admonitio* to examining
specific passages from Augustine that Westphal launches against him. In
response to Westphal's declaration that most of the sacramentarians have
never seen the writings of Augustine or have only looked at them slightly
and from a distance, Calvin returns the challenge by questioning Westphal's knowledge of Augustine. He argues that Augustine refutes the error
of those who take offense at Jesus' discourse in Capernaum because they
imagine that his flesh was to be eaten and his blood drunk in an earthly
manner. Previously, Westphal had compared Calvin and the sacramentarians with the Capernaumites who lacked the faith to accept Christ's
words. Calvin now responds with a much-quoted phrase from Augustine:
"'Why do you prepare your teeth and your stomach? Believe, and you

have eaten.' This passage clearly teaches that Augustine's Capernaumites are those who pretend that the body of Christ is chewed by the teeth, and swallowed by the stomach. How can Westphal deny that he is of this class . . . ?"[12] Calvin argues that, in writing against the Donatists, Augustine wants to show that things that are good do not change their nature by fault of those who use them improperly, so that baptism is not to be considered null simply because unbelievers get no benefit from it: "*In this way, it is not strange for Augustine to say that Judas was a partaker of the body of Christ, provided you restrict this to the visible sign.*"[13] Calvin claims that there is no other way to understand Augustine's distinction (*Tract. in Joann.* 59) that others took the bread, the Lord, while Judas took nothing but the bread of the Lord. Brazenly, he asserts that Westphal himself, as if he were changing sides, "assists us by mentioning that Peter and Judas ate of the same bread."[14] Calvin criticizes Westphal for improperly quoting Augustine, then offers rebuttals for Westphal's objections to his use of Augustine.

Because Westphal denies that Augustine ever interpreted the words of Christ to show that the bread signified Christ's body, Calvin first offers a lengthy discussion about how Augustine's words prove that Scripture often speaks figuratively. He reiterates that Christ's mode of speaking is sacramental, and that the sign must be distinguished from the reality. Hence he infers that Augustine gives his full sanction to the interpretation that Westphal assails. Since neither the substance nor the principal effects of the Supper are taken away by the word "signifying," Calvin tells Westphal to pick another point of quarrel. While Westphal clings to the word "essential," maintaining that the bread is properly called the body of Christ, Calvin relies on Augustine's expression that Christ's body was given when Christ was giving a sign of his body. For Calvin, spiritual eating is held in such a manner as to exclude sacramental eating in no way, as his explanation of Augustine tries to prove. Calvin's study of Augustine requires him to "infer" meaning applicable to the sixteenth-century eucharistic controversies. He argues that although the body of Christ remains in heaven, it inspires life into us by the secret virtue of the Spirit. In addition, he invokes the Holy Spirit as the implicit but central figure in his interpretation of Scripture and the fathers. Since Calvin does not want to separate spiritual from sacramental eating, he infers that spiritual eating takes place when faith is present and declares that there is no ground for Westphal's attempt to sever things that cannot be divided.[15] The dilemma that Calvin sees in Westphal's insistence on a carnal eating is that it leads to the conclusion that when unbelievers rashly and unworthily intrude themselves at the Lord's table, they eat spiritually without faith. Yet, for

Calvin, there is no such eating except in respect to faith.[16] Calvin does not see how an unbeliever can eat the bread of life and not be vivified; without faith, it is just bread.

Next, Calvin makes a condescending remark about the frivolity of delineating all the places Augustine calls the bread the body of Christ, since he does not believe these references prove anything. For Calvin, similar modes of expression function as metonymy, not as synonyms. He accuses Westphal of inconsiderately huddling together those passages in which Augustine indiscriminately calls the holy bread at one time the body of Christ and at another the Eucharist or Sacrament. Calvin is not convinced simply because in one passage the body of Christ is said to be distributed and in another the sacrament of the body and blood is given. Defining whether Augustine meant the actual body or the sacrament of the body was one of the crucial differences in the debate with Westphal. Calvin writes,

> Our Lord himself declared of the bread, "This is my body." The only question is whether he means that the bread is his body properly and without figure, or whether he transfers the name of the thing signified to the symbol? Westphal, interposing the opinion of Augustine with a view to end the dispute, produces nothing more than that the body of Christ is communicated to us in the Supper. What does Augustine himself say? "Had not the sacraments," he says, (*Epist. 23 ad Bonif.*) "some resemblance to the things of which they are sacraments, they should not be sacraments at all. From this resemblance they generally take the names of the things themselves.[17]

Therefore Calvin argues that, although the word "body" occurs a hundred times in Augustine, he understands what the holy man meant by the expression. That is, Augustine acknowledged the metonymy and affirmed that Christ gave the sign of his body and called it his body. Such an interpretation upholds Calvin's understanding of the words of institution. Yet Calvin must also deal with sayings of Augustine that are not as advantageous. He acknowledges that Augustine in his *De Trinitate* says that the body of Christ falls to the earth and enters the mouth. Yet Calvin clarifies this saying by affirming what Augustine says and then specifying that the body of Christ falls to the earth and enters the mouth *in the same sense* in which Augustine affirms that it is consumed. When Westphal quotes from Augustine's *Psalm Thirty-third*, that when Christ instituted the sacred Supper he was carried in his own hands, Calvin points out that he omits a crucial word in quoting Augustine. Augustine had inserted the word *quodammodo* ("in a manner"), which for Calvin meant that the expression is not strictly literal. He then accuses Westphal of deceptively omitting the word *quodammodo* since that word distinctly expresses a figure or similitude.

Thirdly, Calvin discusses the meaning of oblation, a term that Augustine mentions numerous times. He offers a passage that states that the flesh and blood in the passion of Christ was exhibited in reality and, since the ascension, has been celebrated by a sacrament of remembrance.[18] He then challenges Westphal to reconcile Augustine's words, namely that the body which was once exhibited in reality on the cross is celebrated by itself through a sacrament of remembrance.[19] Once again the charge against Westphal is that his omission of *quodammodo* misrepresents Augustine and renders his conclusion useless. Calvin acknowledges that the body of Christ is truly exhibited in the holy Supper; therefore he refutes Westphal's accusations as unfounded and argues that Westphal's caricature of the Reformed view as holding the sacred Supper destitute of its reality is simply false. At this point, Calvin mentions another church father besides Augustine. He writes: "I willingly borrow from Chrysostom—Christ in laying this table, does not feed us from any other source, but gives himself for food."[20] Calvin goes on to do that of which he has accused Westphal—namely citing one father and then generalizing to include all the fathers. For Calvin, the proper explanation of the mode of Communion proves that his view agrees with the holy fathers, "but that their words when adapted to the gross dream of Westphal are in a manner torn to tatters."[21] Calvin pinpoints the crux of this dispute as defining the bread and cup as Christ's body and blood or as a figure of Christ's body and blood.

Related to the question of the mode of Christ's presence, another point of contention is the issue of *manducatio infidelium*, the eating of the sacrament by the unfaithful. Calvin launches this section with a point of agreement, namely that the body of Christ is given indiscriminately to the good and bad because the faithfulness of Christ does not depend on the worthiness of one person alone; Christ truly invites people to partake of his body and blood, and he truly exhibits what he promises.[22] The disagreement is over what is received. Calvin believes that those who partake in faith receive Christ's body and blood and the associated benefits, while those who come without faith receive nothing. Calvin claims that Augustine speaks clearly: "Prepare not your palate, but your heart: for that was the Supper recommended."[23] Meanwhile, Westphal infers that Augustine makes no distinction between the elements given to the good and the bad, but places the whole difference in the effect. Calvin explains that, according to Westphal, unbelievers also receive and yet are not fed, whereas Augustine teaches that there is no receiving except by faith. In arguing over who receives Christ, Calvin's *Admonitio* demonstrates an effort to explain and interpret Augustine differently from Westphal's *Confessio*, which also names Augustine in order to support Lutheran views. In both cases, neither is willing to relinquish Augustine.

For support on his stance, Calvin delves further into Augustine's distinction between a sacrament and its virtue (*Tract. in Joann.* 26). According to Calvin, Augustine says that the fathers understood the visible food spiritually, hungered spiritually, and tasted spiritually, that they might be spiritually filled. Meanwhile, nothing but the bare sign is taken by unbelievers. Therefore the unbeliever receives the bread and the wine without the substance of Christ or his benefits. When Augustine says that unbelievers receive the body of Christ, Calvin declares that it ought to be understood that the wicked do not eat the body of Christ in any other way than in respect of the sign. Because they are deprived of the reality, nothing is conceded to the wicked except the visible sacrament.[24]

While the content of the argument seems to be repetitive, as if sheer volume could lend it weight, one issue that surfaces continuously is the interpretation of Scripture and of the fathers. Westphal contends that the body of Christ is truly and properly eaten because we must believe the plain and literal words of institution, which admit no figure. Calvin's response from Augustine's *Tract. in Joann.* 26 is that a sacrament of the body and blood of Christ is taken from the Lord's table by some unto life and by others unto destruction, whereas the substance of the sacrament is taken by those who partake of it unto life by all and unto destruction by none.[25] The first part of this quote seems to support Westphal's view, while the second seems to agree with Calvin. In places where Augustine's words could be construed either way, Calvin provides additional quotations from other places as further evidence that Augustine speaks for the Calvinist cause:

> Westphal asserts that the twofold communion is nowhere more clearly distinguished than in this sentence, (*Serra. 2, de Verb. Apost.*) "Then will the body and blood of Christ be life to every one, if that which is taken visibly in the sacrament is eaten spiritually in the reality." So willingly do I embrace this passage, that I am contented with it alone to refute Westphal's absurdity.[26]

In many cases, both Calvin and Westphal claim the same passages from Augustine for support. Where they differ is defining what Augustine intended. Their own divergent views naturally lead them to attribute different, usually opposing interpretations. Calvin writes: "Our people, after showing from numerous passages of Scripture that God has taught them this doctrine, have also proved that it is held by Augustine."[27] Since the authority of Scripture is primary, Calvin is careful first to point out that numerous passages in Scripture teach his doctrine, and then to buttress his interpretation of Scripture, presumably with Augustine's words. On the offense, Calvin attacks Westphal's explanation of Christ's body as immense—that is, ubiquitous. When Westphal remarks that Augustine often mentions the power of God concerning miracles, Calvin responds that if Augustine had imagined such a presence as Westphal fabricates, he could never have had a more fit opportunity to proclaim the power of God; thus one may infer from his silence that he had no knowledge of the fiction.[28] Because Calvin's Augustine would not dream of the doctrine of ubiquity, Calvin offers an alternative: summarizing his argument, he says that Augustine plainly asserts that the "Savior with respect to his human nature is in heaven; that with respect to the human nature, he is not diffused everywhere; therefore Christ is omnipresent as God, but with respect to the nature of a real body occupies some place in heaven."[29]

While Calvin does not want to detract from Christ's heavenly glory, he also wants to uphold the humanity of Christ, which Westphal also aims to safeguard. Although both want to ensure the reality of Christ's human nature, they are at odds over what kind of doctrine safeguards this belief. Calvin accuses Westphal of dragging Augustine to his side in a deceptive manner. Based on Westphal's citation from Augustine's *De Civitate Dei* 19.20, Calvin accuses Westphal of a ploy to exclude relevant material when it does not further the Lutheran cause. Calvin's explanation is that without any change of place, Christ's virtue penetrates to believers by the secret operation of his Spirit, so that souls obtain spiritual life from his substance. Calvin assumes that Westphal's perspective diminishes the importance of Christ's humanity. Because Christ has a body like humans' and because it resembles human flesh, Calvin refutes what he calls the "fiction of ubiquity." He cites Augustine, saying that divine nature is everywhere, while human nature is confined to a certain place.[30] When Westphal cites Augustine (*Sermon* 140) and says that humans may possess Christ because he has not withdrawn his majesty from the world, Calvin's rebuttal is to explain how, in speaking of the invisible presence, Augustine always excludes the body, and shows that it is to be looked for only in heaven. Based on Augustine's *Tract. in Joann.* 92, Calvin asserts that Christ left his disciples in corporeal presence, but will always be with his people in spiritual presence.[31] Throughout this section, Augustine is portrayed as a basis for Calvin's view.

*Calvin's Response to the Saxon Confessions*

In the third part of his *Admonitio*, in tackling the *Confessions of the Saxons*, Calvin begins by quantifying Westphal's supporters to perhaps ten percent of Saxony. Nevertheless he devotes a much greater number of pages to his answer to the *Confessions of the Saxons* than to the previous parts of his argument. He also continues to make periodic references to the fathers, including others besides Augustine. Yet Augustine continues to figure prominently in Calvin's references, because Calvin claims that nothing in Augustine is opposed to his own view. With Westphal's publication of the *Confessio*, Calvin realized the lack of support he had from the Lutherans, and he began to employ more references to the fathers. Although the fathers did not have the last word, they could be witnesses to help settle a dispute. Calvin thinks there is no need to call on Jerome as a witness to a point of sufficient agreement;[32] rather, calling on the fathers became necessary in the midst of disagreement. It is not so much that Calvin and Westphal were fighting over the fathers, but that *because* they were fighting, they resorted to the fathers.

Addressing the confession of the Magdeburgians, Calvin portrays them as being confused. They had explained that there is a coupling of the bread and wine, first with the flesh and blood of Christ, and secondly with the promise of salvation and the command to take the sacrament. Calvin accepts the Augustinian phrase that the element becomes a sacrament as soon as the word is added, but Calvin claims that the Magdeburgians erroneously confound the effect or fruit of the Supper with the matter itself.[33] While he agrees with the Magdeburgians that the natural, not spiritual, blood of Christ was shed on the cross and that Christ is given in the Supper, he disagrees with them about the manner of consumption. In defense of his own view, Calvin amasses his references to the early church fathers, beginning with Irenaeus and Jerome:

> Irenaeus says, that whatever is given in the Supper besides bread and wine is spiritual. In the same way I interpret the expression of Jerome (*Cap. 1. ad Ephes.*): "The flesh of Christ is understood in a twofold sense, the one spiritual and divine, of which he says, my flesh is meat indeed, and that which was crucified; not that he makes it twofold in reality, but because the mode of participation raises us above heaven."[34]

Calvin continues to cite other fathers, and often either adds to or qualifies their statements. At times he points to them not only for their theological import but also for their historical import, and he usually elaborates on their struggle against erroneous doctrine. First he writes, "Justin says, that the bread and wine, by the word of prayer and thanksgiving, become the flesh and blood of Christ. We, too, say the same thing, provided the mode of Communion, which was then known to the Church, be added."[35] By "mode of communication," Calvin means that the flesh and blood are the things signified. Calvin then cites Cyril, saying, "When we eat the flesh of Christ, which is vivifying by the conjunction of the word, we have life in us; why then do they maintain that unbelievers eat of it without benefit? If the flesh of Christ gives life when it is eaten it is incongruous to say that it is promiscuously eaten by those who remain in death."[36] In order to lessen the weight of the words about the eating of the flesh, Calvin informs the reader that, since Cyril was contending against the Arians, he was led to hyperbole and was simply trying to teach believers to become substantially one with Christ, just as Christ is one with the Father. In this case, Calvin illuminates the historical context in order to temper the corporeal emphasis of Cyril's words. He adds Hilary and Irenaeus to show that those who partake of Christ's body and blood receive Christ's virtue and benefits. Calvin reiterates Hilary's declaration that these elements, when received and taken, cause believers to be in Christ and Christ to be in them. From this, Calvin concludes that the Magdeburgians are wrong because they say that unbelievers, though they eat the body of Christ and drink his blood, remain in a state of complete alienation from him.[37] Rather than interpreting Hilary's words as expressing the Calvinist view, Calvin simply pits the Lutheran view against Hilary's. He presents the Magdeburgians as maintaining two contradictory propositions. They affirm that unbelievers truly receive Christ, but that they are at the same time completely alienated from the benefits of Christ.

Another strategy employed by Calvin is to question the authorship of an ancient writing cited by the Lutherans. When the Madgeburgians quote the words of Cyprian, for example, he presumes ill motive or wicked guile, since the style of the quotation plainly shows that the expression is not Cyprian's.[38] Even if Cyprian were the author, Calvin claims that the Magdeburgians have only partially presented Cyprian's view; he then offers an explanation amenable to his own views. He also quotes Ambrose through Theodoret and conjectures as to what view Ambrose would have espoused: "Had any one asked Ambrose whether the body of Christ was actually handled in the Supper, he undoubtedly would have abominated the gross delirium. [When] he says that it is handled by the hands, every sober and sensible man sees the metonymy."[39] In case Ambrose alone is not convincing enough, Calvin falls back to his trusted source, Augustine, for support. Because Augustine says that when he handed the Supper to his disciples, Christ was *in a manner* carried in their hands, Calvin judges that Westphal has been dishonest by omitting the expression "in a manner," which, for Calvin, entirely removes any difficulty of interpretation.[40] Meanwhile, Calvin argues that he is not like some fanatics who make the Lord's Supper allegorical. Rather, his objective is to show the significance of the signs so that the meaning may be true and effectual and the reality may be exhibited. With Augustine on his side, Calvin suggests that any attack on his position is an attack on Augustine. For example, when the Magdeburgians criticize the fathers' authority, they claim that the fathers often mixed up human things with divine things, and in this way diluted theology. Calvin responds by upholding the fathers' reputation by praising the teachings of Augustine and commenting that the Magdeburgians' disrespect for Augustine reflects their treatment of himself as well.[41]

As Calvin moves on to tackle a document from the Bremen church, he makes a few more quick references to the fathers, namely Augustine and Jerome. He portrays the ministers of Bremen as enemies of the entire ancient church and claims that when the fathers are correctly understood, they bolster his case. On this basis he condemns the people of Bremen for excluding the spiritual interpretation. He argues that although the true body of Christ is eaten in the Supper, this is no grounds for believing that a spiritual interpretation is excluded:

> Certainly in the age of Augustine and Jerome no man doubted that the body of Christ was one. The former, however, to obviate a gross imagination, introduces Christ as saying, I have committed, an ordinance to you, which, spiritually understood, will give you life. The latter declares more harshly, that the flesh of Christ which we eat in the Supper is different from that which was offered on the cross, and the blood drunk different from that which was offered; not that he really thought the natures of the flesh and blood to be different, but that he might more distinctly express that they are eaten in a mystery.[42]

One of the ways Calvin discredits his opponents is to attack them through the words of the ancient authorities, usually with additional words. The question is not so much about who is truly following Irenaeus, Augustine, or Cyril, since each side believes that the fathers stand with them. Rather, by illustrating his alignment with a respected father in continuity with the early church, Calvin achieves the dual purpose of amassing support from the early church fathers and discrediting a contemporary opponent.

## Westphal's *Confutatio* and *Apologia Confessionis de Coena Domini*

The dilemma that Westphal sees in Calvin's rejection of Christ's corporeal presence is that Christ does not give his body in the Supper and therefore his words of institution are rendered incoherent and need a rational explanation rather than a faithful response to a supernatural event. In 1558 Westphal directs a brief *Answer to Some of the Outrageous Lies of John Calvin* (hereafter referred to by the partial Latin title *Confutatio*)[43] against Calvin's *Admonitio*. Westphal's in-depth answer against Calvin, however, comes in his *Apology concerning the Defense of the Lord's Supper against the Errors and Calumnies of John Calvin* (hereafter referred to as the *Apologia*),[44] which was his counterattack on Calvin's final response. This bulky tome of 462 pages appeared immediately after Easter and Calvin could not be enticed to respond.[45] In the *Apologia*, Westphal dedicates the first thirty-five chapters and the thirty-eighth chapter to the subject of the Eucharist, while the subsequent chapters treat other subjects, such as ceremonies, infant baptism, division of the Decalogue, feast days, and martyrdom. Of the chapters that deal specifically with the Eucharist, chapters 10 through 16, 21, 22, and 28 deal with Augustine's writings. Additionally, Westphal refers to various other church fathers throughout this work, although most of the references are limited to Cyril, Chrysostom, Ambrose, and Cyprian. Part of Westphal's tactic was to introduce a variety of opponents to Calvin, whether Philip Melanchthon, the churches of Saxony, or the early church father Augustine.

In chapter 1 of the *Apologia*, Westphal argues that there is no place in Scripture in which the Lord's Supper is called a sign. He acknowledges Augustine's statement from *Epistle* 5 that when the signs are transferred to the sacred things, they are called sacraments, which are defined as visible signs of invisible grace. Westphal explains, however, that "*more often* the fathers called the Supper the sacrament."[46] Like Luther, Westphal argues that the majority opinion ought to be weighed more heavily. While he is willing to acknowledge other positions, he argues that the majority of the fathers support his view. He deploys Chrysostom's words, for example, for his emphasis on the presence of the body of Christ in the Lord's Supper.[47]

### Westphal's Critique

In chapter 10 of the *Apologia*, after a cursory remark about how the vocabulary used in the Lutheran churches agrees with that used in Augustine's time, Westphal responds to Calvin's charges against him. He extends his criticism back to the debates at the Marburg Colloquy, indicating that the

debates over the Eucharist from the 1520s were never resolved among
Protestant reformers. Westphal questions Oecolampadius' efforts to collect opinions of the ancients, saying, "Why did he labor exceedingly to
drag all the ancients to his figure?"[48] The implication is that such strenu-
ous labor belies a covering up of error. For Westphal, the plain sense
of Christ's words clearly states what ought to be believed. Any effort to
explain otherwise is an attempt fueled by an evil motive to distort both
the sacred Scriptures and the opinion of the fathers. Westphal lists various places that mention the sacred bread, at one time as the body of
Christ and at another time as the Eucharist or the sacrament, in order to
demonstrate that by "sacred bread" Augustine means "body of Christ."
Referring to his own *Collectanea*, he defines other places in Augustine
that reject the notion that the bread signifies or even has similitude with
the signifying thing.[49] He also accuses Calvin of twisting the words of
the "greatest doctor" to fit his meaning in order to boast that Augustine
stands by his side.[50] If there is any ambiguity in Augustine's writings,
Westphal can appeal to the authority of Christ as greater than that of
Augustine, since he has already established a hierarchy of authorities
with Christ at the head.

The point of Westphal's dissent with Calvin revolves around how
Christ's body and blood are present in the Eucharist, even though both
men espouse faith for accepting the mysteries of the sacrament. Appealing to the infrequency of the word "figure" in ancient discussions of the
Eucharist, Westphal argues that Augustine mentions the word "figure"
only twice in relation to the Eucharist, and emphasizes that the word
does not mean what Calvin says. With the purpose of discrediting Calvin, Westphal devotes many pages to delineating how Augustine ought
to be understood correctly. Whatever the fathers taught, Westphal wants
to make sure it is not what Calvin teaches. He trusts that the fathers give
good reasons why they think that the flesh of the Lord is received. Recalling another father, he writes that Irenaeus proves this point after his discussion on the resurrection of bodies when he says, "How do they say
that flesh does not receive life, which is nourished by the body and blood
of the Lord?"[51] For Westphal, the fathers carry weight and value when
their writings are consistent with Christ's words. He perceives Calvin's
use of figurative language as a dismissal of the body of Christ, which in
turn renders Christ absent from the elements. And so he charges Calvin
with deviating from the minds of Scripture and of Augustine, because he
construes the sacrament or figure according to the symbol of the absent
body.[52] Even in the midst of supplying other places in Augustine's writings as evidence, Westphal continues to emphasize that his own view has

been determined first of all by Christ's words in Scripture. Despite Calvin's protests that he is not dismissive of Christ's presence, Westphal has determined that Calvin, along with the rest of the Reformed thinkers, is following in the footsteps of Zwingli and is therefore altogether erroneous. At the end of chapter 10, Westphal includes a reference to Chrysostom as one who strenuously fought against the erroneous beliefs of Berengar[53] by reciting that he truly senses something other than what he perceives. This is not a historical argument, since Chrysostom and Berengar are separated by seven centuries; rather, it is a theological construct in which Berengar represents a heterodox position of symbolic interpretation of the Eucharist. Westphal repeatedly argues that Calvin's assessment of the Supper is based on postulations offered in *one place* from Augustine.[54] By giving the impression that Calvin has chosen esoteric or uncommon passages in Augustine's writings, Westphal can argue that, in many more places, Augustine supports the Lutheran position. Finding no support for Calvin's statement that the unworthy obtain nothing besides the figure, Westphal stresses that Augustine says in many places that the sacraments are the Communion of the good and the bad.[55] Dismissing Calvin's view that the unworthy only receive the bread and wine, not the body and blood of Christ, Westphal recalls the Pauline passages of 1 Corinthians 11 and "the more superior testimonies" of Augustine.[56] For Westphal, the fathers, including Augustine, confirm the testimony of the Apostle Paul, who says that those who eat unworthily, without true faith, eat to their own judgment.

According to Westphal, Augustine expresses both the bodily and the spiritual communication. Yet Calvin, having posited the one and omitted the other, creates a faulty division.[57] Here we see that Westphal has adjusted his argument from his previous citations. Rather than presenting Augustine as a champion of bodily presence in the sacrament, he recognizes that the Augustinian interpretation includes a spiritual communication. Westphal now faults Calvin for what he perceives to be the failure to include both the bodily and spiritual in his interpretation of Christ's presence in the Eucharist. From Augustine's work on Psalm 98, Westphal argues that the spiritual eating ought not to be separated from the bodily. In order to leave no room for Calvin's discussion of metonymy, Westphal clarifies his understanding of the term "mystery" and argues that the word does not refer to a sign and its metonymy, but is to be understood as a hidden and secret thing of faith alone. Three key fathers—Cyril, Chrysostom, and Hilary—are listed as having used the appellation "mystery." Yet there is no discussion of specific references to their writings, as is offered for Augustine, most likely because Westphal has already written the

*Collectanea* and refers to it frequently. Since Westphal also wrote a treatise based on Cyril's writings, Cyril also emerges repeatedly in the *Apologia*.

At the same time, however, Westphal resists the type of cross carnal eating that Cyprian describes of the unbelieving disciples who think that participants in the Eucharist are feeding on human flesh.[58] Returning to Cyril several times on this same point, Westphal argues that Cyril (in *Book 12 in John Ch. 53*) teaches that Christ suddenly enters through closed doors to the disciples by his omnipotence, since he overcomes natural things, and that this type of presence is appropriately applied to the presence of Christ's body in the Eucharist.[59] Westphal states that Chrysostom too stipulates this opinion in *Homily 16*, where he stresses that Christ does not appear as a phantom or a spirit but truly as a body.[60] In addition to Chrysostom, Westphal cites Hilary's *Book 3 Concerning the Trinity* as corroborating the Lutheran assertion[61]—specifically Hilary's statement that we do not apprehend what has been done, but that faith overcomes the lie of what has occurred.[62] In cases where Augustine or the other fathers are silent or comment very little, Westphal argues that Christ's words are clear.

Like Calvin's accusations against Westphal in the *Admonitio*, Westphal's accusations against Calvin are filled with vilification of character in order to diminish any semblance of his opponent's piety. Westphal writes: "First [Calvin] attacks with mad fury that I warn the reader that Augustine makes no mention in the *Epistle to Dardanus* and in *Tract. 30 in Joann.* anything concerning the Lord's Supper. Before me, Philip Melanchthon, a most illustrious man, makes the same point; three times in one work he warns that Augustine has made no mention of the Lord's Supper."[63] Westphal refers to Melanchthon because he knows that Calvin was soliciting Melanchthon's input to provide an alternate Lutheran view. Following Melanchthon's reasoning, Westphal rejects Calvin's reliance on Augustine's interpretation of John because it is not relevant to the Eucharist.

Westphal answers Calvin's main objection to the view of ubiquity with a different interpretation of the creed that places Christ at the right hand of God. Aware of the various debates regarding the locality of Christ's presence, Westphal tries to expand the boundaries of heaven. He notes that Calvin defines heaven as the glorious palace of God and that, similarly, Oecolampadius defines heaven as Christ's most worthy habitation. Yet Westphal prefers Bucer's definition of heaven: "Heaven where God is said to inhabit whence Christ came and to which he ascended, is inaccessible light and the glory of the invisible God."[64] In light of Calvin's explanation from Augustine that heaven is a circumscribed location, Westphal mentions differences of opinion among the fathers themselves:

"If Augustine was dissenting from Cyril and Chrysostom, then it is supposed that Augustine [wrongly] assumed the natural body from the virgin to be resurrected."[65] At the end of this chapter, Westphal excludes Augustine because he can be so easily misconstrued and refers to other fathers, namely Chrysostom, Basil, Ambrose, and Cyril. He writes,

> Chrysostom wrote in *Homily I in Matthew*, that the Apostles were persuaded that the [elements] were beyond nature. Basil in *Ethics* warns that one ought not to hesitate and doubt in these things which were spoken by the Lord, but for the sake of having certainty, the word of God is true and powerful even if it contradicts with nature. Ambrose said in the book *On Mysteries*: the order of nature is not sought in the body of Christ. Thus other catholic doctors divert to the word, to the truth, to the omnipotence of God and to faith. Therefore we have for certainty the word of Christ saying: "This is my body" and we believe this to be true even if philosophy and nature contradict it loudly, [namely] that the body of Christ cannot be distributed present in many places. Cyril said: Because the body of Christ transcends all human things, we therefore believe that he transcends both the extents and dimensions of places.[66]

### Interpretation of John 6

In chapters 27, 28, and 30 of the *Apologia*, Westphal addresses one of the major biblical sources for the Reformed views: the interpretation of the Gospel of John, especially Christ's words in John 6, "the flesh does not profit anything." The Lutheran understanding requires extensive exposition of John 6, since such passages were used by Zwingli as biblical support for his stance. Westphal's arguments are directed against Zwingli, who, by this time, has been dead for over twenty-five years. Doubting the caliber of Zwingli's scholarship, Westphal writes,

> Zwingli wanted to seem that he read all of the writers, especially the ancient Chrysostom noted for his interpretation of scripture, and to persuade [others that] the exposition by which the flesh is received according to a carnal sense is not found in any commentaries. In his *Enarratione super Iohannem*, Chrysostom twice admonishes truly that Christ did not say this concerning his flesh when he said, "That the flesh does not profit anything, he says not concerning *his* flesh . . . but concerning those who receive carnally. . . ." It does not profit anything, not concerning his flesh, but it is spoken concerning the carnal hearing.[67]

By espousing a figurative interpretation rather than a literal one for the word "flesh," Westphal follows Luther's exposition to render a troublesome verse consistent with their eucharistic doctrine.[68] Despite early Lutheran objections to the relevance of John 6 to eucharistic doctrine, Westphal engages those very texts that support the Reformed views, and presents Augustine's interpretation of John as compatible with the Lutheran views. From Augustine's *Tract. 30 in Joann.*, Westphal writes, "Augustine discusses one mode of Christ's presence by which he is present and speaks of his church through the gospel . . . Augustine says, the Lord is above and *the truth of the Lord* is with us. The body can be in one place, truth is, his body is diffused in all places. . . ."[69] From this, Westphal deduces that Augustine could be a supporter of the doctrine of ubiquity.

## Critique of the Questions

Finally, in chapter 35 of the *Apologia*, Westphal returns to his critique of what he calls absurd and perplexing questions. In a previous section, he degrades not only Calvin's response but also his line of questioning. He mentions that Cyril degrades curious questioning and that Chrysostom warns to abstain from questions that ask how God effects a miraculous change, since the reason for asking demonstrates unbelief.[70] Although Calvin has emphasized the importance of faith for partaking of the Eucharist, Westphal points out that this faith is precisely what Calvin lacks. In this section, he offers a list of brief citations from various church fathers, including Basil, Cyril, Chrysostom, Ambrose, Augustine, and Gregory Nazianzus. The idea is that Calvin's line of questioning belongs to the category of unnecessarily absurd questions that demonstrate a lack of faith. Apparently Westphal has a stockpile of citations from the church fathers that discourage overly curious questioning. From book 5 of Basil's *Against Eunomius*, he quotes, "It is necessary to believe in order to come near to God," and then clarifies, "[Basil] says to believe, not inquire faithlessly and curiously."[71] Westphal argues that Cyril, Chrysostom, and Augustine do not lead the wicked to be outside the word of God by curiously inquiring about the mode. For Westphal, the question of mode should not be a question at all, and from Ambrose's *On Faith* he quotes, "Let vain questions be silent, for the reign of God is not in persuasion of words but in the display of power."[72] From Augustine's *Sermon on Time 131*, he quotes, "The Lord does not come to us in thought, just as he is able to become either this or that, so we are commanded to confess his omnipotence."[73] At the end of this chapter, he cites Gregory Nazianzus and returns to Basil's *Epistle 168* to taunt that those who cannot understand small, insignificant things should not presume to fathom divine mysteries.[74] Westphal is using Basil's words to criticize Calvin's intellect and reasoning. In this last chapter, his appeal to the fathers serves to dismiss not only Calvin's answers, but also his questions. The fathers provide a great source of verbal ammunition in his battle with Calvin not only over the right understanding of the Eucharist, but also the right kind of questioning.

## 1559 *Institutes*

While the Calvin-Westphal exchange formally ended with Westphal's *Apologia* in 1558, Calvin wrote his last Latin edition of the *Institutes* in the following year, and his debates with Westphal clearly shaped the expansion of the section on the Eucharist. In this version of the *Institutes*, Calvin includes the highest number of references to the church fathers. Because he is aware of his opponents, including the Gnesio-Lutherans, Calvin's appeal to the church fathers in the 1559 *Institutes* is primarily polemical.[75] Since the work came after the escalating debates with Joachim Westphal, the repercussions of the exchange are apparent. In Calvin's discussion of the Lord's Supper, his references are mostly to Augustine, followed by Chrysostom, and occasionally Cyril of Alexandria and Tertullian, although other fathers are also sporadically mentioned. In chapters 17 and 18 of book 4, Calvin includes thirty-nine specific references to ancient writers and five general references to church fathers.

## Augustine, Chrysostom, Cyril, and Tertullian

Calvin's two key fathers, Augustine and Chrysostom, surface as equally supporting the importance of faith in the participation of the Lord's Supper. Calvin repeats that Augustine highly commends that benefit of faith, "for through the Lord's Supper our souls are as much refreshed by partaking of Christ's flesh as our bodies are by the bread we eat."[76] Because Calvin often employs Augustine's language to discuss the Lord's Supper, it is convenient for him in this last Latin edition of the *Institutes* simply to add Augustine's name in various places. After reiterating a reference to Chrysostom from the 1543 edition, Calvin proceeds to reprove those who do not correctly understand the Lord's Supper. For him, Chrysostom is a springboard for further polemical claims. Building on respected ancient sayings, Calvin rejects the errors of those who, from his perspective, depend too much on the outward sign (Catholics and Lutherans) or partake in spirit only (Spiritualists).

In light of his figurative interpretation of the words of institution, Calvin claims that his view is not a newly devised doctrine. To support this claim, he looks back to the ancients and appeals mostly to Augustine for support. Because Augustine "felt and spoke the same way," Calvin can say that if sacraments did not have a certain likeness to the things of which they are sacraments, they would not be sacraments at all.[77] Thus the sacrament of Christ's body and blood is *in a certain manner* Christ's body and blood. He then adds that there are many similar passages in Augustine that would be superfluous to collect, because this one is enough and Augustine teaches the same thing in his letter to Evodius.[78] Calvin dismisses Westphal's assertion that where Augustine says metonymy is frequent and common in the sacraments, he makes no mention of the Supper.[79] Instead, Calvin's answer is to turn to another place in Augustine, where he says, "Christ, when he gave the sign of his body, did not hesitate to call it his body. And again, Augustine says: 'Wonderful was Christ's patience, because he received Judas at the banquet in which he instituted and gave the figure of his body and blood to his disciples.'"[80]

In discussing the impossibility of a purely literal interpretation, Calvin borrows the polemical language of another church father, Epiphanius, without naming him. By drawing on Epiphanius' attack of the Anthropomorphites, Calvin warns against the dangers of a completely literal interpretation that produces "monstrous absurdities."[81] He employs the ancient rhetoric against "heresies" in his argumentation against any who would not understand the bread as a symbol of the body. In this case, Calvin's tactic is to accuse the Gnesio-Lutherans of returning to the errors of the Roman Catholic Church. Meanwhile, the Gnesio-Lutherans, most poignantly Joachim Westphal and, later, Tilemann Hesshusen, accuse Calvin and other Reformed leaders of lacking faith and being bound to human reason. In response, Calvin repeats the argument that Christ's humanity is in heaven as testified in the Creed and outlined in the first 1536 edition of his *Institutes*, but he adds a short clause in the middle of the sentence: "as Augustine attests."[82] By the time of the 1559 *Institutes*, Calvin was trying to amass increasing support from the fathers because of his debates with Westphal on the subject of the Lord's Supper. Since the crux of the debate revolved around the biblical interpretation of passages on the Supper, Calvin argued that the Gnesio-Lutherans had a method of interpretation like the Anthropomorphites, who made God corporeal, like "Marcion and the Manichees when they devised for Christ either a heavenly or a spectral body."[83] Criticizing transubstantiation as a fairly "new" doctrine, Calvin accuses his Roman Catholic opponents of despising not only Scripture but also the "consensus of the ancient church."[84] At this point, he simply alludes to a common agreement on the Lord's Supper in the ancient church, even though one would be hard-pressed to state exactly what that consensus was. Calvin employs the rhetoric of consensus to delineate who is "inside" or "outside" the agreement of the ancient church.

Concerning the place of Christ's body, Calvin cites Augustine's explanation that "when Christ said, 'you will not have me with you always,' he was speaking of the presence of the body."[85] This explanation was mentioned in the 1543 *Institutes* but in the 1559 edition Calvin introduces this opinion by saying, "Augustine explained it in the same way, with words not in the least ambiguous."[86] Whereas in the earlier editions Calvin felt it necessary simply to offer the ancient opinion, by the time of the 1559 edition, Calvin feels the need to mention the ancient source of this opinion. Continuing his discussion of Christ's presence, he draws on Augustine, who conceives of Christ as present among us in three ways: in majesty, in providence, and in ineffable grace. Calvin explains that the marvelous Communion of Christ's body and blood is included—provided that believers understand that it takes place by the power of the Holy Spirit, not by that feigned inclusion of the body itself under the element.[87] Calvin explains that Augustine ought not to be misunderstood as supporting a corporeal presence of Christ in the Lord's Supper. Based on Augustine, he argues for the spiritual presence in the elements of the Lord's Supper and reaffirms Christ's presence in heaven.

Directed against Westphal, Calvin states his reason for offering his study of Augustine: "since the defenders of this misbegotten doctrine [that Christ never left the earth but remains invisible among his own] are not ashamed to deck it with the approbation of ancient writers, and especially of Augustine, I shall set forth in a few words how perversely they attempt this."[88] Addressing the partaking of the Lord's Supper by unbelievers, Calvin identifies Augustine as affirming that people's unfaithfulness or ill will does not mean that anything is taken away from the sacraments. He employs Augustine's words to support the veracity of his opinion since Augustine's name provides a preapproved ancient endorsement. Afterwards, Calvin continues to mount citations from Augustine as if he can overwhelm his opponents by inundation. In drawing a distinction between eating sacramentally and in reality, he finds confirmation in Augustine's "Do not prepare your teeth but your heart."[89] Claiming that his opponents have misunderstood Augustine in order to feign Augustine's support, Calvin believes that it can certainly be inferred from Augustine's words that, where unbelief closes the door to the reality, sacramental eating has no more value than visible or outward eating. He writes: "[L]est my opponents assert that I fight them by piling up quotations, I should like to know how they can evade this one statement of Augustine, 'In the elect alone do the sacraments effect what they symbolize.'"[90]

In addition to Augustine, Calvin makes a reference to Cyril, who, he says, expresses the same view as Augustine when he states that the wicked are barred from partaking of Christ's body. Calvin particularly aims this depiction of Cyril as supportive of the Reformed cause at the Lutherans, since Westphal had written a tract on the collected sayings of Cyril, as well as Augustine, in support of the Lutheran stance. According to Calvin, it is clear by Cyril's words that those who only sacramentally or metaphorically eat Christ's body are deprived of the true and real eating of it.[91] Although Calvin was accused of being a sacramentarian, he claims to be against those sacramentarians who accept the sacrament without the substance. To guard against any accusations of completely spiritualizing Christ's body, Calvin upholds the nature of a body and the humanness of Christ, and states that Christ rose again and ascended into heaven as Tertullian describes. He then cites Tertullian to argue that, since Christ's body was true and natural, in the sacrament the figure is set before us as a pledge and assurance of the spiritual life.[92] As to the dilemma of how Christ is in heaven and in the Lord's Supper, Calvin repeats Augustine's words, "This mystery, like others is performed by humans, but divinely; on earth but in a heavenly way."[93] At the same time, Chrysostom proves to be a rhetorical resource for Calvin's exegesis on the passages dealing with the Lord's Supper. It is clear that Calvin does not adopt all of Chrysostom's explication on Scripture and, even in the parts he accepts, he does so with clarification or reinterpretation. Nevertheless, his references to Chrysostom serve as a starting point for making polemical claims, clarifying unsatisfactory interpretations, and illuminating the meaning of biblical texts. The other fathers, namely Cyril and Tertullian, are mentioned briefly as references to demonstrate that more than one church father support the Reformed cause.

Calvin's purpose is to show that Augustine is wholly and incontrovertibly on his side. The question fueling the debate over the right understanding of the fathers becomes: Who is on the right side? Like most scholars of the sixteenth century, Calvin agrees that the venerable church fathers are exemplary theologians, but that they are sometimes wrong, and he is willing to correct them. Calvin's purpose is to place himself with those voices who speak "rightly" since authority comes from the perception of being on the "right" side. The citations of respected church fathers, such as Augustine and Chrysostom, provide a type of authorization that is not so much intrinsic to individual church fathers who are centuries removed from the sixteenth-century eucharistic debates, but nevertheless buttress a rhetoric of alignment with correct doctrine in the history of the church. Then the sayings of the fathers serve as building blocks for expanding interpretations of the Eucharist.

# Conclusion

For Calvin and Westphal, the correction of a contemporary opponent looms large over their continuous attempts to substantiate a historical basis for their views. Both claim the church fathers for their sides of the debate and work to prove it. In many cases, both Calvin and Westphal presume to uphold the same passages of Augustine. Where they differ is defining what Augustine means. Despite some points of general agreement, such as supporting frequent Communion and understanding Christ's body and blood as spiritual nourishment, their disagreement over the mode of Christ's presence and reception of unbelievers dominates the debates.

Throughout these debates, Calvin cites the fathers mostly for support but also for correction. Following Westphal's strategy, he devotes more of his references in his second response to Westphal to comparing his opponent with a figure condemned by the ancient church. And, instead of simply citing supportive explanations from the fathers, Calvin, like Westphal, chooses to highlight "bad" ancients as a way to discredit his opponent. Part of the confusion over Calvin's view of the Eucharist comes from the fact that he tries to incorporate both a real and a spiritual component in his explanation of a "true spiritual presence." Yet Westphal judges Calvin's efforts as a disguised form of Zwinglian symbolism. Consequently, Westphal rejects any attempt for consensus as dishonest.

Throughout the *Adversus*, *Confessio*, and *Apologia*, Westphal corrects Calvin and the sacramentarians by delineating his own interpretation of the fathers. In doing so, he offers the fathers in support of his view by interpreting their intentions and by pointing to a majority, or at least frequently stated, opinion. Even though Luther eventually downplayed Augustine in his eucharistic debates, Westphal (together with other Lutherans) labors to redeem Augustine for the Lutheran side. In places where Augustine's words decidedly support Calvin's view, Westphal's tactic is to declare that Augustine is not treating the Lord's Supper. Westphal also includes various ancient quotes unrelated to the subject of the Eucharist, but which are nevertheless useful in embellishing his polemical rhetoric. His tactic is to draw the fathers as close to the Lutheran position as possible, to dismiss difficult passages as irrelevant or infrequently mentioned, and to accuse the Reformed of impious or belligerent questioning. When the fathers seem to fail him, Westphal reiterates that Christ's words are primary. Westphal claims that Augustine's objective was to prevent the reality of human nature from being destroyed. As Westphal sees it, Calvin has no other intent than to deny that Christ is in the Eucharist.

In claiming the support of the fathers, both Calvin and Westphal season their accusations of irrelevance, confusion, and ignorance of the other with insults. Both men claim the truth of the Lord but they differ on what that truth reveals. Both deploy the fathers most frequently in order to contradict each other through the words of an ancient authority. If the denouncement of one another is ambiguous, then it is made clearly antagonistic by further explanation of what the fathers intended. Initially these doctrinal challenges increased the impetus for further patristic study, motivated by subjective interests.

In the last round of the debate between Calvin and Westphal, both men include a greater numbers of references to the church fathers than in their previous exchanges with one another. Where there is consensus, there is no need to establish an authoritative voice for one view over and against another. As both sides claim to have the backing of many Protestant churches, they realize that the debate is not just over the details of eucharistic doctrine but also over the authority to define the church's stance. Therefore, they call on the fathers to testify and give validity to their interpretations or to debunk another's views. They need the fathers to graft their views into an accepted tradition in the midst of disagreement. It is precisely in the midst of polemical debates that ancient authorities such as the church fathers become crucial. Just as this debate manifests the struggle over the authority to dictate doctrine, the use of the fathers is part of an effort to gain an "authoritative voice" in the midst of a highly competitive arena of doctrinal views.

The Calvin–Westphal exchange illustrates two strands of Protestantism that remained divided over the doctrine of the Lord's Supper. The fathers were part of a strategy to define authority among the generation of reformers after Luther. Calvin's letters to other church leaders, such as Laski, Poullain, Bullinger, and Vermigli, show how extensively this debate affected places where Lutheran and Reformed people had to coexist in close proximity. While Calvin resolved that he himself had refuted Westphal more than sufficiently, he also hoped that someone else would refute Westphal. In September 1559, it was his associate, Theodore Beza, who ventured to make such a response in his *Clear and Lucid Treatise on the Lord's Supper in which the Calumnies of Joachim Westphal are Refuted*.[94] Calvin's final piece on the Eucharist against the Lutherans was his response in 1561 to another Lutheran, Tilemann Hesshusen, in *The True Partaking of the Flesh and Blood of Christ*. Through all these debates, Calvin employed the writings and names of the church fathers to shape his view of the Eucharist, to support his view against Lutheran opponents such as Westphal, and to establish an ancestry for the Calvinist view.

## Chapter 5

# Calvin versus Hesshusen
## *The Fathers as a Challenge to Biblical Interpretation*

During the second half of the sixteenth century, Lutheran and Reformed groups produced confessions to define their doctrinal identity while various groups worked toward confessional consolidation, which sometimes led to conflict.[1] Nowhere is this more evident than in those territories that had first experienced a relatively conservative Lutheran reform followed by a second reformation in which Calvinists claimed to discard the remaining "popish relics" and "leftover papal dung."[2] It happened first in the Palatinate (1563), then in Nassau, Bremen, Anhalt (1590), and Hesse-Kassel (1605), and was also attempted in Saxony (1587–1591) and in Brandenburg (1613–1615). After writing *The Last Admonition* in 1557, Calvin had resisted responding to Westphal, a task that was transferred to Theodore Beza. But in 1561 he responded to another Lutheran, Tilemann Hesshusen. These debates over the Eucharist clarified the differences in the Lutheran and Reformed rituals, which publicly confirmed each side's distinctive interpretation. The ritual practices of the Lord's Supper shaped an identity that differentiated Catholic from Protestant, and also Lutheran from Reformed. In many ways, the debates between Calvin and the Lutherans sealed this polarization. In the context of confessional consolidation, the Calvin–Hesshusen debate was part of an effort by Lutherans and Calvinists to express a historical identity by distinguishing themselves first from the Roman Catholic Church, and second from each other as separate Protestant churches.[3]

Tilemannus Heshusius Vesalius, also known as Tilemann Heshus or Hesshusen (1527–1588), was a former student of Philip Melanchthon. As a Lutheran pastor and theologian, Hesshusen opposed the introduction of Reformed theology at Heidelberg and criticized the Palatinate Elector Frederick II's penchant for Calvinist theology. In the controversy over the Lord's Supper, Hesshusen demonstrated his alignment with the Gnesio-Lutherans and was dismissed (at Melanchthon's recommendation) from his post in Heidelberg in 1559. After moving on to Bremen, Hesshusen served as a superintendent and opposed Albert Hardenberg's Reformed understanding of the Lord's Supper. Although Hardenberg was forced out of the city in 1561, in the following year Mayor Daniel von Büren, a supporter of Hardenberg's view, engineered the expulsion of Hesshusen and other Lutheran pastors. From Magdeburg, Hesshusen attacked his Reformed opponents and insisted that Christ's sacramental presence be based only on a literal sense of the words "this is my body," without necessarily arguing for Christ's ubiquity as other Lutherans did.

In 1560 Hesshusen published a polemical treatise against Calvin titled *De Praesentia Corporis Christi in Coena Domini, contra Sacramentarios* (hereafter cited as *De Praesentia*) that was later sent to Calvin via Bullinger. Even though Calvin had stopped writing against his previous Lutheran opponent, Westphal, he decided to answer Hesshusen. In *De Praesentia*, which summarized the heart of the Lutheran case against Calvin's eucharistic theology, Hesshusen claimed to be following the example of the church fathers. His attack evoked from Calvin a one-time response titled *The Clear Explanation of Sound Doctrine concerning the True Partaking of the Flesh and Blood of Christ in the Holy Supper* (hereafter cited by the partial Latin title *Dilucida Explicatio*).[4] In the short treatise that Calvin appended to his *Dilucida Explicatio*, "The Best Method of Obtaining Concord Provided the Truth be Sought without Contention,"[5] Calvin described the original controversy over the Lord's Supper as a controversy between Lutherans who alleged that the grace of the Spirit was tied to external elements and Zwinglians who contended that only bare and empty figures like theatrical shows were left. In Calvin's view, this contention had now ceased. This estimation was, however, only half-true, because Calvin's real presence was neither completely Zwinglian nor Lutheran. Yet, by arguing that the fact of real presence was no longer in dispute, Calvin could deflect one of the strongest criticisms against the Lutherans and, at the same time, appeal to a common ground with them. But the Gnesio-Lutherans saw very little in common with Calvin, because Westphal and Hesshusen argued that Calvin did not espouse a real presence.

Hesshusen responded to Calvin with a defense called *A Pious Defense of the True and Whole Confession concerning the Presence of the Body of Christ in the Lord's Supper against the Jests and Calumnies of John Calvin, Peter Boquinus,*

*Theodore Beza, and William Kleinwitz* (whose actual name was Klebitz).[6] Hesshusen portrayed the debate between Lutherans and Reformed as an echo of the eucharistic controversy of the 1520s leading up to the Colloquy of Marburg. Although this representation provided an inaccurate picture of the controversy, it served his purpose of portraying Calvin as Luther's opponent, like Zwingli or Oecolampadius had done at Marburg. By ascribing Zwingli's position to Calvin, Hesshusen dismissed Calvin's views as a reprise of a misguided symbolic interpretation. He considered Luther's view as normative and his appeal to Luther's authority would have bothered Calvin, since he and other non-Lutheran reformers did not always accept the claims to Luther's adjudicatory authority. By this time, many Lutherans such as Hesshusen had begun to uphold Luther's words, in place of the judgments of popes, councils, and bishops, as a secondary authority concerning the interpretation of the Scriptures.[7]

The debate between Calvin and Hesshusen over the Eucharist was not simply a continuation of the disagreement between Luther and Zwingli. Although Calvin did not abandon altogether the place of figurative language, he devoted his *Dilucida Explicatio* to explaining the reality of Christ's presence. In the controversy over the Eucharist, it was clear that the disagreement between Lutheran and Reformed theologians was not over the fact of the real presence of Christ in the Eucharist but instead how Christ's presence was made real. That is to say, they both acknowledged real presence but argued over what real presence meant. Hesshusen observed in 1585 that the Lutherans were involved in a war on two fronts, with Jesuits and Calvinists.[8] In the latter case, Hesshusen experienced firsthand the struggle in those regions where Lutherans were vying with Calvinists for people's confessional loyalty.

### Hesshusen's *De Praesentia Corporis Christi in Coena Domini, Contra Sacramentarios*

In *De Praesentia Corporis Christi in Coena Domini, contra Sacramentarios*, Hesshusen challenged the claims of patristic authorization by Calvin and the Zwinglians for their eucharistic theology and engaged them in a polemical argument over the correct interpretation of ancient Christian texts. In the four sections of his treatise, Hesshusen devoted the second part to arguments from Scripture and the church fathers. Although Westphal had originally argued that the authority of the fathers was subordinate to Scripture to the point that they did not actually need the fathers to support their doctrine, Hesshusen openly recognized their importance and coupled his references to the fathers with honorific titles and accolades.

In the first section on how the Lord's Supper is instituted, Hesshusen says that the opinions concerning the presence of Christ's body and blood are the chief source of contention between Calvin and the Lutheran churches. He contends that his own view is given without any ambiguity, while Calvin's explanation is so full of contradictions that it fails to convey a clear or correct perspective.[9] Recognizing others of the Reformed confessions, Hesshusen identifies his opponents as John Oecolampadius, Ulrich Zwingli, John Calvin, John Laski, Peter Martyr Vermigli, and Heinrich Bullinger—those who think that Christ's body and blood exist in a certain location in heaven and would therefore argue that it impossible for Christ's body to be offered in the bread and wine of the Lord's Supper.[10] According to Hesshusen, these reformers are sixteenth-century Nestorians who "snatched away the honor of invocation to Christ and weakened the whole foundation of our salvation."[11] While he makes clear that he rejects the papal form of consecration—that is, transubstantiation—Hesshusen claims that the bishops cite Ambrose or other fathers to show that the bread is simply bread before the words of the sacraments, and that it is only after consecration that the bread becomes the body of Christ.[12] In this case, Ambrose is specifically named as one of many fathers who support Hesshusen's repeated point that the consecrated bread is the body of Christ. It does not seem to matter that Calvin would not object to this interpretation. Because Hesshusen sees himself as a genuine representative of Luther and categorizes Calvin as a representative of Zwingli, he depicts the controversy in terms of the Marburg debate over whether Christ is present in the Eucharist. This depiction is, however, outdated, as David Steinmetz has argued, since the debate is no longer over whether Christ is present but over the manner in which Christ is present.[13] By conveying his debate with Calvin as a reprise of Marburg, Hesshusen emphasizes the earlier disagreement between Luther and Zwingli.

Throughout the treatise, Hesshusen continues to argue that there is no obscurity in the words of institution. He claims to be following the teachings of Hilary, although he withholds any direct citation, and argues that he and his Lutheran colleagues use the fathers more appropriately, as opposed to Calvin and his Reformed cronies, who usurp the fathers and force unfitting interpretations upon them.[14] Among his sources Hesshusen cites three main fathers—Augustine, Epiphanius, and Hilary—and, of these, he deems Hilary, who testifies that the Word is truly made flesh and that we truly consume the Word at the Lord's Supper, as the most serious author.[15] With Hilary's testimony, Hesshusen builds his case that Christ's flesh is present in the Supper. He argues that, by eating the bread at the Lord's Supper, believers receive not only power, efficacy, spirit, vigor, and merits of Christ's passion, but also the essence and substance of the body and blood of Christ.[16]

Meanwhile, Hesshusen does not deny that with right faith, charity, and sincerity, believers can be joined spiritually to Christ. Based on Cyril's conjunction of the spiritual and corporeal participation, Hesshusen argues that the Supper is not a rational joining with Christ by way of the flesh, but rather a joining of the spiritual and corporeal by the blessing of mystical power.[17] Following Augustine's words regarding Judas and impious participants in the Eucharist, Hesshusen contends that consuming the flesh of Christ is starkly different from consuming symbols. He adds: "Augustine clearly says that the body and blood of the Lord was in those apostles to whom he spoke. Therefore whoever eats unworthily eats judgment to oneself."[18] Starting with Augustine's words concerning the body and blood, Hesshusen construes a corporeal meaning. He accuses Calvin of espousing an eating that is just spiritual and metaphorical, a simple act of believing without necessarily partaking of the Lord's Supper. When Calvin tries to connect Christ's presence to the Holy Spirit, Hesshusen puts him on the defensive by associating his view of the Holy Spirit in the Lord's Supper with Augustine's enemies, the Donatists. Continuing to rally support for his own case, Hesshusen asserts that the essence of Christ's body is consumed not only with faith in the heart but also with the mouth, just as Hilary testifies.[19] As Hesshusen sees it, Calvin not only misunderstands the Eucharist, but also lacks true faith. Based on the words of Justin Martyr, he argues that asking questions about how something is possible is evidence of doubt about God. It is better, he says, to imitate the modesty of Epiphanius, who knew only what was necessary, than to [demand answers to lofty mysteries].[20] Therefore, according to Hesshusen, those who believe without asking too many questions follow the tradition of the church fathers more closely than Calvin, whose inquiries expose his doubt.

In the second section of the treatise, Hesshusen's use of the fathers is coupled closely with his biblical exposition. In addition to offering "illustrious" arguments from Christ and the Holy Spirit, Hesshusen introduces the testimonies of the church fathers as his defense. He begins by elevating the fathers' authority and particularly praises those fathers whose opinions most closely reflect his own views. He says: "We affirm truly that there is no difference between the fathers and our spiritual eating, that is, the reception of Christ's benefits. [And] in true corporeal eating which is in the Lord's Supper . . . the fathers are the experts."[21] He then claims these "experts" for his own perspective. Based on the Apostle Paul, Gregory Nazianzus, and Theophylact, Hesshusen argues that the bread is the body of Christ, which is given not only in its fruit or efficacy but also in its substance.[22] As additional support, he includes several other fathers, such as Basil and Ambrose, who testify to the judgment and condemnation of Judas in the last Supper for unworthy eating. Hesshusen identifies his view with that of the Apostle Paul, as well as the plain words of Augustine and the testimonies of other fathers.[23] With his army of witnesses, he argues that it is necessary to conclude that the true body and blood of Christ are offered in the Supper.

Hesshusen's use of the fathers involves one of two things: either elevating their words as true, or relegating their views as inferior and faulty. What becomes clear is that Hesshusen assumes the role not only of deciding correct eucharistic doctrine but also of establishing a hierarchy of the fathers[24] (an action that builds on Luther's willingness to divvy up the fathers), and follows Melanchthon's distinction of more esteemed and less respectable fathers. The dichotomy of righteous and faulty fathers allows Hesshusen to argue either that a reputable church father supports his view or that a disreputable father supports Calvin's view. He can deflect an issue by arguing that a church father clearly does not support Calvin, while not necessarily claiming the father for his own opinion. In essence, Hesshusen aligns the Lutherans with the righteous fathers and the Reformed with the inferior ones.

In his estimation of the fathers, Hesshusen establishes Irenaeus as a bishop who taught the church faithfully, and therefore recalls his teachings. Portraying a direct link from Irenaeus to the Lutheran position, he writes that Irenaeus taught straightforwardly on the holy supper as "we teach it today."[25] Because Irenaeus does not speak of the body of Christ through allegory or metonymy, but corporeally, Calvin's allegorical view necessarily abandons the teachings of the orthodox fathers and is, by extension, fundamentally unorthodox. As Westphal had done before him, Hesshusen describes his own struggle against Calvin in terms of ancient *personae*. Setting Tertullian and Hilary against Marcion and the Manicheans, Hesshusen compares himself to the former and Calvin to the latter. He also approves of Athanasius, "whose writing above all others emanates as if light. For he was in his time a true defender of religion against the greatest Arian blasphemies."[26]

A key component of the exemplary fathers, for Hesshusen, is their fervor against "false" doctrine. His own alliance with respected ancient fathers is thus meant to highlight his opponent's alignment with faulty ones. He calls Origen, for example, a second-rate theologian and understands him to have much in common with the opinions of Calvinists and Zwinglians. According to Hesshusen, Origen follows his teacher, Clement, when he philosophizes that Christ's body in the Supper is the word of God and the prayer of the gospel, which through allegory or metaphor is named the food and drink of the soul.[27] Hesshusen criticizes Origen, who derides the doctrine of the resurrection of bodies, just as Epiphanius claims, and obscures the truth by playing with silly and untimely allegories.[28] For Hesshusen, Epiphanius stands as the herald of orthodox doctrine and righteous condemner of heresies, while Origen is the corrupter of doctrine and the propagator of absurd allegories. Although Hesshusen concedes that Clement and Origen are not on his side, he is not completely willing to hand them over to Calvin either. Instead, he implies that the Reformed thinkers do not even have the support of Clement and Origen, when he says, "Oecolampadius also who alleges Origen as a serious witness, nevertheless thinks differently from him."[29] By denying the substantial support of even the lesser fathers, Hesshusen endeavors to depict the Reformed position as lacking any historical support. Even when he admits that Calvin is not entirely without witnesses, he presents Calvin's use of those witnesses as a concession, saying, for example, "Lo, *we give you* both [your] patron and witness Origen."[30]

Hesshusen's main strategy in the first two sections of the *De Praesentia* is to assemble as many church fathers as he can to support his own views. First, he raises as his champion Hilary, who, he believes, sums up the authority and testimony of the holy fathers most clearly.[31] According to Hesshusen, Hilary confirms that the flesh of Christ is eaten not only spiritually through faith but also corporeally, but Oecolampadius and his followers misuse the testimonies of Cyprian in defense of their own errors. Thus, if readers are diligent and will examine Hilary's entire position, they will understand that Hilary certainly thinks differently from the errors of the sacramentarians such as Calvin.[32] Secondly, Hesshusen returns to Epiphanius concerning the substance of the bread, and teaches that it ought to be believed by faith that the bread is Christ's body, even if seen and experienced otherwise. Third, he adds Ambrose to the list as pronouncing judgment on those who consume the body of Christ negligently. Fourth, he enlists Jerome as one who asserts the true presence of Christ's body in the Supper. Fifth, he includes Chrysostom as supporting his view that participants in the Eucharist eat and receive the whole Christ, while the apostle Paul and all the orthodox fathers deny whatever the Zwinglians say.[33] Therefore, when Calvinists and Zwinglians oppose Hesshusen's views, he implies, they deviate from a "great consensus of holy fathers."[34] As further evidence of this "great consensus," Hesshusen appeals to the weighty opinion of Augustine and uses excerpts from Augustine's homilies, letters, and *Against the Donatists* in order to show that Calvin tries to persuade with violently contorted opinions that Augustine agrees with Zwinglianism.[35] Overall, Hesshusen's references to the fathers do not include their historical context but instead give a theological assessment of the current debate. He says, for example, that Cyril "is the bitterest enemy of the Zwinglians."[36] He also writes that the Eucharist consists of two things: earthly and heavenly, as Irenaeus and Theodoret describe.[37] Lamenting on how the words of the holy ancients are misused, Hesshusen points to Calvin as the one who obscures and dilutes the proper wisdom of the church,[38] and blames Calvin and his followers for reviving the positions of Pelagius and Origen and producing a new theology from the Platonic Academy. By denying Christ's ability to be present bodily, he argues, Calvin correlates Christ's presence to the Holy Spirit. According to Hesshusen, these new Sabellians who deny the distinction of persons and refuse Athanasius' profession of faith also deny that the body of Christ truly and substantially exists in the holy Supper.[39]

The final section of Hesshusen's treatise is devoted to refuting the objections of Zwingli and Calvin, and ultimately guiding the pious reader to shun Calvin's corruptions. The key fathers cited in this section are Athanasius, Epiphanius, Cyril, Hilary, and Augustine. Hesshusen claims that the testimonies of most of the church fathers strengthen his view and that his adversaries the Zwinglians have two patrons: Clement of Alexandria and Origen. He describes Clement as an erudite but impious philosopher who is, in most serious points, shamefully hallucinating, while Origen, a disciple of Clement, is more inept than his teacher because he criticizes Epiphanius, who recognizes that Origen corrupts the words of Christ with absurd allegories.[40] Because Hesshusen believes that most of the fathers support the Lutheran position, he sees his own view as truly Christian because it is within the tradition of the church. He also portrays his work as reproducing points made by "the most excellent men who educated the church with fidelity, of whom a great part of faith and the right spirit were constantly demonstrated with martyrdom and who were clearly with the universal church of God: Ignatius, Justin Martyr, Tertullian, Irenaeus, Cyprian, Eusebius, Pamphilius, Athanasius, Basil, Gregory Nazianzus, Epiphanius, John Chrysostom, Jerome, Augustine, Cyril. These testimonies even our enemies cannot reject."[41] Because, in his opinion, various writings of the church fathers support a corporeal eating of the elements, Hesshusen asserts that those who do not accept the words of institution lack faith. Faithful acceptance of the correct interpretation of the Eucharist is made synonymous with salvation. He recognizes differences in the church fathers and willingly divides up the fathers between those worthy of praise and those deserving of censure. He then applies the division he sees in the early church to himself and Calvin, who represent righteous and faulty fathers, respectively, in their debates over the Eucharist. By demonstrating his own agreement with the best church fathers by and criticizing other ancient writers whom he has already associated with his Calvinist opponents, Hesshusen defines Calvin's view as outside the tradition of the church and therefore not truly Christian.

## Calvin's *Dilucida Explicatio* (1561)

Calvin begins his *Dilucida Explicatio* by recognizing the division among the Lutherans, a tactic used by Westphal years earlier. He claims that Melanchthon, who died the previous year, had lamented the "madness and fury" of his Saxon neighbors and had desired to be on Calvin's side, but had been reluctant to join in the debate because of his "mild temper desirous of peace and rest."[42] Calvin points out that not all Lutherans agreed with Hesshusen, including Melanchthon, his former teacher. Calvin also recognizes two other opponents, Nicolaus Gallus of Köthen, nicknamed "The Cock," and Friedrich Staphylus of Osnabrück. In his brief response to them, he notes that Staphylus has classified Luther, Melanchthon, and Calvin, as well as many others, as new Manichees. Identifying opponents with ancient heretics was obviously a popular rhetorical technique, and Calvin finds no use in working to clear his name because he likens the accusations to stones thrown from the street at the heads of unoffending passersby. He then moves on to address Hesshusen.

First, Calvin puts Hesshusen in a category with his previous nemesis, Westphal, and claims that Hesshusen ostentatiously repeats Westphal's follies in order to portray him as someone who obstructs all attempts at compromise.[43] Calvin blames Hesshusen's contentious spirit and argues that if Hesshusen has directed his anger at the Calvinist view for maintaining that the sacrament is conferred by Christ, then he ought to be angry with Augustine and Chrysostom as well.[44] By mentioning these two notable fathers, Calvin positions Hesshusen in opposition to the early church authorities. Moreover, Calvin says he agrees with Augustine "that there may be invisible sanctification without the visible sign, just as on the other hand there may be the visible sign without true sanctification."[45] Thus, whenever Hesshusen stresses a text that supports the physical real presence of Christ in the Eucharist, Calvin counters with an interpretation or a text that distinguishes the spiritual reality from the physical sign.[46] On the question concerning the mode of Christ's presence, Calvin summarizes,

> Although I distinguish between the sign and the thing signified, I do not teach that there is only a bare and shadowy figure, but distinctly

declare that the bread is a sure pledge of that communion with the flesh and blood of Christ which it figures. For Christ is neither a painter, nor an actor, nor a kind of Archimedes who presents an empty image to amuse the eye; but he truly and in reality performs what by external symbol he promises. Hence I conclude that the bread which we break is truly the communion of the body of Christ.[47]

Second, and more importantly, Calvin criticizes Hesshusen's biblical interpretation according to the letter as unnecessarily limiting. For Calvin, the presence of the divine essence is not excluded when the name of God is applied by metonymy to the symbol by which God represents himself;[48] Hesshusen, however, does not see how the divine essence can be present in a symbol, even if it signifies something magnificent. Calvin realizes that the crux of this dispute is not about the fact of presence or substantial eating, but rather how both of these are to be understood. Although Hesshusen denied the ubiquity of Christ in principle, he admitted that the bread is properly the body, and is therefore one and the same with the body. To support this claim, he made a reference to Irenaeus' statement that there are two different things in the Supper: an earthly and a heavenly component, respectively the bread and body. But Calvin denies that Irenaeus' statement can be applied to support the idea that Christ's body and the bread have the same essence.[49] Instead, he agrees with Augustine that believers receive Christ in the bread, "but I utterly abhor the delirious fancy of Hesshusen and his fellows, that it is not received unless it is introduced into the carnal mouth. The Communion of which Paul speaks does not require any local presence."[50] Augustine's comparison of the bread to Christ's body on the cross does not obviously support Calvin's view, yet he accepts Augustine's quote and rejects Hesshusen's use of Augustine. Likewise, in discussing the debate over the "eating of the unfaithful," the point of contention revolves around Augustine's words, as well as the interpretation of 1 Corinthians 11. When Hesshusen asserts that the body of Christ is taken by the wicked, Calvin rejects this view with his interpretation of Augustine.[51] If Scripture is the primary authority, why does Calvin not just say that the Bible supports his argument? Why have Augustine say these words from Scripture? Once again, Calvin realizes that the contention is not about the fact of Scripture's truth but how to understand Scripture and how to apply that interpretation properly to Christian practice: Calvin's Augustine challenges Hesshusen's biblical interpretation. In other words, Calvin reads Augustine's words in light of the Pauline text in order to expand the possible ways of interpreting Augustine. He does not want to confine Augustine to Hesshusen's interpretation, which he finds too limiting and exclusive.

Third, Calvin finds it intolerable for Hesshusen to represent himself as an imitator of the fathers. In fact, this claim may have been the impetus for Calvin to reply to Hesshusen when he had already passed on to Beza the task of responding to Lutherans two years earlier. Because Calvin sees himself as a faithful follower of the church fathers, the bulk of his response resists Hesshusen's claims on the fathers, and he challenges Hesshusen's references to Cyril, Justin Martyr, Irenaeus, Tertullian, Hilary, Cyprian, Athanasius, Epiphanius, Basil, Ambrose, Gregory Nazianzus, Augustine, Jerome, and Chrysostom. In the interpretation of selected ancient fathers, Calvin first mentions Cyril's words against the Arians. In describing the historical context of these words, he explains that Cyril's words "we are essentially one with Christ" were offered to dismiss the Arians, who denied that Christ was one with the Father in reality and essence, in order to prove that the sacrament carries the force of the mystical benediction.[52] Although Hesshusen quoted Cyril to show how Christ is present essentially in the bread, Calvin emphasizes Cyril's words against the Arians and argues that Cyril did not espouse a momentary Communion. He then adamantly argues that Augustine is diametrically opposed to Hesshusen by reiterating references to Augustine, including the contentious passage on Augustine's admission (*Ser. 2 de verb. Dom.*) that there are different modes of eating the flesh and that Judas and other hypocrites ate the "true flesh" of Christ. Calvin finds fault with the word "true" as an addition by Hesshusen and argues that Hesshusen has forged the phrase "true flesh."[53] Since Augustine employs the terms "flesh" and "sacrament of flesh" indiscriminately in the same sense, Calvin recites Augustine's explanation that the sacraments often receive their names from things that share a resemblance. He explains Augustine's sense of a twofold eating, namely that while some receive the virtue of the sacrament, others receive only a visible sacrament—that it is one thing to take inwardly, another outwardly; one thing to eat with the heart, another to bite with teeth.[54] In order to show his complete agreement with Augustine, Calvin refers to the passage in which Augustine says that Judas ate the bread of the Lord against the Lord whereas the other disciples ate the bread of the Lord (59 *Tract. in Joann*). Claiming the entire ancient tradition, he adds, "Not one of the fathers has taught that in the Supper we receive anything but that which remains with us after the use of the Supper."[55] Thus Calvin extends the observations of a single father to make a universal claim about the fathers in general.

In the ongoing debate over the Lord's Supper, the church fathers functioned as rhetorical weapons in the struggle to determine the meaning of Scripture, especially when all reformers did not recognize Luther's interpretation as authoritative. The diminishing possibility of any consensus between Lutherans and Calvinists in the strife over the Lord's Supper forced Calvin to claim the support of more fathers than Augustine alone, who represented the dominant voice in Calvin's first two writings against Westphal. Both sides claimed their doctrine as approved by the early church because the early church still represented the true church. Reacting to Hesshusen's assertion that a plethora of ancient writers favors his opinion, Calvin stresses his own agreement with antiquity even though he says that the agreement between the ancient writers and the Reformed view has been proven "with accuracy and skill by Oecolampadius, who clearly showed that the figment of a local real presence was unknown to the ancient Church. He was succeeded by Bullinger, who performed the task with equal felicity. The whole was crowned by Peter Martyr [Vermigli], who left nothing more to be done."[56] Calvin mentions that Hesshusen has repudiated the authority of John of Damascus, Theophylact, Clement of Alexandria, and Origen, and uses the rejection of these figures as a gauge for Hesshusen's ulterior motive to select at will from antiquity whatever writers suit his purpose. Calvin then offers his counterarguments to Hesshusen's presentation of the fathers.

*Ignatius, Justin Martyr, and Gregory Nazianzus*

Beginning with the early church authorities, Calvin wishes that Ignatius' writings were extant in order to prevent the father's name from being so frequently employed as a disguise by imposters like Hesshusen. Calvin faults Hesshusen for employing the name of a church father, only to misconstrue the father's words to his advantage. Raising doubts about the authorship of a letter cited by his opponent, Calvin questions whether the epistle is genuine and posits a fictitious Ignatius. This questionable Ignatius says that some rejected the Supper because they denied that the Eucharist was the flesh of Christ, which was sacrificed for mankind. Calvin says, "The name of Eucharist is taken from the action of thanksgiving or from the whole Sacrament . . . certainly the literal meaning cannot be urged."[57] Calvin asserts that early writers everywhere called the consecrated bread the body of Christ just as Christ spoke of it, "but how very different is this from the barbarous fiction that the bread is literally the body which is corporeally eaten . . . [Hesshusen] classes us with Messalians and enthusiasts, who denied that the use of the Holy Supper does either good or harm."[58] He also asserts that Justin Martyr has great authority and does not damage the Reformed cause.[59] This kind of rhetoric demonstrates that the fathers only had as much authority as the reformers were willing to give them.

Calvin offers alternate interpretations of patristic writings in order to debunk Hesshusen's presentation of the church fathers as spokespersons for the Gnesio-Lutherans. While Hesshusen cited Justin Martyr as affirming that the mystical consecration of the Supper is equally miraculous as the incarnation, Calvin asserts that all Justin meant is that the flesh that Christ once assumed is given to believers as daily food. Calvin reclaims Justin with a new interpretation of the father's unspoken intentions. By confirming this opinion, Calvin is content simply to quote the words of Christ and to contend that the Supper's benefit is imparted only to the disciples who have been initiated into true piety.[60] By proposing to describe what a particular church father meant, Calvin is free to formulate his interpretation of that father's words. He writes,

> Because Gregory Nazianzen [*sic*] says that priests carry in their hands the image of the great God, Hesshusen boldly infers that the bread is properly the body of Christ. My answer, which I am confident will be approved by all men of sense, is simply this, that Gregory meant nothing more than what Augustine has expressed somewhat more familiarly, when speaking of Christ holding forth the bread to his disciples, he says, Christ bore himself in a manner in his hands, an expression by which the difficulty is completely solved . . . Hesshusen absurdly wrests his words to a meaning foreign to them, since Gregory is not there speaking of the ordination of the Supper, but of our Savior's incarnation and death, though I deny not that Gregory, in the words eating and drinking recommends faith and alludes to the Supper.[61]

Calvin now turns to a strategy that he had used implicitly in his earlier writings but finally makes explicit in this treatise. He employs a grouping strategy in which he lumps two or more fathers together and attributes one opinion to them. In this case, he takes Gregory's words, likens them to Augustine's expression, and then presents them both as saying the same thing. Calvin uses this technique most often with Augustine as the father who eclipses all the others.

### Jerome, Chrysostom, Irenaeus, Hilary, and Cyril

The next father up for discussion is Jerome, since Calvin says that Jerome supports his view. Calvin's references to Jerome are particularly numerous in his post-1550s writings, with Jerome being second in frequency after Augustine. Although he is critical of Jerome's doctrine of free will, penance, and marriage, and even deems Jerome's view of the Lord's Supper unclear, Calvin repeatedly interprets Jerome as being consistent with his own opinion in his writings against Hesshusen (and Westphal).[62] He claims that Jerome speaks clearly when he distinctly denies that the wicked eat the flesh of Christ or drink his blood,[63] and asserts that Jerome's words undercut Hesshusen's opinion, based on Jerome's saying (*Ep. ad Eph. c. 1*) that "the flesh and blood of Christ is taken in a twofold sense."[64] Calvin claims that Jerome could not have imagined a twofold flesh, and presumes that Jerome took notice of a spiritual, and therefore different, mode of communication, to guard against the fiction of a corporeal eating.[65] In this way, Calvin manages to turn Jerome's words into an attack on Hesshusen's emphasis on corporeal eating. On the more troubling passages in Jerome's writings, Calvin explains how to understand Jerome when he says that (1) the bread is the body of Christ; (2) the clergy make the body of Christ; and (3) they distribute his blood to the people. In light of such sayings as these, Calvin thinks that the problem can be easily solved if it is understood that Christ's body and blood are taken "in a mystery." For Calvin, the controversy is over, since it is clear that "in a mystery" and "corporeally" are antithetical.[66] This distinction is the underlying difference between Calvin's view of presence and Hesshusen's, for Hesshusen understands "in a mystery" and "corporeally" to be synonymous.

Because Hesshusen has produced a passage from Chrysostom, Calvin recognizes Chrysostom as a pious teacher who teaches believers to approach the sacrament with faith and a clean heart. In doing so, Calvin essentially argues that the ancient father is unlike Hesshusen, who not only infers that some receive the sacraments without faith and with an unclean heart but also further misconstrues Chrysostom, as if he had hinted at the corporeal reception of a substantial body, which, according to Calvin, he did not.[67] Calvin also presents Chrysostom as a faithful expositor of Paul so that, once he demonstrates Chrysostom as a representative for his own side in the debate, he can also include the support of the Apostle Paul. Related to this grouping strategy, Calvin also recalls one father to clarify another seemingly ambiguous authority. In this case, Calvin agrees with Hesshusen that Irenaeus is a clear expounder of Justin's brief statement. Calvin argues that Irenaeus is not discussing whether we eat Christ corporeally, but that he only contends that flesh and blood become meat and drink to us so as to infuse spiritual life into our flesh and blood. Hesshusen tried to prove from the words of Irenaeus that the body of Christ is received not only in a spiritual manner, but also corporeally by the mouth, but Calvin takes up Irenaeus' words to conclude that there is no distinction between corporeal and spiritual eating, which Hesshusen contends is the central point of the controversy.[68]

In regard to other church fathers, Calvin continues to assert that his view is not damaged by what is affirmed in Tertullian, Hilary, and

Irenaeus, namely that the flesh of Christ nourishes the believer's flesh in the hope of eternal life. He argues that the fathers were clear when they referred to the perpetual union with Christ and taught that this spiritual union is the effect of faith. In light of Hilary's statements that support Hesshusen, Calvin reorients Hilary's view by arguing that although Hilary repeatedly says that believers are naturally united to Christ, it is apparent that his only object is to prove that the life of Christ abides in believers, because they are one with him.[69] For further support, Calvin argues that Irenaeus clearly shows that the perpetual union of which he speaks is spiritual[70] and adds Cyril's interpretation of John, in which "[Cyril] distinctly maintains that the flesh of Christ is made vivifying by the agency of the Spirit, so that Christ is in us because the Spirit of God dwells in us."[71] This repeated reinterpretation of the fathers demonstrates Calvin's role in establishing the historicity of the Calvinist view of the Eucharist.

In addition to neutralizing or appropriating the fathers as Zwingli and Bucer do,[72] Calvin works at accruing the fathers in opposition to Hesshusen. Because Hesshusen relinquishes a few fathers, Calvin takes his opponent's selective censure of a few fathers and enlarges the numbers of fathers that oppose him. Describing Tertullian's historical context as addressing the Marcionite challenge, Calvin argues that the figure of Christ's body is not an empty thing, but carries the reality, according to Tertullian. Thus, to hold that the bread was crucified would contribute to the vanity of Marcion. Because Tertullian proved that the bread was the true substance of the flesh of Christ, Calvin claims that the bread could not be a figure without being the figure of a true substance.[73] He surmises that Hesshusen's quibbles cannot wrest Tertullian's support from the Reformed position, and, addressing Hesshusen's quote from Tertullian's tract on the Lord's Prayer, he claims that the quote supports his own view. Therefore, Hesshusen has little support from antiquity.[74] Throughout this treatise, there is a sense that Calvin is trying to set the record straight. He gives the impression that because Hesshusen has misrepresented Tertullian, he most likely misrepresents other fathers as well. By noting that Hesshusen obtains the support of Cyprian "with similar dexterity," Calvin inadvertently recognizes Hesshusen's skill of argumentation and depicts Cyprian (as well as Athanasius) as confirming the Reformed doctrine.[75]

In these rebuttals, Calvin works tirelessly to portray Hesshusen's attacks through the words of the fathers as unfounded, and he judges Hesshusen's efforts to oppose him with the fathers as dishonest. Although Hesshusen cites Hilary against him, Calvin claims that when Hilary distinctly treats the vivifying participation of Christ, such participation does not demand the external use of the Supper, but maintains a perpetual vigor in believers. In Calvin's view, Hesshusen was spurred by an evil motive to provide a misguided interpretation of the fathers in his treatise. Referring to Epiphanius, Calvin says, "[N]othing is less accordant with the mind of this writer than the dream of Hesshusen, that the bread is truly and substantially body. Hesshusen asks, why does Epiphanius insist on faith in the words of the Supper, if the bread of the Eucharist is not the body? It is only by faith we comprehend that corruptible food is the pledge of eternal life."[76] For Hesshusen, faith is necessary to believe that the elements are truly Christ's body and blood; for Calvin, faith is nec-essary to eat Christ's body and blood. In Calvin's view, Hesshusen is at fault because he argues that the body of Christ can be eaten without faith, and assails the Reformed position for requiring faith in the eating. By depicting Hesshusen as attacking the requisite faith for Communion, Calvin can recall any church father who speaks of the necessity of faith. He believes, for example, that Ambrose speaks in the same way he does when Ambrose says, "Having been redeemed by the death of Christ, we commemorate this event by eating the flesh and blood which were offered for us . . . The covenant was therefore established by blood, because blood is a witness of divine grace, as a type of which we receive the mystical cup of blood."[77] By highlighting Ambrose's covenant language in relation to the mystical elements of the Eucharist, Calvin feels justified in his position. He finds it incredulous that Hesshusen would have the audacity to cite this passage against him because it is as if "we had actually borrowed the expression of our doctrine from it."[78]

*Augustine Again*

Finally, Calvin returns to his beloved father, Augustine. Since he is convinced that Augustine is on his side, he criticizes Hesshusen's use of Augustine as the height of impudence. Calvin's use of the fathers is undoubtedly selective—as this study confirms and other scholars have already pointed out—but what is noteworthy is his continued efforts to find the significance and relevance of ancient Christian writings for his own context. Indeed, the search for significance explains why Calvin's use of the fathers would be selective and why he would make Augustine sound Reformed. He writes: "When Augustine says, in his *Epistle to Januarius*, that the order of the Church should be approved, requiring us to go fasting to the sacred table, in order that the body of Christ may enter the mouth before any other food, if we add, 'in a mystery,' or 'sacramentally,' all contention will cease."[79] As long as Calvin can add these words, "in a mystery" or "sacramentally," he finds Augustine historically significant, as well as consistent with his own views. He argues that if Augustine had approved of the fiction of Hesshusen, he would have said "he eats the body corporeally." Calvin explains that by the expression "sacramental," Augustine shows that good and bad communicate in the signs of the Supper.

Both Calvin and Hesshusen saw the fathers as faithful, even if occasionally mistaken, expositors of Scripture. Both also continued to claim that the fathers supported their views of the Lord's Supper, and sought to strengthen their theological positions, even if the effort to cite the fathers meant further explanation. In a treatise titled "The Best Method of Obtaining Concord," Calvin reiterates that insistence on the swallowing of Christ's flesh and blood is foolish because it is not supported by the authority of Scripture or the testimony of the early church.[80] He also accuses Hesshusen of pronouncing a lofty encomium on the ancient writers only to find out that they give him no support.[81] Interestingly enough, Hesshusen's abundant praise of the fathers, which appeared throughout his *De Praesentia*, is somewhat tempered in his next treatise against Calvin, the *Pia Defensio*.

## Hesshusen's *Pia Defensio*

Hesshusen formulated his response to Calvin in *A Pious Defense of the True and Whole Confession concerning the Presence of the Body of Christ in the Lord's Supper* (hereafter cited by the partial Latin title *Pia Defensio*), in which he also addressed Peter Boquinus, Theodore Beza, and William Klebitz. In this treatise, Hesshusen asserts that his objectives are to explain clearly the true and steadfast reasons concerning the presence of Christ's body in the eucharistic sacrament, to defend his explanations by the firm and doubtless testimony of the sacred Scriptures, and to confute plainly the truly impious jesting of his adversaries.[82]

First, Hesshusen mentions the fathers in the rhetoric of concord and peace when he responds to the claim that the Lutherans maintain the peace while their enemies detract from it because of their ill motives. He describes himself as desiring peace in line with the universal church and says, with Jerome, that, "[w]e desire both peace and truth . . . but the peace of Christ . . . peace which is not such that it subjugates adversaries but so that it joins friends."[83] Therefore, by implication, Calvin and the Reformed side are the ones disturbing the peace. According to Hesshusen, they are schismatics who pretend to seek peace, but hide war.[84] Hesshusen rightly recognizes Calvin's language of peace as superficial. After the testimony of Paul, Hesshusen adds that if Irenaeus, Athanasius, Augustine, Cyril, and innumerable others considered their tranquility and "bore with the raging corruptions in their time either through sloth or concealment, would there be any trace of pure religion remaining on the earth? Or would not the weed of errors and corruption strangle the whole harvest of divine words?"[85] Hesshusen uses the fathers to justify a self-righteous attack against corruption and continues to uphold the fathers as champions of faith willing to fight for the maintenance of "pure religion," so that he can then place himself with those who combat error. He trusts that the most holy fathers have left to posterity "the deposit of blameless faith accepted by the majority"[86] and includes a specific reference to Cyril, who "rightly and piously [says] when faith is harmed and perverted, how can we be silent?"[87] Although Hesshusen asserts that he wants peace, it is obvious that the conflict has escalated. Therefore, at this point, he admits that he is willing to disturb the peace and justifies his attack as the correct thing to do, based on the model of the righteous fathers who could not be silent for the sake of true doctrine.

## Testimonies of the Fathers

Turning to the specific issue of the Lord's Supper, Hesshusen addresses several recurring issues, namely the nature of the sacraments and the eating of the unworthy. He devotes a section of his *Pia Defensio* to the "Undoubtable Testimonies of the Fathers on the Presence of Christ's Body in the Holy Supper."[88] In this section, he argues that if Calvin thinks his opinion is well-known in the world, then he understands the world as bewitched by Calvinist error. Reflecting the growing sense of national identity, Hesshusen says that the Germans, especially the Saxons, are surely the church, since they follow the sound opinions of the ancient doctors. According to Hesshusen, among the least respected are Clement and Origen, because they only understood Christ's flesh and blood spiritually, allegorically, and divinely, and did not take into consideration the word as it is. He also denigrates Jerome, who derived defects from his teacher, Origen, and spoke deceitfully about taking the blood and flesh of Christ.[89] For these fathers, Hesshusen omits any accolades.

Meanwhile, Hesshusen considers the more "respectable fathers"—Augustine, Chrysostom, Irenaeus, and Ambrose. In the case of Augustine, Hesshusen's intent is to explain that Augustine testifies that the same body that hung on the cross is eaten in the Communion bread, and that, by testifying to this, Augustine accepts the term "body."[90] By excluding Calvin's interpretation of the fathers, Hesshusen can carve out who is inside and outside the tradition of the church. In the continued effort to relegate Calvin's view to the margins, he claims that Chrysostom in his *Homily on 1 Corinthians 11* does not describe a spiritual eating. He also presents Irenaeus as a defender of the faith against the phantasms of Marcion, and writes, "Irenaeus refutes this falsehood concerning twofold blood, which Calvin remembers from Jerome. For [Irenaeus] testifies that the wine of the Eucharist is the communication of a substance, not of a symbol or of an allegory of the blood."[91] Hesshusen then mentions Ambrose as explaining that, just as the doctrine of the virgin birth goes beyond the order of nature, likewise it is Christ's extraordinary body that is given in the Eucharist. Hesshusen explains that the expositions of these fathers are clear and they have more strength than other early church authorities because they agree with the declaration of Christ. Therefore he hopes to expose Calvin and his associates as attempting to contort and elude the sayings of the fathers.[92]

*Eating by the Unworthy*

Concerning the eating of the unworthy, Hesshusen asserts that the testimony of the fathers endorses his view. He writes: "If Augustine defends Calvin, it would be necessary for him to say: that nobody who is deceitful with the heart eats Christ's body, but just bread."[93] Here Hesshusen follows Calvin's tactic of setting up a hypothetical statement of Augustine in order to prove that, since Augustine did not say it in such a way, it can be concluded that Augustine did not support such a view. For Hesshusen, to reject the bodily presence of Christ is to deny the sacrament's holiness and ultimately to lack faith. Hesshusen notes how often the fathers mention how mysteries ought to be received by believing the word of God and neglecting rational falsehoods.[94] Because the importance of the eating of Christ's body corporeally depends on the "unbelievable" presence of Christ, Hesshusen disqualifies Calvin's view as a position of faithlessness. In addition to Epiphanius, Hesshusen cites Chrysostom's sermon, saying, "[O]ur eyes ought to understand with faith not only to perceive the fruit from the Eucharist but also to understand this mystery . . . for sense and reason cry out against the word of Christ who says that the bread is his body which hung on the cross. It is necessary for us to apply faith and mistrust our senses [rather] than to mistrust Christ."[95] He points to the malicious intent of the Calvinists since it is visibly clear that his adversaries, in fact, have a greater desire for contention than for truth.[96]

The central focus of this debate, for both authors, is to transfer the source of their views on the Eucharist to well-respected church fathers. In this transference, Hesshusen wants to reiterate that the fathers do not substantiate Calvin's view, while claiming for himself the testimonies of the fathers, particularly Augustine, Cyril, Cyprian, Theodoret, Ambrose, and Chrysostom. Concerning the interpretation of John 6, Hesshusen follows Luther and other Lutherans by describing how the words of Augustine, Cyril, and Chrysostom ought to be understood by redefining the word "flesh" as meaning "carnal hearing," not Christ's flesh. Noting the two forms of the sacrament, the visible elements and the invisible flesh and blood of Christ, Hesshusen claims the support of Irenaeus and Augustine. Since he has already explained Irenaeus' support as a defender of faith, he turns to Augustine's battles against the Manichees and the Donatists. By setting up the dichotomy of good fathers versus wayward heretics, Hesshusen wants to identify himself not only with Augustine's doctrine but also, and perhaps even more so, with his position as "defender of the faith" against all who oppose him. By continuing with the rhetoric of orthodoxy versus heresy, Hesshusen suggests that Calvinist views are not simply at the margins of Christian belief and practice but even outside the acceptable boundaries.

## Conclusion

In the debate over the Lord's Supper, both Calvin and Hesshusen appealed to the church fathers to authorize their views defining distinct Lutheran and Reformed traditions. While the fathers were not decisive authorities in all things, they could be treated as such in order to exclude other views that threatened to stretch the boundaries of orthodox belief. The fathers also provided a way to build up newly defined views of the Eucharist and were considered valuable enough that they had to be taken out of the hands of adversaries. They were part of the multifaceted tug-of-war to determine church doctrine. The words of the ancient fathers became a primary way to reject or relegate competing interpretations as misguided, unfaithful, or—worse—not even Christian. By recalling negative examples from antiquity, Calvin and Hesshusen used the tactic of comparing the other to an ancient heretic. When one tried to claim the support of a church father whom the other was also claiming for support, strategies to interpret the works of that father came into play. Both appealed to the authority, clarity, and intent of the fathers to either emphasize or minimize the impact of a father's words. In this eucharistic conflict, Calvin and Hesshusen dealt with a number of disputed texts from the church fathers, as both sought to wrest the fathers out of their opponent's hands. In addition to Scripture, the fathers had also become an instrument of criticism and correction.

For Calvin and Hesshusen, the church fathers were respected human authorities because they were considered faithful expositors of Scripture. If they wanted to uphold the authority of the fathers, they portrayed them as conveyors of biblical truth. If they wanted to diminish the importance of the fathers on a particular point, they leaned on the primacy of Scripture or the preference for better fathers or sometimes even reason.

References to patristic writers accomplished several purposes. First, alignment with the church fathers could establish the antiquity of a view and dismiss the charge of innovation. Second, the church fathers were called on as defenders of the Christian faith against heresies so that reformers could connect their opponents' views to ancient views already marginalized by the tradition of the early church. Third, the fathers opened up the possibility of an alternate church tradition, a tradition that followed a lineage of faithful expositors of Scriptures that rivaled the late medieval Roman church tradition.

Calvin and Hesshusen devoted a great deal of their debate about the words of church fathers to comprehending, interpreting, and at times imposing on the fathers' words a sixteenth-century doctrinal stance on the Eucharist. Another way the fathers entered the dialogue was by being introduced as supporters of whatever had already been presented. After discussing a view, Hesshusen simply attached a phrase such as "Epiphanius thinks in the same way,"[97] and in a list of supportive fathers, he could include any fathers whose works he had explained, even if their writings were not clearly supportive of his views. As long as Hesshusen presented these fathers as not clearly voicing his opponents' views, he could claim them for his side in the debate. A little ambiguity provided the room for maneuverability. Furthermore, whenever his adversaries seemed to attack him with the writings of the fathers, especially Augustine, he responded with a different interpretation or emphasis.

Meanwhile, Calvin's references to the fathers had increased and diversified by the time of his response to Hesshusen, even though references to Augustine continued to be the most popular on both sides. Ancient writers could be called on to discount views already marginalized by the tradition of the early church. To this end, Calvin and his opponents called on as many fathers as they could to help them frame acceptable doctrine and dismiss false teachings. Their use of the fathers was by no means inclusive of all the patristic writers, despite their language professing it to be so. Because Hesshusen compelled Calvin to elaborate on other patristic arguments, their debate included a detailed discussion of the sayings of Pseudo-Ignatius, Justin Martyr, Irenaeus, Tertullian, Cyprian, Hilary, Ambrose (actually Ambrosiaster), Jerome, and Cyril.[98] While Calvin and Westphal spent a great portion of their debate over the right interpretation of Augustine, Calvin and Hesshusen were competing for a broader spectrum of the fathers who were needed to authorize their views.

*Chapter 6*

# Use of the Fathers
# at the Colloquy of Montbéliard (1586)
## *Theodore Beza versus Jacob Andreae*

By the time of the Colloquy of Montbéliard in 1586, Luther, Zwingli, Oecolampadius, Melanchthon, Calvin, and Westphal were deceased and a new generation of Lutheran and Reformed leaders had emerged. By 1580 German Lutherans had published and disseminated the *Formula of Concord* in a large-scale attempt to promote confessional unity. In the midst of defining boundaries, both national and theological, Theodore Beza and Jacob Andreae debated their theological differences concerning the Eucharist. When Beza and Andreae met early on in their careers as representatives of Reformed and Lutheran sides, respectively, they were both amenable to drawing up the Göppingen document to establish common ground and reach a compromise between the adherents of Zürich and Wittenberg theology.[1] When other leaders on both sides rejected this compromise document, however, Beza and Andreae identified their loyalties to their respective groups. By the time the two men faced each other at the Colloquy of Montbéliard, they were mature theologians who had become spokespersons for their doctrinal stances. They delineated their views by incorporating their understanding of the fathers, since the consent of the ancients meant belonging to the proper tradition.

## Introduction to the Authors

*Theodore Beza*

Theodore Beza (1519–1605), known as Calvin's successor and head of the Genevan church, was born into a Catholic family of Vézelay in Burgundy.

121

In 1548 Beza officially renounced the Catholic religion and in 1549 became a professor of Greek at Lausanne. In 1558 Calvin offered him a professorship at the newly founded academy in Geneva, a post that Beza held until 1595. Regarding Beza's life, Paul Geisendorf's monumental work was the first modern endeavor to chronicle a complete biography of Beza, a culmination of previous partial studies of the man and his work.[2] With the sources available to him, Geisendorf established the early influence exerted by Melchior Wolmar on Beza, traced Beza's development in the Evangelical cause, and portrayed his leadership role from an ecumenical viewpoint, including his part in the religious discussion at Poissy.[3] Since Geisendorf, other studies on Beza have continued to fill out the portrait of this church leader.[4] In her essay, Jill Raitt describes Beza's frustrated attempts at cross-confessional relations and credits his work among the Reformed for avoiding the internal conflict experience by the Lutherans.[5] In addition to his academic duties, his publications, and his involvement with France and its refugees, Beza undertook diplomatic journeys to gain support among German princes for the French Protestants. From the late 1550s to the late 1580s, Beza's efforts at diplomacy would be frustrated by differences between Lutheran and Reformed theologians concerning the Lord's Supper.[6]

When Calvin's ill health limited his duties, including his ability to write against Gnesio-Lutherans such as Joachim Westphal and Tilemann Hesshusen, it was Beza who picked up the debates with them. In defending the view that the Holy Spirit makes Christ's divine nature present to the faithful in the Eucharist, Beza produced a series of writings between 1559 and 1593 against the proponents of the Lutheran doctrine of ubiquity—notably Brenz, Westphal, and Andreae. In the 1560s, Beza was summoned to Poissy, where Catherine de Medecis hoped to unite her fractured kingdom by means of a colloquy between Roman Catholics and the Reformed. The conciliatory sentiments at the Colloquy of Poissy, however, soon soured because of disagreements over the doctrine of the Lord's Supper. On that occasion, the French Catholic Claude de Sainctes (later bishop of Évreux) accused Beza of incorrectly reading Tertullian, Chrysostom, and other fathers of the church whom Beza had cited to support his statements.[7] References to the fathers had been part of the Reformed line of argumentation since the beginning of the sixteenth century against the Catholics and the Lutherans. Following the publication of the *Formula of Concord* in 1577, the French Reformed refugees in the lands of Lutheran princes were in varying degrees subjected to increasing pressure to conform to Lutheran church practice and discipline. In 1586 the Colloquy of Montbéliard was called to settle this problem in the duchy of Württemberg. The principal disputants were Beza and Jacob Andreae, the latter of whom had, with Martin Chemnitz, written the *Formula of Concord*.[8]

## Jacob Andreae

Jacob Andreae (1528–1590) was born into a blacksmith family in the Swabian town of Waiblingen, and at age six became an Evangelical when his duke, Ulrich, converted the people of his lands to Lutheranism. Initially, Andreae was attracted to the Genevan model of the church. When a synod of Lutherans decided against him in 1554, however, he accepted its judgment and continued to propagate the Evangelical practice and doctrine.[9] Andreae focused the peak years of his career on the establishment of doctrinal harmony among the Lutherans. From 1568 to 1570 and from 1575 to 1580, Andreae traveled extensively to build support for his plans for concord.[10] His efforts yielded the composition and adoption of the *Formula of Concord* and had a significant impact on the developing orthodoxy of the early modern period.[11] Commenting on Andreae's contribution to theology, Robert Kolb notes, "Perhaps Andreae's most significant theological stance concerned the person of Christ, particularly as Christology relates to the understanding of the real presence of Christ's body and blood in the Lord's Supper."[12]

Early on in his pastoral ministry, Andreae attempted to find a basis for solving the eucharistic disputes that had separated Zürich and Wittenberg. After Beza and William Farel led an embassy to Bern and Zürich, where Heinrich Bullinger helped them in successfully persuading authorities to intercede with the French for the Waldensians who had adopted Protestant Reformed teaching and as a result was encountering further persecution in France, Beza and Farel went to Germany. They encountered growing fears among German Protestant authorities that theological deviations, particularly in defining and interpreting the sacraments, could lead to dangerous types of religious radicalism.[13] The onus was on Beza and Farel to prove that the French Protestant party did not endorse any of the revolting heresies on matters of sacramental theology developed by the more radical groups, such as the Spiritualists and the anti-Trinitarian Rationalists. With Beza and Farel, Andreae sought to formulate a common document on which the Lutherans and Reformed could agree. At their meeting in 1557, Beza and Andreae drafted a statement to achieve a precarious consensus, but Bullinger and Johannes Haller (a Reformed leader in Bern) looked upon the Göppingen confession, drafted in part by Beza, as a flagrant breach of the *Consensus Tigurinus* signed in 1549. Calvin and Beza sent apologetic letters to Bullinger and his colleagues so that

Bullinger, Vermigli, and Haller would finally agree to pardon Beza for his imprudence.[14] Consequently, the potential compromise of the Göppingen formula faded into oblivion soon after it was concluded. Two years later at a synod in December 1559, Andreae wrote into a confession the position of his mentor, Johannes Brenz, who disagreed with the Calvinist stance that at the ascension Christ's human nature ascended to the right hand of God and was located there and nowhere else.[15] Between 1557 and 1559, Andreae aligned his views on the Eucharist with the Gnesio-Lutheran position, and from that point he never turned back.

The importance of Andreae's career, specifically upon German Lutheranism, consisted in his ability to consolidate the Lutheran church around key doctrinal positions and solidify a Lutheran Christian identity. Andreae, one of the architects of Lutheran orthodoxy, combined the ideas of others with his own driving energy. Although he was not considered a creative thinker, he organized the concepts of other Evangelical theologians in such a way that he was able to overcome the differences that separated them. While divisions with the Reformed became more pronounced, Andreae was able to assist in shaping a common confession for German Lutherans (which both theologians and princes longed for) and in establishing models for the structure of church government.[16] Andreae became involved in the polemics over the Lord's Supper when he became the Lutheran representative at the Colloquy of Montbéliard in 1586 to discuss with Beza and other Reformed theologians their points of difference. In the end, the two sides could not come to an agreement on the Lord's Supper or on the person of Christ, baptism, the use of images, and predestination. In effect, they secured the distinct theological traditions of Lutherans and Calvinists.

## The Colloquy of Montbéliard

*Setting the Stage*

The Peace of Augsburg in 1555 set the boundaries for each local government and prince within the Holy Roman Empire to choose either the Catholic confession, which was in the process of being codified at the Council of Trent, or the Augsburg Confession, the first edition of which, called the *Invariata*, was drafted in 1530. Yet not all adherents to the Augsburg Confession were Lutheran. Many towns and areas, especially along the Upper Rhine and near the Swiss and French borders, considered themselves simply Evangelical and had not differentiated themselves as either Lutheran or Reformed. They understood the Augsburg Confession in the form of Melanchthon's edition of 1540 known as the *Variata*, or as it was interpreted by the signers of the Wittenberg Concord of 1536, including Melanchthon and Martin Bucer.[17] Divisions within the Protestant camp became apparent with the growth of the Calvinist movement within the empire and the German-speaking territories. Calvin and his associates claimed to accept the Augsburg Confession but they preferred the later version, Melanchthon's *Variata*.[18] While some German states supported this later version, other states insisted upon the more restrictive *Invariata*, which was later elaborated in an inter-Lutheran confessional statement called the *Formula of Concord* that explicitly excluded Calvinists and Zwinglians. Since the *Formula* sought to mark out the limits of Lutheran orthodoxy, Reformed thinkers in Germany such as Zacharias Ursinus and Caspar Olevianus argued that the Book of Concord, published in 1580, should not be considered on the same level of authority as the ancient creeds or above other Protestant confessions.[19] In the face of mounting, empire-wide opposition in the late 1570s through early 1580s, the general Reformed strategy worked to preserve a place for Reformed Protestantism.[20] Lutherans rejected Zwinglians (who did not espouse the Augsburg Confession) and Calvinists (who followed the revised Augsburg Confession). More than simply a religious distinction, the legal residence of Calvinists within the Holy Roman Empire was at stake. Meanwhile, in France, wars of religion erupted in 1562 that would disrupt the country for over thirty years until Henry of Navarre, with Reformed sympathies, succeeded to the throne as Henry IV in 1593.

Three competing confessions were vying for the allegiance of the French-speaking county of Montbéliard, which became the center of the controversy on account of its geographical, political, and religious situation. In this instance, Montbéliard provided "a paradigm for many of the religio-political problems of [late sixteenth-century] Europe."[21] It was flanked on one side by the duchy of Lorraine, which was Roman Catholic and defended its faith in alliance with the papacy and the French Catholic Holy League. On the other side, it bordered the electorate of the Palatine, which was primarily Calvinist and defended its faith in alliance with French Protestants, the Swiss cantons, and the Netherlands. To add to the brewing tensions, Montbéliard was ruled by the duchy of Württemberg, which was committed to strict Lutheranism and defended its faith in alliance with Gnesio-Lutheran powers in eastern and northern Germany. The resulting divisions were apparent, with three competing governments upholding a different confession and each aiming to assert its own identity and independence.[22] Since Montbéliard's reform had been Swiss in origin, with William Farel's work from 1524–1525, it had been converted to a largely Calvinist version of Protestant Christianity. Yet Montbéliard itself was ruled by the dukes of Württemberg, and they became determined that it should become an integral part of their Lutheran territories. In the 1540s and 1550s, Lutheran leaders wanted to impose the Württemberg Ordinances as well as the Württemberg Confession, written by Brenz, with its doctrine of corporeal presence that reinforced the doctrine of ubiquity. When the French wars of religion broke out in 1562, French Reformed refugees filtered into the French-speaking border town of Montbéliard, and again in 1572, the Saint Bartholomew's Day massacre resulted in a new influx of French refugees. In 1577 Frederick, who vacillated between the Swiss Reformed position of his father, Count George, and the Lutheranism in which he had been educated at Tübingen, came to Montbéliard and signed the *Formula*, which not only set out Lutheran doctrine but also condemned "Zwinglians."

The immediate impetus for the Colloquy of Montbéliard reflected the struggle in France in 1585 when Henry II issued the Treaty of Nemours, which declared that only Catholics would be tolerated in France. Huguenots had to convert to Catholicism or leave France within six months. In late October and November of 1585, many French fled to Montbéliard and Frederick permitted residence to those who wished to remain. Since the Marburg Colloquy failed to establish theological unity between the Lutherans and the Swiss Reformed in regard to the Lord's Supper, debates over this issue continued to exacerbate Lutheran–Reformed ties, such as the polemics between Calvin (and eventually Beza) and Westphal/ Hesshusen. In the late sixteenth century, the small town of Montbéliard briefly captured the center of European attention when the Colloquy of Montbéliard attempted to resolve the ongoing tensions between the Reformed and Lutherans, which carried political ramifications for the conduct of the wars of religion.

## Leaders of the Colloquy

The colloquy involved a debate between Beza and Andreae over the announced topic of the Lord's Supper, although other related topics, such as the person of Christ, also surfaced.[23] Published successively in Tübingen and Geneva, Andreae's *Acta* and Beza's *Responsio* supplied the recorded protocols and accounts of the discussion. As Andreae reported and Beza admitted, the colloquy had been called for the sake of the French exiles living in Montbéliard. The French nobles who were refugees from the French wars of religion often asked for such a meeting concerning some articles of religion and the use of the French language in the liturgy. Frederick had apparently forwarded their petition to Duke Ludwig of Württemberg, who responded by sending his court theologian and several politicians to participate in the colloquy. No remark was made by either side about the place of Count Frederick among the German theologians.[24] While Beza sought an international conciliation that would transcend national boundaries since pockets of Reformed congregations were scattered throughout various regions in Europe, Andreae focused on uniting the German people in a theological agreement as outlined in the *Formula of Concord*, which included the *Catalogus Testimoniorum* appended to it by Andreae and Chemnitz. In the debates at Montbéliard, Beza and Andreae were committed to different theological stances, particularly on the Lord's Supper but increasingly on other matters as well.[25] At the same time, both groups of theologians accepted the councils of the first five centuries as true to the Word of God, and appealed to the Scriptures and the early church fathers, as well as their own confessional statements, in confirmation of an increasingly important claim: orthodoxy.[26]

## Use of the Fathers in the Debate over the Lord's Supper

Both collocutors claimed that the Word of God was to be the sole norm—the declared principle of Scripture alone (*sola scriptura*). Beza, for example, believed that his use of a trope to understand how Christ was present in the elements of bread and wine suggested that the concept belonged to Scripture (not to the originality of the Reformed theologians), and he further testified to its antiquity by quoting Virgil and Homer.[27] The emphasis on the principle of *sola scriptura* did not diminish the use of the church fathers throughout the sixteenth century; rather, it did just the opposite. In the search for the "correct" interpretation of Scripture, the fathers had a pivotal role in intra-Protestant tensions.[28] The Reformation's insistence on *sola scriptura* in no way excluded a reformer's endeavor to prove connections to the fathers;[29] in fact, the polemical context encouraged the recognition of other authorities. These intra-Protestant debates over the Eucharist provided the impetus for further study of the church fathers. Although the fathers were initially recalled for support, when the words of an ancient father challenged a reformer's view, even the fathers had to be reinterpreted to fit the shape of Lutheran or Reformed views. There is no doubt that the ancient fathers played an integral role in the sixteenth-century debates over the Eucharist. In those cases, however, the fathers failed to gain any absolute power,[30] and their sayings did not cause many reformers to change their views in light of ancient evidence to the contrary. Nevertheless, the reformers' new interpretations of the fathers became normative for each respective confessional tradition, both Lutheran and Reformed.

By 1586 the major confessions had been ratified. The *Second Helvetic Confession* (1566) had been adopted by the Swiss and also by the French at

La Rochelle (1571) in harmony with their own *French Confession of 1559*. The Lutheran *Formula of Concord* was first published in 1576, with subsequent editions following closely. Each church considered its confession to be the correct interpretation of the Word of God, drawn from Scripture. Although these reformers would not admit that any of the confessions had the unique authority of Scripture itself, they in fact believed that their confessional statements stood as the standard for deciding "orthodox" doctrine. Furthermore, it became clear that each of these confessions was meant to define a religious identity based on an interpretation of Scripture that would be distinct from other interpretations.

At the Colloquy of Montbéliard, Andreae and his followers presented two groups of theses. The first group of Württemberg theses listed points on which the Lutherans judged there was no controversy. The second set considered controversial topics and included Reformed ideas that the Lutherans considered contrary to Scripture.[31] Beza's response did not follow the order of questions or topics in Andreae's work, but rather a sequence of arguments already formulated in his own *Confessio fidei* and his theses at the Colloquy of Poissy. These arguments were repeated in his 1593 *De Controversiis in Coena Domini*, and thereby established a blueprint for the Reformed understanding of the Eucharist.

### Andreae's *Acta Colloquij Montis Belligartensis*

In recording the discussions at Montbéliard, Andreae does not simply recite Beza's theses and responses but accompanies them with his own refutations in the form of marginal notes. On the topic of the Lord's Supper, Andreae lists his arguments under five subjects: (1) the words of institution, (2) Christ in the Old and New Testaments, (3) Christology as it appears in this section, (4) sacramental principles, and (5) the use of philosophical terms. He sums up the controversy under two principal points, however: (1) the true and real presence of the body and blood of Christ, and (2) the true and sacramental reception of that body and blood.[32] For Andreae, the words of institution ought to be accepted literally, while the words of John 6 are to be understood figuratively because they refer to faith and believing, not to the sacrament of the Eucharist. Andreae emphasizes that the Lord's Supper has to be for both soul and body, since the whole person, body and soul, is refreshed spiritually and redeemed. One explanation he offers for Christ's ubiquity is found in the Lutheran interpretation of what the fathers called the *communicatio idiomatum*. One of Beza's main objections is that if Christ's body is set to be simultaneously in many places, it is not anymore the true body because it has relinquished the properties of a body. According to Andreae's records, Beza argued that John of Damascus' explanation on the deification of Christ's body cannot be understood such that deification means that Christ disperses his properties and is made divine, since "John Damascus says that what Christ once assumed, he no longer throws away."[33] According to Andreae, John of Damascus properly granted deification to Christ's body on account of his personal union with the Son of God and attributed divinization to the body of Christ in such a way that Christ supersedes the angels because this action is unique to him and does not apply to angels. With further support from Gregory Nazianzus and Cyril for his claim concerning the deification of Christ,[34] Andreae denies that the Lutheran Württembergers taught consubstantiation of the body with the bread, but rather a sacramental conjunction of the body and the bread.[35]

Andreae now turns his attention to another father whom he mentions for the first time: Chrysostom. He argues that Chrysostom says that spiritual things are dispensed mysteriously, although not necessarily carnally, through corporeal things in the sacraments,[36] and that Christ descended in order that his flesh, too, could give life and truly vivify. According to Andreae, this is a doctrine that the orthodox fathers (especially Cyril) taught with one voice and unanimous consensus.[37] Andreae then claims that such fathers not only ascribed relational gifts to the humanity of Christ through personal union (in agreement with Beza's view of relational gifts), but openly testified that divinity proper is truly and really communicated to Christ's body.[38] Such an explanation would lead to the subsequent discussion on the person of Christ.

On the question of ubiquity, Andreae offers the Lutheran explication of how Christ's body can simultaneously be in heaven and on earth—that Christ's presence in heaven does not preclude his presence on earth. And while he recognizes some common ground with Beza over sacramental eating, he repeatedly objects to the ascent of Christ, as if Christ was sent to a place and is now in heaven. Rather than dwell on the premise of such questions, Andreae reverts to the ecclesiastical writings that explain three states of Christ: when Christ (1) came in the flesh, (2) comes in grace, (3) and will come in glory. Since Christ comes in grace in the Eucharist, two things are required: the sign and the thing signified (to use Augustine's terms), or, as Irenaeus says, things earthly and heavenly. The earthly things are the bread and wine, while the heavenly things are the body and blood of Christ.[39]

Beza reiterates one point of agreement that the sacrament of the Lord's Supper encompasses not only bread and wine, but also Christ's body and blood. He adds: "From Augustine, sacraments are visible words which make use of God's words as if visible signs and confirm their power.

Since the same is true of the reception of Christ in the sacrament, the pure word differs in external forms but not in the very thing signified and offered."[40] Meanwhile, Andreae dismisses any point of agreement since a partial agreement is not, in fact, an agreement at all, just as occasional fidelity is not fidelity at all. What is surprising is not Andreae's refusal to acknowledge any basis of unity with the Reformed (opportunities for any religious or political partnership between the Lutherans and Reformed had eluded them for generations), but his appeal to the fathers, in this case Irenaeus, for his rejection of the Reformed stance. He writes,

> Irenaeus testifies that the sacrament consists of two things, namely earthly and heavenly. Irenaeus did not say [that] the sacrament consists in one thing, namely bread and wine that is joined in relation and form to the absent body of Christ. For bread and wine are not the sacrament, body and blood of Christ is also not the sacrament, but these two joined simultaneously in a mystery . . . And this is the unanimous opinion of all the orthodox fathers who simultaneously define all sacraments not in one part only but in two.[41]

In this case, fidelity to a church father was the reason for rejecting Beza's opinion. Meanwhile, another more frequent form of argumentation was to debate the meaning of the fathers' writings. Among the early church fathers named, Augustine, the father par excellence in the previous debates between Calvin and the Gnesio-Lutherans, not surprisingly arises early in the discussion. Beza asserts that when Augustine says, "Take this in the bread which hung on the cross. Drink this from the cup which flowed from Christ's side," it refers to the reception of things offered, not to the presence of Christ's body in the place where the bread is.[42] Andreae counters that since Augustine commands to drink from the cup that flowed from Christ's side, he is not speaking about a spiritual receiving, but rather a physical eating. After all, Augustine commands to drink from the cup, not to believe from the cup.[43]

Andreae claims that he does not ignore Augustine's concerns about the abuse of the sacrament, often in one part of the sacrament, namely the bread and wine. But Augustine nevertheless openly testifies that the sacrament of the Eucharist consists of two things: "we receive his flesh, which is in the form of bread working in the sacrament and we drink his blood which is under the species and flavor of wine. Likewise the sacrifice of the church consists of two, in the species of the visible elements and in the flesh and blood of the invisible Lord Jesus Christ."[44] According to Andreae, the consensus of all the orthodox fathers suggested that the nature of divinity cannot be exhausted (which is common to human nature).[45] In the late sixteenth century, the *Consensus Orthodoxus* often referred to a specific document published in 1574 and reprinted several times. This work used the fathers to defend other Reformed doctrines against the Lutheran formulation.[46] In response to the 1574 documents supporting Reformed views, Andreae was quick to associate ancient figures accused of heretical or heterodox views with Reformed views. He writes that in the emptying and glorification of Christ, all these sayings ought to be understood as concerning Christ from his humanity. Anyone who interprets these things as relating to his divinity is a follower of Arius, he argues.[47]

Andreae then offers a short rationale for his rejection of the *Consensus Orthodoxus*:

> For what does the so-called *Consensus Orthodoxus* discuss so that it teaches against Luther, Brenz and us; first in the Lord's Supper the body of Christ is not present locally and circumscriptively? Then Christ's body is not eaten Capernaitically in the Supper? . . . It is proper to silence this fancy creation. Therefore occupation with the local and physical presence of Christ's body in the Lord's Supper and the Capernaitic eating of Christ's body is most brief and solid refutation of this whole book called *Consensus Orthodoxus*.[48]

Andreae realizes that his debates with Beza at the Colloquy of Montbéliard fall within a larger context of deteriorating relations between the Lutherans and the Reformed. Beza claims that the fathers who say that the body of Christ falls to earth and is crushed by teeth do not properly approach the body of Christ.[49] To answer this accusation, Andreae refers to Chrysostom: "When Christ showing the bread said take, eat, this is my body, not the bread without his body, nor his body without the bread, but this spiritual thing through a corporeal thing, just as Chrysostom says, is dispensed in this mystery."[50] To avoid any notion of cannibalistic or Capernaitic eating, Andreae says that Chrysostom recognizes that the body of Christ, whose presence is spiritual, means that teeth can by no means be stuck to it.[51] According to Andreae, the teachings from Irenaeus, Augustine, and Chrysostom support the bodily presence of Christ in the Lord's Supper without falling into any error.

### Beza's *Responsio ad Acta Colloquii Montisbelgardensis*

The heart of Beza's doctrine, as he developed it out of Calvin's theology of the Lord's Supper, is the conjunction of the signs and the thing signified (*res*), for it answers the difficult question of how Christ is present sacramentally.[52] Since the body of Christ must remain circumscribed and localized, it requires a presence by habit or relation rather than by substance. Beza rejects the notion of ubiquity, saying, "I myself do not see how the flesh of Christ can be omnipresent . . . The fathers have many errors which we nevertheless just on that account do not abandon."[53] Beza is clear that the Lord's Supper is more than a symbolic act, because the sacraments call believers away from the earthly to the spiritual and heavenly. From Augustine he learns that Christ brings the sacraments as the most excellent sign perfectly accommodated to humans.[54] Yet Andreae understands these words from Augustine differently: when Augustine says that the sacraments of the New Testament are the most excellent signs, Andreae claims that Augustine did not look at the bare sign, but rather that he meant the display of the things promised, the body and blood of Christ.[55]

Beza records his theses and his responses to Andreae's marginal refutations in his *Responsio ad Acta Colloquii Montisbelgardensis*. He organized his answer into six subjects or themes: (1) the signs, (2) the signified, (3) the conjunction of the signs and the signified, (4) the reception of the signified, (5) the effects of Communion, and (6) the causes of the salutary effects.[56] For Beza, a sacrament is a visible sign divinely instituted for the church through which Christ and his benefits, by a certain analogy of correspondence, are really sealed in the souls of believers.[57] The sacramental signification is even more efficacious because it is totally dependent on the action and promise of God. Nevertheless, the mode of presence is not substantial but sacramental, not local but relational: therefore the *res* is spiritually perceived and able to be grasped only by faith.[58]

The first theme had been a fundamental difference between the Lutherans and the Reformed over the interpretation of the words of institution since the Colloquy of Marburg in 1529.[59] The debate at Montbéliard, however, does not simply repeat the Marburg debate over the correct translation of the words of institution, but conjures up more sophisticated distinctions, as the discussion moves from the question about whether the verb "is" means "signifies" to the effectiveness of Christ's presence as relating to his two natures. The Lutherans insist that the words have to be taken literally, but the Reformed teach that the words involve a trope or figure of speech that upholds Christ's humanity and divinity, which require clarification from other scriptural passages, notably John 6. For Beza, the final arbiter in the interpretation of all Scripture is the analogy of faith contained in the Apostles' Creed.

Of the church fathers named at the Colloquy of Montbéliard, five are cited by both Beza and Andreae: Irenaeus, Augustine, Chrysostom, Cyril, and John of Damascus. Yet Beza and Andreae disagree in their interpretation of these fathers. They exemplify their problem when they discuss the fathers' use of the terms "substantially," "corporeally," "essentially," and "in, with, and under" the bread and wine. Both agree that the fathers used these terms, but they disagree as to what the terms meant. Andreae sees the fathers as affirming the Lutheran interpretation of the words of institution, while Beza argues that the fathers meant that Christ is truly offered to the faith of the communicants, not to their mouths. The terms "orally" and "sensually" are not in patristic vocabulary; therefore Beza simply rejects them.[60] In speaking of the fathers, Beza is primarily preoccupied by the usefulness of the early church fathers, who themselves resorted to the authority of Scripture.[61] Because they did not believe that the humanity of Christ is converted to divinity, the fathers spoke of the personal union in which the Son of God unites the assumed body to himself.[62]

Revealing the tension over biblical interpretation, Beza cannot make sense of Andreae's dismissal of John 6 as pertaining to the Lord's Supper. Developing his argument from his reading of Augustine, Cyril, and Chrysostom, Beza describes how the passage in the Gospel of John informs his understanding of Christ's flesh. Both he and Andreae claim that, just as the Scriptures are variously interpreted, so are the fathers of the church. And both sides claim the same authorities for upholding opposing positions.[63] While Andreae cites Irenaeus to demonstrate that the bread and body are joined in a mystery, Beza refers to Irenaeus to explain that Christ's body and blood are heavenly things not with regard to their substance, but with regard to their sacramental use. Beza sees himself as protecting the human nature of Christ from the kind of divinization that would destroy its human reality.[64]

Overall, Beza offers an interpretation of the early fathers that represents the view of the Calvinist tradition. He claims that the ancients who used vocabulary concerning the presence of Christ's body did not mean that the substance of the thing signified is established to be present in the same place; rather, that faith grants the body and blood itself, which the words of institution certainly promise and the external symbols testify.[65] He identifies the source of this view when he quotes Augustine's saying that "he who does not believe does not eat the body nor drink the blood but only the symbols of them . . . not discerning the body of Christ."[66] Attacking the vocabulary of the Lutherans as the debate over the choice of words intensified, Beza argues that none of the ancient fathers explained the words of institution with these phrases, but used them to show that the power of the sacramental promise is not empty. He also fires off an arsenal of church fathers who are on "his side" on this point:

Augustine responds for us [*Lib. de Civit. Dei* 5.10] . . . And Tertullian *Against Praxeam Sabellianum*, [says] nothing is difficult for God . . . And he does not say this . . . Take, eat, so that he returns concerning the body on earth, the real and essential one, nevertheless not following the mode of the body presently explained. Cyril says, Christ, who ascended to the father, cannot with his flesh dwell somewhere else.[67]

Since the point of contention revolves around defining the kind of presence, Beza strenuously claims that the Lord's Supper is a sacramental presence by relation or habit, rather than by substance. He compares his debate with Andreae to the early church's christological debates and claims that Vigilius confutes Eutyches, because the flesh of Christ is in heaven, not everywhere on earth.[68] Beza then depicts Andreae as Eutyches, upholding the Monophysite cause that Cyril himself later backed away from. In his response to Andreae's marginal annotations, Beza says, "Vigilius concluded against Eutyches, 'just as he who was on earth, this flesh was not in heaven, therefore also he who now ascended into heaven and there remains, is not on earth'; Augustine [says], 'now he is not on earth, since he ascended into heaven and hereafter we await his coming.'"[69] Beza's implication is that Andreae represents Eutyches, who stands against the affirmations of Vigilius and Augustine.

When the related question arises regarding Christ's presence according to his humanity and divinity, Beza draws from multiple church fathers. Since the church fathers had their own conflicts over Christology, Beza accrues more fathers from the rich supply of sources:

Cyril [says], "God's power fills all and passes through all and . . . is not of another nature than what ought to be conceded of the divine." And Vigilius [says], "One and the same Christ is . . . everywhere following the nature of his divinity and satisfied in a place following the nature of his humanity." This is . . . a confession which the apostles handed down, [and] martyrs strengthened. And Tertullian [says], "Everywhere called to be present, he is not of the human nature but of God so that he can be present in all places." Likewise, Vigilius [says], "When the flesh was on earth it was not in heaven and now that which is in heaven, is surely not on earth, which is expected to be coming from heaven." And Augustine [says], "As long as time is ended [and] the Lord whose body in which he resurrected will be upward [above], it is necessary to be in one place." And Fulgentius [says], "Christ following human substance was absent in heaven when [humanity] was on earth and left earth when he ascended to heaven."[70]

The point of difference revolves around the question of where the mystery exists. While, for Andreae, the mystery is in the union of the body of Christ and the bread (on which one does not need to speculate), for Beza, the mystery lies in the union of Christ and the faith. This point is set in the context of Beza's covenant theology. Beza also appeals to Augustine to defend the Reformed statement that "Christ is not more present to participants in the Eucharist than he was to Abraham," which the Lutherans considered to be contrary to Scripture. On the relationship of the Hebrew Bible with the New Testament, Beza states, "We confess that Christ, God and man was not man in act before the real incarnation. Nevertheless we teach that he was present to the faith of Abraham not by an illusory opinion but truly and efficaciously, just as he was present to the other holy patriarchs."[71] In summary, Beza recalls a reference to Augustine: "the sacraments of the old times were equal to ours in things, but different in their signs."[72]

According to Beza, the mode by which the signified thing (*res*) is joined to the signs by divine ordination explains the naming of the signs, and shows it to be dependent on God's pact. But the mode of reception of the signified thing is a great mystery, and therefore to be believed and adored. Beza argues that if Christ's body and blood are essentially present with the bread and wine but differ from the latter merely by being invisible, then there is no longer a presence in mystery, but a purely natural presence. Behind these arguments lies an understanding of essence as another term for nature. Beza therefore introduces the category of relation, which allows for things essentially unlike to be brought together in a relationship that may be either natural or supernatural.[73] He appeals to the fathers to counter Lutheran criticisms against Reformed points considered contrary to Scripture. One contentious point heavily criticized by the Lutherans, called the "Calvinist extra" (*extra-Calvinisticum*), refers to the tenet according to which believers through faith ascend toward heaven. In defense of this concept, Beza recalls Augustine, Ignatius, and Justin to justify Christ's presence in heaven:

> Augustine [says]: ". . . Sense his presence to be sure . . . Put on and hold onto faith . . . His body carries to heaven, his majesty that is his divinity is not carried from the world." Ignatius [says], "Having conversed for forty days with the Apostles, he was raised up to the right seat of the father where he remains permanently, while his adversaries are subjected to his feet." And Justin [says], "However, while Christ having been raised up from his death, God the father of all was prevailing in heaven and there while he was detained, he struck down the demons of his enemies."[74]

Such statements make room for the Reformed cause, since it supports Calvin's position of hypostatic union and the presence of Christ's divinity in the Lord's Supper.

In his answer to Andreae's marginal refutation, Beza continues with further support from Augustine's words in *Tract. in Joann.* 26: "For they eat the same spiritual food indeed; for another corporeal thing: because to them it is manna to us it is another thing, and all drink the same spiritual drink. To them, one kind to us another: but indeed in a visible form."[75] Based on this explanation, Beza accuses Andreae of separating Christ's benefits from Christ himself in the old sacraments. As Beza sees it, Andreae's stance is against the words of Christ because of a faulty interpretation of John and a denial of Christ's command to eat spiritually. Beza believes that he has the support of Origen, Jerome, and Augustine. He then jabs at Andreae with a taunt: "[I]f Andreae does not believe us, let him believe the *Swabian Synagram*, it is from Brenz himself not yet an ubiquitarian, whose these words are."[76] (Despite Beza's assertion, Brenz afterwards focused on the difference between the fathers and the Reformed.) Beza recognizes that there is a distinction between the sacraments of things promised in the Hebrew Bible and the sacraments instituted in the New Testament, since Augustine says, "[O]ur sacraments are evidently clearer and more majestic, and [Christ] himself binds these together in the presence of faith."[77] Yet faith is the common aspect of both types.

In the context of his refutation to Andreae's marginal annotations, Beza's references to the fathers appear more frequently. The use of the fathers provides a greater service in Beza's defensive responses, for he appears to be defending not just himself or the Reformed cause but also the tradition of the "orthodox" fathers. He claims, for example, that the appeal to the sacraments is related to the signs in particular, but Andreae denies this interpretation. Beza therefore accuses Andreae of rejecting a definition that was received without controversy when the fathers said that the sacraments are visible words. Augustine, for example, identified signs as things attached to divine things and Cyprian located the effect of eternal life in the visible sacrament.[78] Beza's explanations continue to include various church fathers. After describing how Christ is present in the Eucharist through his divinity and what the communicants receive, Beza asserts that his view has the support of Athanasius, Hilary, and Augustine.[79] He also mentions John of Damascus' explanation of Christ's presence as partly from the hypostatic union of natures, partly from properties.[80] For Beza, the analogy of a cogently articulated Christian faith is given by Augustine, who followed the body upward so that hope came from heaven, and by Athanasius on the body of Christ, who also speaks of glorification.[81]

Concerning Beza's theme on the conjunction of the signs and things signified, Andreae cites Chrysostom in his marginalia: "Chrysostom testifies that Christ dispenses the spiritual through the bodily."[82] To this, Beza writes: "Andreae ought to give the citation of Chrysostom so that whether he cites him appropriately or falsely would be evident. Yet I affirm that it is not less absurd to say, Christ is essentially eaten and drank by the mouth in the Lord's Supper."[83] Having already worked on an edition of ancient Christian works for combating anti-Trinitarian heresies,[84] Beza counters with his own interpretation, namely that other fathers such as Theodoret and Augustine understood the name of the thing signified as figuratively transferred to the sign.[85] On this point, Beza's argument is built on Calvin's eschatology against the Lutheran notion of ubiquity: he emphasizes the localization of Christ's body in heaven according to the account of the ascension and the promised return of Christ on the last day.

Since the debate on the Lord's Supper brings Christ's presence under scrutiny, the discussion consequently leads to a debate over the person of Christ. While all the details of this second point of contention will not be presented here, a few points as they relate to the use of the fathers will be highlighted. In both Andreae's *Acta* and Beza's *Responsio*, there are extended references to early christological heresies, particularly to the doctrine of Nestorius. Beza and Andreae accuse each other of repeating Nestorius' error, and each interprets the Council of Chalcedon as a historical basis for his own Christology. Beza claims that Nestorius would not have made the mistake he did, had he been able to discern the difference between abstract and concrete terms.[86] Beza explains that Nestorius, a man both subtle and gifted with natural eloquence, neither took away the reality of the Son of God with Paul of Samosata, or the distinction of persons with Sabellius and Photinus, nor denied the truth of human nature. On the contrary, Nestorius was not ignorant in joining the two natures in Christ but was misrepresented, as John of Damascus testifies.[87] According to Beza, it was Cyril of Alexandria, Nestorius' bitter adversary, who argued (at the Council of Ephesus) against the assertion that two natures also established two persons. From *Epistle 2* of Nestorius to Cyril, Beza cites that Nestorius indeed believed in two natures, but that he did not confess the hypostatic union, only conjunction.[88] Beza tries to show that Andreae does not even correctly understand the early church figures of the christological controversy in order to show that Andreae's use of the fathers is based on a misunderstanding of them. Against the errors of

Nestorius and Eutyches, Beza teaches that, just as there are two natures, so there are two essential properties, two wills, and two operations tending to one common and final effect that is attributed to one single person, because Jesus Christ is but one being subsisting in two natures.[89] Beza writes that, whether Nestorius thought that the word was truly made flesh or that it constituted just as many persons as are in Christ's nature, neither is enough to excuse Andreae's claim that the word does not separate from the flesh of Christ. Beza sees this point as a theological stumbling block, since misunderstanding the two distinct natures of Christ leads people astray from orthodox views. He praises Cyril for opening people's eyes to Christ, who "is not God-bearer but God-man."[90]

Reminiscent of Calvin's previous writings against Westphal and Hesshusen, Beza wants to make sure that Cyril is depicted as a supporter of the Reformed view. According to Beza, he himself has already cited Andreae's additional explanation from Cyril and other places of Andreae's writings for many years.[91] Beza reiterates his belief in the real substance of Christ's humanity, and upholds it in the administration of the sacrament, especially in the Lord's Supper. He then asserts that these are "not our words but [the words] of all the orthodox antiquity," and cites the sayings of Augustine, Cyril, Vigilius, and Fulgentius in support of his claim.[92]

## Conclusion: Montbéliard and the New Significance of the Fathers

In the end, the Lutheran and Reformed sides could not agree on the Lord's Supper and their differences continued to be one of the key dividing points between Lutherans and Calvinists for succeeding generations.[93] The debate between Andreae and Beza continued beyond the Colloquy of Montbéliard. Andreae published his *Epitome* in 1588 as well as a vernacular version titled *Kurzer Begriff*, but Beza had the last word when he responded, after Andreae's death, with *De Controversiis in Coena Domini* (1593), an appeal not simply to Andreae and his followers but to all Lutherans who adhered to the Augsburg Confession. Andreae demonstrated impatience with the eucharistic controversy, as is evident in the last of his resumes of the colloquy, the *Kurzer Begriff* of 1588, while Beza's *De Controversiis* of 1593 returned to a more conciliatory tone. Although Beza's literary style may have reflected a more amenable tone, however, it is clear that Beza himself was not willing to budge in his beliefs any more than Andreae. In addition, since Calvin's death, Beza's polemical attacks on Lutheran theologians had become increasingly ferocious and frequent. At the Colloquy of Montbéliard, for example, Andreae cited six fathers—Augustine, John of Damascus, Gregory Nazianzus, Cyril, Chrysostom, and Irenaeus—and Beza cited fourteen—Augustine, Cyril, Chrysostom, Ignatius, Justin, Origen, Irenaeus, Cyprian, Athanasius, John of Damascus, Vigilius, Jerome, Fulgentius, and Theodoret. This was a dramatic increase from Calvin's appeal to Augustine in his first two treatises against Joachim Westphal (1555–1556). As a defensive strategy, Beza's use of the fathers demonstrated his confidence in the historical validity of his view even as he was assailed by accusations of deviating from the Word of God. While Beza referred to many more fathers than Andreae, both cited five of the same fathers, including Irenaeus, Augustine, Chrysostom, John of Damascus, and Cyril.

In the case of Marburg, the political leader Philip of Hesse aimed to gain a united Protestant front of German and Swiss reformers against powerful Roman Catholic threats. In the case of Montbéliard, Henry of Navarre looked to the international colloquy in hopes of proving that theological differences between Reformed and Lutheran sides were less important than their common opposition to the pope and the Roman Catholic Holy League. Both Philip of Hesse and Henry of Navarre considered the basis of political alliance and their aggregate political strength to be the top priority over what they saw as minor theological differences, and urged theologians to reach a consensus. Both were disappointed. In both cases, theologians and church leaders resisted the formation of a common doctrine on several key issues, and thereby dissolved the potential bonds of a Protestant league.

Tensions arose in the forging of confessional identities in a time and place that valued neither religious diversity nor innovation. While the Lutheran governing members listened to the concerns of the French Reformed living among them, they also wanted civic tranquility and theological unity. As theologians from both sides resisted the formation of a common doctrine on several key issues, including the Eucharist, they created distinctive confessional identities that contributed to establishing regional and national identities. And as debates over the Eucharist intensified, reformers cited the fathers more frequently by adapting the rhetoric of early church polemics against each other. Citing the fathers as authorities to override other opinions was not a new tactic and, in fact, had been the predominant method of using the fathers since the medieval period. Since some medieval commentators had already pointed out inconsistencies in the works of the fathers, it was not new for reformers to point out the fathers' errors, although they were willing to notice more of them than their medieval forebears had acknowledged. What was new in the reformers' use of the fathers was that they redefined what the fathers meant and offered new interpretations of the ancient texts that had immediate applications to the sixteenth-century context. As the reformers sought the sayings of the fathers that supported Lutheran or Reformed doctrine, the actual voices of the fathers were limited to speaking only those words that the reformers gave them.

This elaborate, repetitive process of incorporating cues to the church fathers guided reformers in building up authoritative, albeit contested, confessional traditions. In other words, while interest in the early Christian writers was not new, their works were being recalled in a new way—to provide ancestral roots for a newly consolidated Lutheran or Reformed tradition that could compete simultaneously with the formation of other churches. The significance of the use of the fathers is that they became the primary way of authorizing new views, through claims that these views were not new at all, but in fact had an ancient historical heritage. By interpreting a new ancient tradition, both Andreae and Beza could derive their religious identities from the beginning of Christian history.

# Conclusion

Up to the present, many scholars have argued that the fathers did not have absolute authority for the reformers. This continues to be true, but what needs to be added to this point is that the reformers' interpretations of the fathers did carry an authority that supported each confessional tradition and excluded others, particularly on divisive issues such as the Eucharist. These newly authorized views set boundaries and defined the limits of orthodoxy for the Lutheran and Reformed traditions. While the Protestant reformers initially appealed to the church fathers for authorization to deviate from the late medieval church, it is noteworthy that they continued and often intensified their appeal to the fathers in intra-Protestant debates. Although the Protestant reformers claimed Scripture as their primary authority, it was nevertheless important to have a tradition that would demonstrate a history of correct interpretations of God's Word. Lutherans and Calvinists turned to the ancient tradition to show that their views had the consent of past authorities. They strove to establish "true religion" by interpreting Scripture and defining biblical doctrine. When differences arose in defining this doctrine, they turned to the early church fathers because they were considered faithful expositors of the Bible. While Luther's approach was to follow the spirit of the fathers who recognized their own sayings as subject to the word of God, Calvin's approach was to consider certain preapproved sayings of the church fathers just as authoritative as Scripture, provided that he had already established those particular sayings as faithful expositions of Scripture.

Lutheran and Reformed leaders strove to distinguish their particular views of the Eucharist as the orthodox or "right" belief even in the fine points of their theological differences. Their appeal to ancient authorities was an attempt, on the one hand, to find alternative sources of authority against the established authority of the early modern Catholic Church, and, on the other hand, to subvert the authority of competitors in an expanding arena of religious choices. Their followers demonstrated their allegiance by following distinctly Lutheran or Reformed modes of liturgy and practice of the Lord's Supper. In some cases, Lutheran and Reformed leaders tried to work toward consensus when they felt their mixed communities were threatened. As lines of denominational division grew deeper, the fathers were part of an effort by the reformers to establish a historical foundation for their emerging branch of Protestantism. To varying degrees, the reformers attempted to graft their confessional belief onto historic Christianity by attempting to root many of their views of the Lord's Supper in the ancient church.

Since Scripture was the primary authority, Luther and Zwingli followed the principle of explaining the meaning of Scripture by referring to other passages within it.[1] Zwingli noted that the church fathers had used the same method in order to deal with heretical opinions. While at Marburg, the reformers simply divided up the fathers by determining which ones supported Luther and which supported Zwingli and Oecolampadius. Augustine was a star witness mostly for the latter. The fact that the various reformers could not reach an agreement even at this early stage set the tone for their antagonistic relationships with one another in the future, initially for the Lutherans and later for the Reformed. Just as Luther's association of Zwingli and Oecolampadius with Karlstadt tainted his view of them, so Westphal's association of Calvin with Zwingli prejudiced his view of Calvin.

During the debates of the 1550s, Calvin and Westphal initially fought over Augustine, and their debates resembled a tug-of-war to claim Augustine for their side. Yet Westphal started to claim other fathers besides Augustine, and although Calvin claimed to hold the fathers in high esteem, he initially cited very few of them. Meanwhile, Westphal claimed many more fathers, such as Cyril, Chrysostom, Gregory Nazianzus, Ambrose, Justin Martyr, Hilary, Irenaeus, Cyprian, and Theodoret, even though he claimed the authority of God's word to be sufficient. In Calvin's last response to Westphal, and by the time of his debate with Hesshusen, a greater number of fathers were cited by both sides. Hesshusen was willing to divide up the fathers when he granted that Calvin had at most two possible ancient supporters, Clement of Alexandria and Origen. In the writings between Hesshusen and Calvin, the array of fathers discussed by both sides included Justin Martyr, Irenaeus, Tertullian, Cyprian, Ambrose, Augustine, Jerome, Chrysostom, Hilary, Cyril, Basil, Gregory Nazianzus, Epiphanius, Athanasius, and John of Damascus, as well as Clement and Origin.

Often a list of several patristic writers would be presented as representative of the general opinion of the church fathers as a whole, or one or two names would be listed, followed by the phrase "and many others" to portray an ambiguous but large number of supporters. At the Colloquy of Montbéliard, Beza and Andreae both claimed to have some of the same key fathers on their sides. Of the six fathers mentioned by Andreae, Beza claimed five but also made references to nine others not mentioned explicitly by Andreae. Therefore Beza's approach to the fathers was not merely to divide up the fathers or simply claim Augustine for his side, but to apply all the strategies used before him—to deploy as many fathers in support of the Reformed view as possible and to fight for the "correct" interpretation of those key fathers whom Andreae also tried to claim.

The Protestant reformers considered the theological differences over the Lord's Supper to be important because a correct understanding of how Christ is present in the Eucharist meant a correct understanding of who Christ is and who the church is. Because Scripture was considered a reliable source of God's revelation, it was vitally important to know what Scripture meant in order to know what to believe and how to be saved. Misunderstanding Scripture led not only to heresy but also to damnation. By the end of the sixteenth century, the Lutheran and Reformed views of the Lord's Supper were solidified in their respective confessions, and the ancient fathers were an important component of the reformers' theology. While the use of the fathers was initially meant to persuade and convince others to accept particular points of view in the eucharistic controversies, the fathers became the building blocks used to define and refine the differences between opposing sides in the argument. In other words, the fathers, newly interpreted by the Protestant reformers, became authenticators of the Protestant tradition. By interpreting the ancient tradition as the heritage of the Protestants, the reformers created a "new" ancient tradition. With this reinterpretation, they claimed to be legitimate heirs of the early church and faithful interpreters of God's word. Perhaps by creating multiple Christian traditions that all claimed to stem from the early church, the reformers genuinely inherited the spirit of theological diversity of the early church itself.

# Appendix I

## The Württemberg Theses

The first set of theses are points about which the Lutherans deemed there was no controversy. The second set was considered controversial, and the third set lays out the Lutherans' summary of those Reformed points that they considered contrary to Scripture.

### The First Set

The following four points of agreement are:

(1) All the faithful, even outside the liturgy, eat the flesh of the Son of Man spiritually, by faith for salvation, as John 6 makes clear. But the eating of the sacrament is another kind of eating and is not always salutary. Andreae concluded that although the two eatings are not the same, spiritual eating is necessary if sacramental eating is to be salutary.
(2) Capernaitic eating of Christ's flesh is a damnable doctrine.
(3) Roman Catholic doctrine of transubstantiation is rejected.
(4) Lutherans as well as the Reformed deny that the presence of Christ's body and blood is physical, local, or inclusive.

### The Second Set

The six Lutheran theses unacceptable to the Reformed may be summarized as follows:

(1) The true body and blood of Jesus Christ are truly and substantially present and distributed with the bread and wine and taken orally by all who use the sacrament, whether worthy or unworthy, faithful or infidel, the former to life and the latter to judgment.

(2) The words "in," "with," and "under" the bread indicate the presence of the true body. The same thing is indicated by the terms "substantially," "corporeally," "really," "essentially," and "orally."

(3) The words of institution declare the presence of Christ's real body.

(4) Christ is not a liar.

(5) Christ is God-man in one inseparable person to whom nothing is impossible. What he wished to do, he could do: *Quod vellit, posit ergo fecit.* He wished to give himself to be eaten; therefore he did so.

(6) The mode of Christ's presence is not expressed in Scripture. But this much can be said: it is supernatural and incomprehensible to human reason and therefore it is not to be disputed. God can find many ways to make the body and blood of Christ everywhere available other than the natural and physical mode, which is the only mode understood by human reason. Christ's words are simply to be believed.

## The Third Set

The third set which the Württemberg theologians judged to be contrary to Scripture:

(1) That the words of Christ are not to be taken simply as they sound but must be interpreted in the light of other passages.

(2) That the mouth receives only bread and wine, while Christ is eaten by faith. That by faith believers ascend to heaven and there are made partakers of his body and blood since Christ's body is in heaven and will remain there until the last day.[1]

(3) That God is not able by his omnipotence to make the body of Christ present in more than one place at a time.

(4) That Christ is not more present to participants in the Eucharist than he was to Abraham of old.

(5) That in the Supper the virtue, operation, and merit of the absent body and blood of Christ are dispensed.

(6) That among those eating unworthily (and therefore taking judgment to themselves) are numbered those also who are weak or stupid in faith or suffer other weaknesses but who nevertheless have true faith.

(7) That oral manducation leads to stercoranism.

# Appendix II

## The Swiss Theses

*The Signs*

Beza began by distinguishing two uses of the word "sacrament." The narrower meaning refers to those things that the senses perceive, that is, bread and wine. By the Lord's institution and commandment, the bread and wine are removed from their common and natural use and given a spiritual and sacred signification. This signification is not bare and empty, nor is it a mere remembering, but it really attains to God; what is signified, namely Christ's body and blood, is offered to souls. Beza then asserted that he and Andreae agreed on the foundation of this thesis, the words of institution, with one exception: for the Reformed, what is offered is received by faith, not by the mouth. Oral manducation had been the major point of contention from the beginning of the Protestant disagreements about the Lord's Supper.

*The Signified*

Thesis II says only a little more than the first in listing those things that are signified. Besides the signification of the body and blood by the bread and wine, the Passion of Christ is signified by the breaking of the bread and the pouring out of the wine. The foundation of Thesis II is Christ's command to do as he did so that the rites as well as the elements are part of the institution of the Lord's Supper and must be observed lest the signification be vain and empty.

## The Conjunction of the Signs and the Signified

With regard to this point, Beza repeated his application of the narrower meaning of the word "sacrament" and introduced the Aristotelian category of "relation," or habit: "Since sacraments by their narrower signification are signs, we put the sacramental conjunction in the mutual relation and habit of the signs and the things signified by which as these things impinge upon the sense, from Christ's ordination, they are taken from their common and natural use and applied to signifying and offering to us sacred and divine realities." This is the heart of Beza's doctrine as he developed it out of Calvin's theology of the Lord's Supper and answered the difficult question of how Christ is present sacramentally. The foundation of this thesis is the truth of Christ's body. Since that body is a human body and is therefore circumscribed and localized, it requires a sacramental presence by relation or habit rather than by substance. Beza employed the Aristotelian categories to explain his sacramental theology but not to provide its foundation, which remained the witness concerning Christ's human nature as given in Scripture and expressed in the creeds of the apostolic church. Beza held that the more one insists on the truth of the body of Christ, the more one must give up the notion of consubstantiation. The rest of Beza's argument on this point dealt with the localization of Christ's body in heaven according to the account of the Ascension and the promised return of Christ on the last day.

## The Reception of the Signified

Beza explained the reception of the signs and the signified through the analogy of eating ordinary food. The purpose of sacramental eating, he said, is to nourish the soul. Therefore, just as the mouth of body eats physical food, so the mouth of the soul eats spiritual food. The mode of receiving the body of Christ is therefore spiritual. This is the basis of what Beza called "sacramental metonymy," whereby earthly elements signify heavenly realities that are offered to the soul and received through the instrument of faith by the power of the Holy Spirit.

## The Effects of Communion

Beza said that the Lord's Supper was not instituted for the sake of the bread and wine but for the salvation of human beings. The mystery therefore lies in the union of Christ and the faithful, not in the supposed union of the body of Christ with the bread. Through the sacrament, which requires and confirms penitence and faith, a spiritual conjunction with Christ is deepened and strengthened through which Christ gives all his gifts and benefits to the faithful. The Holy Spirit effects this mystical union so that Christ is the head of the members of the body united to him and is the source of their increasing unity and spiritual growth into eternal life.

*The Causes of the Salutary Effects*

The Causes of the Salutary Effects are, first, the Holy Spirit, who, with ineffable power, effects the union of the faithful with Christ, a union that St. Paul called a "great mystery." The Holy Spirit, who is the Spirit of Christ, does so through the life, suffering, death, resurrection, and ascension of Christ, in whom the faithful believe. The instrumental causes are the minister doing as Christ commanded, the words of institution, the sins themselves, and the sacramental rites. Faith given by God is the principal instrumental cause. None of these instruments, however, has any intrinsic efficient power apart from the working of the Holy Spirit and the command of Christ.

# Abbreviations

CCSL   Corpus Christianorum: Series latina

CO     *Ioannis Calvini opera quae supersunt omnia*

CR     *Corpus Reformatorum*

CT     *Selected Works of John Calvin: Tracts and Letters*

FC     Fathers of the Church

GCS    Die griechischen christlichen Schriftsteller der ersten drei
       Jahrhunderte

LCC    *Theological Treatises,* Library of Christian Classics (Calvin)

LW     *Luther's Works*

MBW    *Melanchthons Briefwechsel: Kritische und kommentierte
       Gesamtausgabe*

NPNF   *Nicene and Post-Nicene Fathers*

OS     *Opera Selecta* (Calvin)

PG     Patrologiae cursus completus: Series graeca

PL     Patrologiae cursus completus: Series latina

WA     *D. Martin Luthers Werke*

WABr   *D. Martin Luthers Briefwechsel*

# Notes

## Introduction

1    Gerald R. Evans, *Problems of Authority in the Reformation Debates* (Cambridge: Cambridge University Press, 1992), 86.

2    Gordon Rupp, *Patterns of Reformation* (Philadelphia: Fortress, 1969), xvii.

3    Anthony N. S. Lane, *John Calvin, Student of the Church Fathers* (Grand Rapids: Baker Books, 1999). For Luther and Athanasius, see Bernhard Lohse and Gabriele Borger, *Luther und Athanasius, Evangelium in der Geschichte* Series, vol. 2 (Göttingen: Vandenhoeck & Ruprecht, 1998). For studies on Melanchthon's use of the fathers, see Pierre Fraenkel, *Testimonia Patrum: The Function of the Patristic Argument in the Theology of Philip Melanchthon* (Geneva: Droz, 1961); E. P. Meijering, *Melanchthon and Patristic Thought: The Doctrines of Christ and Grace, the Trinity and the Creation* (Leiden: Brill, 1983) and Timothy Wengert, *Philip Melanchthon's "Annotationes in Johannem" in Relation to its Predecessors and Contemporaries* (Geneva: Droz, 1987).

4    See Nicholas Thompson, *Eucharistic Sacrifice and Patristic Tradition in the Theology of Martin Bucer, 1534–1546* (Leiden: Brill, 2005).

5    See David Steinmetz and Robert Kolb, introduction to *Die Patristik in der Bibelexegese des 16. Jahrhunderts*, ed. David Steinmetz (Wiesbaden: Harrassowitz, 1999).

6    Leif Grane, "Some Remarks on the Church Fathers in the First Years of the Reformation (1516–1520)," in *Auctoritas Patrum: Contributions on the Reception of the Church Fathers in the 15th and 16th century*, ed. Leif Grane, Alfred Schindler, and Markus Wriedt (Mainz: von Zabern, 1993), 21.

7    Grane, "Some Remarks," 22.

8    For instance, some scholars claim that in the Middle Ages less than a quarter of the genuine works of Chrysostom were accessible. While it is hard to measure the veracity of this statement, the new interest in the fathers prompted the search for ancient sources to make them available.

9     Rupp, *Patterns of Reformation*, xviii.
10    Rupp, *Patterns of Reformation*, xviii.
11    Philip Melanchthon, *Melanchthons Briefwechsel: Kritische und kommentierte Gesamtausgabe*, vol. 1, no. 40, ed. Heinz Scheible (Stuttgart: Frommann-Holzboog, 1977), 55. (*Melanchthons Briefwechsel* is hereafter cited as *MBW*.)
12    Evans, *Problems of Authority*, 83, notes that one of the factors in bringing about a gradual change in the old patterns of respect from authority seems to have been wider reading.
13    See Melanchthon, *Epistola de Lipsica disputatione* in *Melanchthons Werke*, ed. Robert Stupperich, Studienausgabe 1 (Gütersloh: Bertelsmann, 1951), 5; idem, *Defensio Phil Melanchthonis contra Joh. Eckium*, in Melanchthon, *Melanchthons Werke*, 20.
14    Beatus Rhenanus and Ulrich Zwingli, *Huldreich Zwinglis sämmtliche Werke, Briefwechsel I*: 1510–1522 [*CR* 94, no. 49]. Beatus Rhenanus showed initial support for the Reformation but remained in the established church as the Protestant churches took on distinct identities, beliefs, and practices. Wolfgang Capito thought along the same lines when, in June 1519, he asked Georg Spalatin to greet Luther and Karlstadt and to tell them that he would be on their side against the arrogance of the scholastic theologians, namely by continuing his translations of the fathers. Oswald Myconius, then schoolmaster at Lucerne, greeted the same Capito as a renewer of theology and true Christianity, precisely because he was translating the fathers. Capito, in his greeting to Luther and Karlstadt just before the Leipzig disputation, suggests the close connection between fighting the sophists and translating the fathers: both activities pull in the same direction. In the preface to his *Rhetoric* from January 1519, Melanchthon does more than suggest the connection. He complains about the way in which young people are being indoctrinated with bad dialectic, and indicates a position that was shared by many in these years: the church fathers are of a different and higher order than scholastic doctors, and to praise them is the same as being open-minded and listening to Erasmus, Reuchlin, and Luther (*MBW* 1, no. 40: 38–48). The expression "the fathers" has become a battle cry for those who are engaged in the ongoing fight against scholasticism by joining forces with these three great leaders.
15    Rhenanus, "Letter to Zwingli," *CR* 94, no. 49.
16    Lane, *John Calvin*, 154–55.
17    Lane, *John Calvin*, 155. Currently there is no evidence that Calvin compiled his own book of quotations, although it is certainly a possibility. At the least, he had access to Bucer's *florilegium*.
18    Willem Van't Spijker, *Calvin: A Brief Guide to his Life and Thought*, trans. Lyle D. Bierma (Louisville, Ky.: Westminster John Knox, 2009), 61.
19    Carter Lindberg, *The European Reformations* (Oxford: Blackwell, 1996), 181.
20    John Foxe, *Book of Martyrs*, ed. W. Grinton Berry (Grand Rapids: Baker Books, 2003), 318–22; A. G. Dickens, *The English Reformation* (New York: Schocken Books, 1964), 171–72.
21    I fully acknowledge the diversity of late medieval schools of thought within early modern Catholicism in the years prior to the Council of Trent. At the same time, it is also understood that the late medieval Catholic theologians to

varying degrees accepted the doctrine of the Mass as a sacrifice, transubstantiation and the doctrine of concomitance. See David Bagchi, "Catholic theologians of the Reformation period before Trent," *The Cambridge Companion to
Reformation Theology*, eds. David Bagchi and David C. Steinmetz (Cambridge:
Cambridge University Press, 2004), 220–32.

22  Gottfried Hoffman examines the patristic argument in the eucharistic controversy between Oecolampadius, Zwingli, Luther, and Melanchthon, but
confines a discussion of the Marburg Colloquy to a four-page excursus at the
end of his work. See Hermann Gottfried Hoffmann, *"Sententiae Patrum*: Das
Patristische Argument in der Abendmahlskontroverse zwischen Oekolampad,
Zwingli, Luther und Melanchthon" (Ph.D. diss., Ruprecht-Karl Universität zu
Heidelberg, 1971). Ralph Quere's book includes a brief but helpful section
on Oecolampadius and Luther on the fathers, but in a subsequent section on
the Marburg Colloquy, Quere's mention of the fathers is summed up in a dis-
appointing brief paragraph. See Ralph Walter Quere, *Melanchthon's Christum
Cognoscere: Christ's Efficacious Presence in the Eucharistic Theology of Melanchthon*
(Nieuwkoop: de Graaf, 1977). Irene Dingel broaches the role of the fathers
in the intra-Lutheran eucharistic debates by focusing on an anonymous 1574
document from Heidelberg called the *Consensus Orthodoxus*. Dingel's essay discusses Luther's and Melanchthon's views about the authority of Scripture and
the fathers as they relate to the struggle for an orthodox consensus among the
fathers. See Irene Dingel, "Das Streben nach einem 'consensus orthodoxus'
mit den Vätern in der Abendmahlsdiskussion des späten 16. Jahrhunderts," in
Steinmetz, ed., *Patristik in der Bibelexegese*, 181–204.

23  Kenneth Hagen argues that the historical development of modern Western
Christianity seems to have been the closing of more and more theological
doors. Sixteenth-century churches were determined in their confidence about
the essential truths of the gospel, and intolerant of those who begged to differ.
See Kenneth Hagen, *Foundations of Theology in the Continental Reformation: Questions of Authority* (Milwaukee, Wis.: Marquette University Press, 1974).

24  Hagen, *Foundations of Theology*, 119.

25  Thompson, *Eucharistic Sacrifice*, 75.

26  See Ronnie Po-chia Hsia, *Social Discipline in the Reformation: Central Europe,
1550–1750* (New York: Routledge, 1989). In the seventeenth century, the
denominational polarization of the post-Reformation era that had pushed
supporters of the old and new faiths into increasingly militant stands, and
ultimately plunged all of Germany into a war, had finally reached its limits,
at least for German Lutherans and Calvinists. The crisis precipitated by the
Thirty Years' War caused Germany's Evangelicals to seek closer ties at Leipzig.
Confronted with the overwhelming Catholic victories of the late 1620s and
the possibility of total annihilation, the political and religious spokesmen of
Germany's two major Reformation churches came together to focus more on
their common Protestant interests. See Bodo Nischan, *Lutherans and Calvinists
in the Age of Confessionalism* (Aldershot, UK: Ashgate, 1999).

27  The concept of confessionalization is a much-debated subject. Heinz Schilling
argues that in the 1580s there was an increasingly confessional polarization of
all three kinds (Lutheran, Catholic, Reformed), and that these were princely

confessionalizations. Some scholars, such as Walter Ziegler however, have seen Schilling's thesis as particularly relevant for the Lutheran model rather than for all of Europe. See Wolfgang Reinhard and Heinz Schilling, eds. *Die katholische Konfessionalisierung: Wissenschaftliches Symposion der Gesellschaft zur Herausgabe des Corpus Catholicorum und des Vereins für Reformationsgeschichte*. Gütersloh: Gütersloher Verlagshaus, 1995; and Heinz Schilling, "The Reformation and the Rise of the Early Modern State," in *Luther and the Modern State in Germany*, ed. James Tracy (Kirksville, Mo.: Sixteenth Century Journal Publishers, 1986), 21–30. In sketching the historical development of the three confessions, Hsia, *Social Discipline*, offers a more balanced view by stressing the distinctiveness of each without losing sight of the significant structural similarities among them.

28    Craig S. Farmer, "The Johannine Signs in the Exegesis of Wolfgang Musculus" (Ph.D. diss., Duke University, 1992), 62–63.

29    Farmer, "Johannine Signs," 64 (emphasis added).

30    Rupert E. Davies, *The Problem of Authority in the Continental Reformers* (London: Epworth, 1946), 10.

31    See David V. N. Bagchi, *Luther's Earliest Opponents: Catholic Controversialists, 1518–1525* (Minneapolis: Fortress, 1991).

32    See Susan Schreiner, "Calvin and the Exegetical Debates about Certainty," in *Biblical Interpretation in the Era of the Reformation*, ed. Richard A. Muller and John L. Thompson (Grand Rapids: Eerdmans, 1996), 199.

*Chapter 1*

1    In the 1525 *Enchiridion of Commonplaces: Against Luther and Other Enemies of the Church*, ostensibly directed against Philip Melanchthon's *Loci Communes*, Johannes Eck, a Catholic theologian from the University of Ingolstadt, claimed the church fathers for the Roman Catholic side in his reply to Lutheran objections. See Johannes Eck, *Enchiridion locorum communium adversus Lutherum et alios hostes ecclesiae* [1525–1543], ed. Pierre Fraenkel (Münster: Aschendorff, 1979).

2    The Wittenberg Ordinance codified modifications to the Mass, such as offering Communion in both kinds, meaning both the consecrated bread and wine, delivering the words of institution in the vernacular, and eliminating the host's elevation. While Luther encouraged many of the reforms set out in the Wittenberg Ordinance, he later named Karlstadt and Zwilling as authors of the "monstrosity." Whatever comradeship Luther and Karlstadt had shared as colleagues in the Wittenberg movement eroded quickly. Karlstadt's sermons and his speed in implementing reforms in the Mass, despite the Elector's instructions prohibiting any innovations, were seen as the cause for subsequent confusion and rabblerousing in Wittenberg. Because Karlstadt and Zwilling claimed to be advocating the teachings of Luther, Luther felt a need to distance himself from these men as a practical matter of reputation. See Mark U. Edwards Jr., *Luther and the False Brethren* (Stanford, Calif.: Stanford University Press, 1975), 12–24.

3    Karlstadt introduced this reform for evangelical worship on January 1, 1522. Concerning the words of institution in the Lord's Supper, he argued that Jesus was pointing to himself (i.e., his own body) when he spoke, "This is my body."

4    Edwards, *Luther and the False Brethren*, 24.

5    Martin Brecht, *Martin Luther: Shaping and Defining the Reformation* (Minneapolis: Fortress, 1990), 295.

6    Martin Luther, D. *Martin Luthers Briefwechsel* (Weimar: Böhlaus, 1930), 3:373 (hereafter abbreviated *WABr*). See also *WABr* 3:397, 422, 437; and *Luther's Works*, American edition, edited and translated by Gottfried G. Krodel (Philadelphia: Fortress, 1955–), 49:88–90 (hereafter abbreviated *LW*).

7    Edwards, *Luther and the False Brethren*, 82.

8    Brecht, *Martin Luther: Shaping and Defining*, 293.

9    Luther, *Letter to the Christians at Strasbourg in Opposition to the Fanatic Spirit*, *WABr* 3:422.

10   Luther, *Letter to the Christians at Strasbourg in Opposition to the Fanatic Spirit*, *WABr* 3:422.

11   Martin Luther, *Against the Heavenly Prophets in the Matter of Images and Sacraments*, in *Karlstadt's Battle with Luther: Documents in a Liberal-Radical Debate*, ed. Ronald J. Sider (Philadelphia: Fortress, 1978), 1.

12   W. P. Stephens, *The Theology of Huldrych Zwingli* (New York: Oxford University Press, 1986), 21.

13   Walther Köhler, *Zwingli und Luther: Ihr Streit über das Abendmahl nach seinen politischen und religiösen Beziehungen*, vol. 1: *Die religiöse und politische Entwicklung bis zum Marburger Religionsgespräch 1529* (Leipzig: Eger & Sievers, 1924), 314.

14   Ulrich Zwingli, *Commentary on True and False Religion*, ed. Samuel Macauley Jackson and Clarence Nevin Heller (Durham, N.C.: Labyrinth, 1981); translated from Zwingli's *De Vera et Falsa Religione* (Zürich: Froschauer, 1525). For example, Tertullian says in his first book against Marcion, "Nor did God disdain the bread by which He represents His own body." The initial response to Zwingli came from Luther's colleague, pastor, and friend Johannes Bugenhagen in July 1525, when he wrote the first Wittenberg publication against Zwingli, titled *Open Letter Against the New Error Concerning the Sacrament of the Body and Blood of Our Lord Jesus Christ*. Bugenhagen rejected the interpretation of "is" as "signifies" in the words of institution, as well as the spiritual interpretation of the Lord's Supper on the basis of John 6. In response, Zwingli's defended his own position and made it widely known in *An Addition or Summary on the Eucharist* (August 1525) and *The Lord's Supper* (February 1526).

15   Johannes Brenz, *Syngramma Suevicum* in *Frühschriften*, vol. 1, eds. Martin Brecht, Gerhard Schäfer and Frieda Wolf (Tübingen: J.C.B. Mohr, 1970), 244–45.

16   Brecht, *Martin Luther: Shaping and Defining*, 295.

17   Brecht, *Martin Luther: Shaping and Defining*, 304. The next generation of Gnesio-Lutherans, such as Joachim Westphal, projected the same accusations that Luther had made against the Reformed side. Accusations of disunity and a misguided regard for reason continue in the tradition of Lutheran polemic against the Reformed.

18   Lindberg, *European Reformations*, 192.

19   W. P. Stephens, "Zwingli on John 6:63," in Muller and Thompson, *Biblical Interpretation in the Era of the Reformation*, 161.

20   Ulrich Zwingli, *And Martin Luther with His Latest Book Has by No Means Proved or Established His Own and the Pope's View*, CR 92:819–24.

21    Zwingli, *And Martin Luther*, CR 92:848–49; Edwards, *Luther and the False Breth-ren*, 101.
22    Edwards, *Luther and the False Brethren*, 101.
23    Such terms as "Protestant," "Lutheran," and "Reformed" are in some cases used prematurely. I note when such designations become officially recognized, but at times, for the sake of clarity, I refer to these terms as a categorization in hindsight.
24    Heiko Oberman, *Luther: Man between God and the Devil* (New Haven, Conn.: Yale University Press, 1989), 237.
25    Edwards, *Luther and the False Brethren*, 105.
26    See Philip's letter to Melanchthon, CR 2:96–100.
27    See William J. Wright, "Philip of Hesse's Vision of Protestant Unity and the Marburg Colloquy," in *Pietas et Societas: New Trends in Reformation Social History*, ed. Kyle C. Sessions and Philip N. Bebb (Kirksville, Mo.: Sixteenth Century Essays and Studies, 1985), 163–79.
28    Wright, "Philip of Hesse's Vision," 171.
29    Walther Köhler does not believe that the report is based on notes made by Zwingli, as is assumed by the editor in Martin Luther, D. *Martin Luthers Werke* (Weimar: Böhlaus, 1883), 30.III:101 (hereafter abbreviated WA). See also LW 38:11–12; and Walther Köhler, *Das Religionsgespräch zu Marburg 1529* (Tübin-gen: Mohr, 1929).
30    Köhler, *Das Religionsgespräch zu Marburg*, 7–37.
31    Hermann Sasse, *This is My Body: Luther's Contention for the Real Presence in the Sacrament of the Altar* (Minneapolis: Augsburg, 1959). Sasse argues that the con-troversy between Luther and Zwingli is an event that deeply influenced the political and cultural development of Europe and demonstrated the struggle to understand correctly the word of God among those who accepted the primacy of the authority of Scripture.
32    Hoffmann, "*Sententiae Patrum*," 2–4. While Hoffman presents a cohesive por-trait of each reformer's use and knowledge of the fathers, the drawback of his study is that the development of the use of the fathers in the discussions and disagreements among the reformers cannot be discovered, especially on such a divisive issue as the Lord's Supper, and therefore the reason for citing the fathers is lost.
33    Kent A. Heimbigner, "The Evolution of Luther's Reception of the Early Church Fathers in Eucharistic Controversy: A Consideration of Selected Words, 1518–1529," *Logia: A Journal of Lutheran Theology* 7 (Epiphany 1998): 3–11.
34    Köhler, *Das Religionsgespräch zu Marburg*, 41.
35    Köhler, *Das Religionsgespräch zu Marburg*, 42.
36    Marburg Colloquy, *LW* 38:17 (Hedio).
37    Marburg Colloquy, *LW* 38:24 (Hedio).
38    Marburg Colloquy, *LW* 38:18 (Hedio).
39    Marburg Colloquy, *LW* 38:20 (Hedio).
40    Marburg Colloquy, *LW* 38:21 (Hedio).
41    Marburg Colloquy, *LW* 38:36 (anonymous).
42    Marburg Colloquy, *LW* 38:50 (anonymous).

43  Fulgentius, *Libri tres ad Trasimundum* II.17, as recorded in the account of the Marburg Colloquy, *LW* 38:50 (anonymous).
44  Marburg Colloquy, *LW* 38:51 (anonymous).
45  Marburg Colloquy, *LW* 38:53 (anonymous).
46  Marburg Colloquy, *LW* 38:26–27 (Hedio).
47  The conflict over the correct view of the Eucharist between the Gnesio-Lutherans and the Philippists revolved around the earlier and later revised versions of the Augsburg Confession.
48  Marburg Colloquy, *LW* 38:64 (Osiander).
49  Marburg Colloquy, *LW* 38:27 (Hedio).
50  Marburg Colloquy, *LW* 38:28 (Hedio).
51  Lindberg, *European Reformations*, 191.
52  Marburg Colloquy, *LW* 38:51–52 (anonymous).
53  Marburg Colloquy, *LW* 38:52 (anonymous).
54  Synecdoche is a figure of speech by which a part of something is used to express the whole (e.g., "fifty sail" for "fifty ships"), the whole for a part (e.g., "society" for "high society"), the species for the genus (e.g., "cutthroat" for "assassin"), the genus for the species (e.g., "creature" for "man"), or the name of the material for the thing made (e.g., "silk" for "robe"). Earlier, Zwingli uses a similar definition for the word "metonymy." Yet technically metonymy is a figure of speech by which one term is replaced by another that is *closely related to* it, but not necessarily a part of it (e.g., "Washington" for "the government"). Despite Zwingli's confusing understanding of metonymy, in which he includes synecdoche, Luther correctly notes the difference when he supports synecdoche, while Zwingli and Oecolampadius support metonomy.
55  Marburg Colloquy, *LW* 38:30 (Hedio).
56  Marburg Colloquy, *LW* 38:31 (Hedio).
57  Marburg Colloquy, *LW* 38:31 (Hedio).
58  Marburg Colloquy, *LW* 38:33 (Hedio).
59  Marburg Colloquy, *LW* 38:33 (Hedio).
60  Marburg Colloquy, *LW* 38:33 (Hedio).
61  Marburg Colloquy, *LW* 38:33 (Hedio).
62  Marburg Colloquy, *LW* 38:33–34 (Hedio).
63  *Das Marburger Gespräch und die Marburger Artikel von 1529*. WA 30.III:142c, 33.
64  Around the third century, Cyprian spoke of "representation" to describe the metaphorical meaning for the Christian eucharistic celebration as the sacrifice of Jesus, not of animals or food. Other ancient Christian writers, such as Origen, pointed out that the reception of the Lord's body and blood was a purely spiritual affair. At the same time, early Christians were also worried about the growing gnostic groups that valued spiritual things and denounced all material substances. Against the Gnostics who denied the value of the Lord's Supper, Irenaeus, for example, used strong "realistic" language. Subsequent controversies within the early church prompted other emphases of the Lord's Supper to arise. Conflicts with the Manichees, Donatists, and Pelagians shaped the teachings of Augustine, who addressed some aspects of the Eucharist in his conflict with the Donatists. For Augustine, the sacraments did not rely on the

purity of the priest but were defined as belonging to and given by Christ. In the "Nestorian" controversy in the fifth century, Cyril, patriarch of Alexandria, wished to demonstrate the unity of the divine and human natures of Christ against Nestorius, patriarch of Constantinople. In his commentary on the Gospel of John, Cyril insisted that the body of Christ was so inseparably linked to the second person of the Trinity that, through contact with Christ's body in the Eucharist, believers shared in divine immortality. For Cyril, the sharing of immortality could only happen if there was an insoluble union between the human and divine natures in Jesus Christ. Responding to controversies in their time, the church fathers often discussed the Eucharist to address particular issues concerning Christology (e.g., the humanity and divinity of Christ) and ecclesiology (e.g., the efficacy of the sacraments).

65    Marburg Colloquy, *LW* 38:34 (Hedio).
66    Marburg Colloquy, *LW* 38:34 (Hedio).
67    Marburg Colloquy, *LW* 38:35(Hedio).
68    Marburg Colloquy, *LW* 38:35(Hedio).
69    Marburg Colloquy, *LW* 38:76 (Brenz).
70    Marburg Colloquy, *LW* 38:68 (Osiander).
71    Marburg Colloquy, *LW* 38:68 (Osiander).
72    Marburg Colloquy, *LW* 38:69 (Osiander).
73    Johannes Brenz, *Grundt der heiligen geschrifft, darvon ungeverd in dem gespech zu Martburg in des Sakraments sach gehandelt worden* [1529], in *Frühschriften*, vol. 2, ed. Martin Brecht, Gerhard Schäfer, and Frieda Wolf (Tübingen: Mohr, 1974), 424–27.
74    Marburg Colloquy, *LW* 38:78 (Brenz).
75    Marburg Colloquy, *LW* 38:80 (Rhapsodies).
76    Marburg Colloquy, *LW* 38:83 (Rhapsodies).

*Chapter 2*

1    See Amy Nelson Burnett, "Basel and the Wittenberg Concord," in *Archive for Reformation History* 96 (2005): 33–56.
2    Rorem argues that Calvin took a Chalcedonian *via media*, affirming the sacrament as a means of Communion with Christ's body and blood over against the Zwinglian separation of sacramental sign and reality, and denying a corporeal presence of Christ over against the Lutherans' closer identification of the sign and the thing itself, Christ's body. See Paul E. Rorem, "The Consensus Tigurinus (1549): Did Calvin Compromise?" in *Calvinus Sacrae Scripturae Professor: Calvin as Confessor of Holy Scripture*, ed. Wilhelm H. Neuser (Grand Rapids: Eerdmans, 1994), 74–75.
3    Lane, *John Calvin*, 48.
4    See R. J. Mooi, *Het Kerk-en Dogmahistorisch Element in de Werken van Johannes Calvijn* (Wageningen: Veenman, 1965), 365–97.
5    In the chapter *De sacramentis*, Calvin feels the need to defend himself against Roman Catholic views. It is in this context that he appeals to the testimony of the fathers. See Johannes van Oort, "John Calvin and the Church Fathers," in *The Reception of the Church Fathers in the West*, ed. Irena Backus (Leiden: Brill Academic, 2001), 667.

6    John Calvin, *Christianae Religionis Institutio* [1536], CR 29:103 (= CO 1:103).
7    *"Sacramenta mosaicae legis Christum praenunciasse, nostra vero annunciare"* (Calvin, *1536 Institution*, CR 29:106 [= CO 1:106]).
8    Calvin, *1536 Institution*, CR 29:121 (= CO 1:121).
9    Calvin, *1536 Institution*, CR 29:122 (= CO 1:122).
10   Calvin, *1536 Institution*, CR 29:131 (= CO 1:131). Calvin echoes Luther's criticism of the Roman Catholic practice of withholding the cup from the laity in *The Babylonian Captivity of the Church*, since Luther gives a general reference to the fathers who served Communion in both kinds, followed by a specific example from Cyprian.
11   Calvin, *Institutio 1536*, in *Opera Selecta* 1:151–52. (*Opera Selecta* hereafter abbreviated OS)
12   Calvin, *Institutes of the Christian Religion 1539*, ed. Richard F. Wevers (Grand Rapids: The Meeter Center for Calvin Studies, 1988), 293 (= CR 29:999, CO 1.18.14). (hereafter cited as *1539 Institutes*)
13   Calvin, *1539 Institutes*, 297 (= CR 29:1009, CO 1.18.28).
14   Calvin, *1539 Institutes*, 299 (= CR 29:1014, CO 1.18.35).
15   Calvin, *1539–1554 Institutes*, CO 1:1033.
16   Calvin, *1539–1554 Institutes*, CO 1:1034.
17   See tables in Mooi, *Het Kerk-en Dogmahistorisch Element*.
18   A major share of additional references to the fathers also stems from his debate with Albert Pighius. See Lane, *John Calvin*, 179–89.
19   See Hugh Oliphant Old, *The Patristic Roots of Reformed Worship* (Zürich: Theologischer Verlag, 1975), 155.
20   John Calvin, *Institutio Religionis Christianae, 1539–1554* [hereafter cited as *1543 Institutes*], CO 1:999–1000 (= *Institutes* 4.17.6, CO 2:1006); Augustine, *On Christian Doctrine* III.16.24, in *NPNF*, First Series, vol. 2, ed. Philip Schaff (Grand Rapids: Eerdmans, 1956), 566.
21   Calvin, *1543 Institutes*, CO 1:999–1000 (= *Institutes* 4.17.6).
22   Calvin, *1543 Institutes*, CO 1:1000 (= *Institutes* 4.17.6, CO 2:1006).
23   Calvin, *1543 Institutes*, CO 1:1000 (= *Institutes* 4.17.6, CO 2:1006).
24   Calvin, *1543 Institutes*, CO 1:1020 (= *Institutes* 4.17.46, CO 2:1048).
25   Calvin, *1543 Institutes*, CO 1:1019 (= *Institutes* 4.17.45, CO 2:1047).
26   Calvin, *1543 Institutes*, CO 1:1019 (= *Institutes* 4.17.45, CO 2:1047).
27   Calvin, *1543 Institutes*, CO 1:1021–22 (= *Institutes* 4.17.48).
28   Calvin, *1543 Institutes*, CO 1:1022 (= *Institutes* 4.17.49).
29   Calvin, *1543 Institutes*, CO 1:1022 (= *Institutes* 4.17.49).
30   Calvin, *1543 Institutes*, CO 1:1033–34 (= *Institutes* 4.18.10); Augustine, *Contra Faustum* 20.18 (= PL 42.382, NPNF 4:260–64).
31   Calvin says, "There is memorable passage in *On the Trinity*, book 4, chapter 24, where after [Augustine] has discussed the unique sacrifice he concludes thus: '. . . that same one true Mediator, reconciling us to God through the sacrifice of peace, remains one with him to whom he has offered; [and] has made those for whom he offered one in himself'" (Calvin, *1559 Institutes*, CO 2:1058–59).
32   Calvin, *1543 Institutes*, CO 1:1034 (= *Institutes* 4.18.10); Chrysostom, *Homilies on Hebrews*, hom. 17.3, PG 63.131; Augustine, *Against the Letter of Parmenianus* II.8 (= PL 43.59).

33 See Fraenkel, *Testimonia Patrum*; Quere, *Melanchthon's Christum Cognoscere*; Meijering, *Melanchthon and Patristic Thought*; Wengert, "Philip Melanchthon's Patristic Exegesis."

34 Philip Melanchthon, letter to Oecolampadius on the Lord's Supper (1529), CR 1:iv . See *Melanchthon: Selected Writings*, trans. Charles Leander Hill (Minneapolis: Augsburg, 1962), 126-27.

35 Melanchthon, *De Ecclesia et Autoritate Verbi Dei* [1539], CR 23:585-642.

36 T. H. L. Parker, *Calvin's New Testament Commentaries* (Louisville, Ky.: Westminster John Knox, 1993), 87. Bucer, on the one hand, wrote massive commentaries in an attempt to satisfy all medieval and humanist models of interpretation. His commentaries include a paraphrase of the passage, a running commentary addressing the theological import of the passage, an analysis of special issues often of linguistic character, and a topical explanation of various questions arising from the text. Melanchthon, on the other hand, strove for rhetorical clarity in his biblical exposition and offered the overall argument and disposition of an entire book. He did not discuss the entire text, but rather the theological topics contained within it in order to emphasize the text's broad rhetorical forms. See Richard A. Muller, "Biblical Interpretation in the Era of the Reformation: View from the Middle Ages," in Muller and Thompson, *Biblical Interpretation in the Era of the Reformation*, 3-22.

37 John Calvin, "Dedication to Simon Grynaeus of Basel," in *Calvin's New Testament Commentaries*, vol. 8: *Romans and Thessalonians*, trans. Oliver and Boyd Ltd., (Grand Rapids: Eerdmans, 1995), 3.

38 Parker, *Calvin's New Testament Commentaries*, 88-89.

39 Calvin, "John Calvin to the Reader," in *1559 Institutes*, CO 2:1-4.

40 Calvin, "Dedication to Simon Grynaeus," 4.

41 The precise date of the *Preface* is unknown. I believe that W. Ian P. Hazlett's dating of 1538-1540 is the best estimation offered, although some (such as Mooi) use an earlier date of 1535 and others (such as Walchenbach) offer a later date of 1559.

42 Calvin, *Preface to the Homilies of Chrysostom*, CO 9:834-35. Interpretation based on the translation in W. Ian P. Hazlett, "Calvin's Latin Preface to His Proposed French Edition of Chrysostom's Homilies: Translation and Commentary," in *Humanism and Reform: The Church in Europe, England and Scotland, 1400-1643* (Oxford: Blackwell, 1991), 145-46.

43 Hazlett, "Calvin's Latin Preface," 130.

44 Lane believes that disapproving remarks should be understood an indication of respect since Calvin feels the need to justify departure from the stance of a respected precursor and sees the fathers as important voices to be reckoned with (*John Calvin*, 4).

45 Pontien Polman, *L'élément historique dans la controverse réligeuse du XVIe siècle* (Gembloux: Duculot, 1932), 73-75.

46 Calvin does not see a dogmatic necessity to take the fathers as a starting point, as Polman argues. Calvin does not want to return to the state of the ancient church, but to the Scriptures alone, which are the single standard of all reform. He does not look to revive the past, but has to bring the Gospel up to date, to readjust the current Church's view on Scripture alone. See Danielle Fischer,

"L'histoire de l'Eglise dans la pensée de Calvin," *Archiv für Reformationsgeschichte* 77 (1986):79–125.

47   Calvin, "Letter to Grynaeus," *CR* 38:405.
48   Calvin, "Letter to Grynaeus," *CR* 38:403.
49   Hans-Joachim Kraus, "Calvin's Exegetical Principle," *Interpretation* 31 (1977): 10–11.
50   Lane, *John Calvin*, 54.
51   David C. Steinmetz, *Calvin in Context* (New York: Oxford University Press, 1995), 136.
52   Steinmetz, *Calvin in Context*, 136.
53   Emphasis added. See Calvin, *Commentary on the First Twenty Chapters of the Book of the Prophet Ezekiel*, trans. and ed. Thomas Myers, vols. 1–2 (Grand Rapids: Eerdmans, 1948), ad loc. Ezek. 20:18-19 in *John Calvin's Commentaries*, The Comprehensive John Calvin Collection, ([CD-ROM] Rio, Wis.: AGES Digital Library, 2002).
54   John Walchenbach, "John Calvin as Biblical Commentator: An Investigation into Calvin's Use of John Chrysostom as an Exegetical Tutor," (Ph.D. diss., University of Pittsburgh, 1974).
55   After writing his commentary on Romans, Calvin began his exegetical work on 1 Corinthians. He revised his commentaries on the Pauline epistles in 1551 and again in 1556.
56   John Calvin, *Commentarius in Epistolam Pauli ad Corinthios I* ad loc. 11:19 (= CR 77:480, CO 27:480); *Opera Exegetica et Homiletica*, CO 27:480
57   Calvin, *Comm. ad Cor. I* ad loc. 11:19 (= CR 77:480-81, CO 27:480-81).
58   Calvin, *Comm. ad Cor. I* ad loc. 11:19 (= CR 77.481, CO 27:481).
59   Calvin, *Comm. ad Cor. I* ad loc. 11:19, (= CR 77.481, CO 27:481).
60   Hazlett, "Calvin's Latin Preface," 133.
61   Walchenbach, "John Calvin as Biblical Commentator," 54. Modern day scholars have debated the distinction between the Alexandrian and Antiochene schools of biblical interpretation. Nevertheless, sixteenth-century reformers such as Calvin perceived of allegorical interpretation, the caricature of the Alexandrian school, as straying from the plain sense of Scripture.
62   Walchenbach, "John Calvin as Biblical Commentator," 58.
63   Irena Backus, "Calvin and the Greek Fathers," in *Continuity and Change: The Harvest of Late Medieval and Reformation History* (Leiden: Brill, 2000), 256.
64   Calvin, *Comm. ad Cor. I* ad loc. 11:19 (= CR 77.481, CO 27:481).
65   Calvin, *Comm. ad Cor. I* ad loc. 11:19 (= CR 77.481, CO 27:481).
66   "*Non erat illa mensa tunc ex argento nec aureus calix, ex quo sanguinem proprium Christus suis dedit discipulis; preciosa tamen erant illa omnia et tremenda, quoniam erant spiritu plena.*" See Ganoczy and Müller, *Calvins Handschriftliche Annotationen zu Chrysostomus. Ein Beitrag zur Hermeneutik Calvins*, 152. See Backus, "Calvin and the Greek Fathers," 261.
67   Backus, "Calvin and the Greek Fathers," 262 (emphasis in original).
68   *Comm. ad Cor. I* ad loc. 11:21 (= CO 27:482).
69   *Comm. ad Cor. I* ad loc. 11:21 (= CO 27:482).
70   Walchenbach, "John Calvin as Biblical Commentator," 199.
71   Walchenbach, "John Calvin as Biblical Commentator," 101.

72    Walchenbach, "John Calvin as Biblical Commentator," 101–2.
73    John Chrysostom, *Homily 27: I Corinthians 11:17*, in *Homilies on Hebrews*, ed. J. P. Migne (Paris: Garnier Frères, 1844–1890), PG 61:223–32.
74    *Comm. ad Cor. I* ad loc. 11:21 (= CO 27:483).
75    *Comm. ad Cor. I* ad loc. 11:20 (= CO 27:482).
76    Walchenbach, "John Calvin as Biblical Commentator," 100.
77    *Comm. ad Cor. I* ad loc. 11:23 (= CR 77:484, CO 27:484).
78    *Comm. ad Cor. I* ad loc. 11:23 (=CR 77:484, CO 27:484).
79    *Comm. ad Cor. I* ad loc. 11:24 (= CR 77:488, CO 27:488).
80    *Comm. ad Cor. I* ad loc. 11:24 (= CR 77:486, CO 27:486).
81    *Comm. ad Cor. I* ad loc. 11:24 (= CR 77:487, CO 27:487).
82    *Comm. ad Cor. I* ad loc. 11:24 (= CR 77:492, CO 27:492).
83    Eleanor B. Hanna, "Biblical Interpretation and Sacramental Practice: John Calvin's Interpretation of John 6:51-58," *Worship* 73, no. 3 (1999): 224–25.
84    Hanna, "Biblical Interpretation," 228.
85    John Calvin, *Commentarius in Evangelium Ioannis* ad loc. 6:51 (= CO 25:153).
86    Calvin, *Comm. in Ioann.* ad loc. 6:53 (= CO 25:154); John Calvin, "The Gospel according to St. John 1–10," trans. T. H. L. Parker, in *John Calvin's Commentaries* (Edinburgh: Oliver & Boyd, 1959), 169.
87    Calvin, *Comm. in Ioann.* ad loc. 6:51 (= CO 25:152); Calvin, "The Gospel according to St. John 1–10," 167.
88    Calvin, *Comm. in Ioann.* ad loc. 6:54 (= CO 25:155).
89    Calvin, *Comm. in Ioann.* ad loc. 6:54 (= CO 25:155).
90    Concerning Calvin's use of the Greek Fathers in his *Commentary on the Fourth Gospel*, Backus notices that Calvin's sources, though unnamed, are obviously Augustine and Cyril. When commenting on the phrase *in principio* at the beginning of the Gospel, Calvin attributes to Augustine a statement that actually seems to come from Cyril. Calvin is willing to give Augustine more credit than he has rightfully earned. See Backus, "Calvin and the Greek Fathers," 274.
91    Calvin, *Comm. in Ioann.* ad loc. 6:55 (= CO 25:155).
92    Calvin, *Comm. in Ioann.* ad loc. 6:56 (= CO 25:156). Given Calvin's exegetical principle that exegesis should be clear and based on the most natural or simple meaning of the actual words of the biblical text, it is surprising, according to Eleanor Hanna, that Calvin does not accept "what to many will seem the most natural interpretation" of Jesus' words, that the bread he gives is his flesh, given for the life of the world (Hanna, "Biblical Interpretation," 211–30). Yet some scholars have explained Calvin's reticence on the Lord's Supper in his treatise on John 6 as a consistent effort to provide the "natural" meaning. Brian Gerrish, for example, suggests that the future tense ("shall give") indicates the most natural interpretation—i.e., "that Jesus was speaking only of the crucifixion that awaits him and that to have life is to believe in the saving efficacy of his death" (Brian A. Gerrish, *Grace and Gratitude: The Eucharistic Theology of John Calvin* [Minneapolis: Fortress, 1993], 130). It seems that, in light of the controversy surrounding this passage, Calvin is doing more than just looking for the "natural" meaning, whatever that might be.
93    Calvin, *Comm. in Ioann.* ad loc. 6:54 (= CO 25:155).
94    "*Caro non prodest quicquam.*"

95   Calvin, *Comm. in Ioann.* ad loc. 6:63 (= CO 25:159).
96   Calvin, *Comm. in Ioann.* ad loc. 6:63 (= CO 25:159).
97   Backus, "Calvin and the Greek Fathers," 275.
98   John Calvin, *Commentarius in Harmoniam Evangelicam* ad loc. Matt. 26:26 (= CO 23:704).
99   Calvin, *Comm. in Harm. Evang.* ad loc. Matt. 26:26 (= CO 23:706).
100  Calvin, *Comm. in Harm. Evang.* ad loc. Matt. 26:26 (= CO 23:706). See also Thomas J. Davis, *The Clearest Promises of God: The Development of Calvin's Eucharistic Teaching* (New York: AMS Press, 1995), 204.
101  Calvin, *Comm. in Harm. Evang.* ad loc. Matt. 26:26 (= CO 23:706).
102  Calvin, *Comm. in Harm. Evang.* ad loc. Matt. 26:26 (= CO 23:707).
103  Calvin, *Comm. in Harm. Evang.* ad loc. Matt. 26:26 (= CO 23:707).
104  Chrysostom, *Homily 82: Matthew 26:26-28*, NPNF 10:491.
105  Kraus, "Calvin's Exegetical Principle," 11.
106  Calvin, *Praefatio in Chry. Hom.* (= CO 9:836).
107  Calvin, *Institutes* 4.17.48 (= CO 2:1050).
108  He is referring to the medieval type of ritual, in which sometimes the priest's words could not be heard by the congregants.
109  Calvin, *Institutes* 4.17.39 (= CO 2:1042).                                    .

*Chapter 3*

1   The Gnesio-Lutherans pressed the doctrine of ubiquity not only against Calvin but also against Melanchthon, since both sides solicited his support. See also Gordon E. Pruett, "Protestant Doctrine of the Eucharistic Presence," *Calvin Theological Journal* 10 (1975): 142–74.
2   W. P. Stephens, "Bullinger's Defense of the Old Faith," *Reformation & Renaissance Review* 6, no. 1 (2004): 35–55.
3   See Thompson, *Eucharistic Sacrifice and Patristic Tradition.*
4   For example, despite his immense respect for the fathers, Wolfgang Musculus, reformer in Bern and Augsburg, reasoned that the fathers' opinions had weight because of their erudite scholarship and because of the sanctity of their lives, but that their views did not have any kind of absolute authority.
5   According to Rorem, a historical record of the actual progress of the meeting is not available; therefore hardly anything about the session can be reconstructed. In a letter to Bucer, however, Calvin later wrote that things seemed hopeless at first but that light suddenly broke out. Calvin also revealed that some Zürichers were reluctant to agree, whereas Bullinger much later recalled that Calvin tried to promote some terminology that was suspiciously Bucerian. Rorem sees the formation of the *Consensus Tigurinus* as a compromise between Calvin's view of the Lord's Supper as an instrument of God's grace and Bullinger's view of the Supper as a testimony to or an analogy of God's grace (although Calvin also uses the word "analogy"). See Paul E. Rorem, *Calvin and Bullinger on the Lord's Supper* (Bramcote, Nottingham: Grove Books, 1989), 80, 84.
6   Joseph N. Tylenda, "The Calvin–Westphal Exchange: The Genesis of Calvin's Treatises against Westphal," *Calvin Theological Journal* 9 (1974): 183.
7   "*Neque enim minus absurdum iudicamus, Christum sub pane locare, vel cum pane copulare, quam panem transubstantiare in corpus eius.*" John Calvin, *Defensio Sanae*

et Orthodoxae Doctrinae de Sacramentis eorumque natura, vi, fine, usu & fructu: quam pastores & ministri Tigurinae Ecclesiae & Genevensis antehac brevi Consensionis mutu formula complexi sunt: una cum refutatione probrorum quibus eam indoctri & clamosi homines infamant (Geneva: Oliva Roberti Stephani, 1555), 25.

8   Andrew Pettegree, "The London Exile Community and the Second Sacramentarian Controversy, 1553–1560," *Archiv für Reformationsgeschichte* 78 (1987): 228.

9   Joachim Westphal, *Farrago confusanearum et inter se dissidentium opinionum de Coena Domini, ex Sacramentariorum libris congesta* (Magdeburg: Christian Rödlinger, 1552). This *Farrago* is not to be confused with Timann's *Farrago*.

10  Westphal also quotes portions of his *Short Treatise on the Lord's Supper* (1541), his *Catechism* (1542), his *Commentary on 1 Corinthians 11* (1546), and the *Consensus Tigurinus*.

11  Westphal, *Farrago*, 2.

12  Davis, *Clearest Promises of God*, 30.

13  Pettegree, "London Exile Community," 226.

14  Pettegree, "London Exile Community," 230.

15  Calvin, letter to Bullinger, May 3, 1554, CR 43:124.

16  Pettegree, "London Exile Community," 245.

17  Pettegree, "London Exile Community," 248.

18  Calvin, *Defensio Sanae et Orthodoxae Doctrinae*, CR 37:1.

19  Calvin, *Defensio Sanae et Orthodoxae Doctrinae*, CR 37:21.

20  In his *Defensio Sanae et Orthodoxae Doctrinae*, Calvin provides a deeper discussion of Augustine's writings, primarily those from *Homilies on the Gospel of John*, but also from *Against the Donatists* and *The City of God*.

21  Joachim Westphal, *Adversus cuiusdam sacramentarii falsam criminationem iusta defensio* (Frankfurt: Petrus Brubacchius, 1555).

22  Although Luther had been willing to relinquish Augustine to the Reformed side and eventually referred to the fathers more sparingly in the Eucharistic controversies, Westphal is energetic about reclaiming the fathers for the Lutheran cause. He needs to reclaim Augustine in particular since the Reformed thinkers assumed Augustine's support for their position.

23  Westphal, *Collectanea sententiarum D. Aurelii Augustini ep. Hipponensis de Coena Domini. Addita est confutatio vindicans a corruptelis plerosque locos quos pro se ex Augustino falso citant adversarii* (Regensburg: Ioannis Carbonus, 1555). Westphal wrote this treatise in September 1554 and it was published in early 1555.

24  See Tylenda, "Calvin–Westphal Exchange," 197.

25  Westphal, *Fides diui Cyrilli episcopi Alexandrini de praesentia corporis & sanguinis Christi in sacrae coenae communione* (Frankfurt: Petrus Brubacchius, 1555), 30–31.

26  Westphal, *Fides diui Cyrilli*, 12.

27  Tylenda, "Calvin–Westphal Exchange," 198.

28  Westphal, *Adversus cuiusdam sacramentarii falsam criminationem*, 5.

29  Westphal, *Adversus cuiusdam sacramentarii falsam criminationem*, 10.

30  Westphal, *Adversus cuiusdam sacramentarii falsam criminationem*, 126.

31  Westphal, *Adversus cuiusdam sacramentarii falsam criminationem*, 137.

32  While the Zürich ministers, including Bullinger, had reviewed and edited

Calvin's first response, they were not given such an opportunity the second time. Although Bullinger was in agreement over the *Consensus Tigerinus*, he apparently felt the need to voice additional comments; soon after the publication of Calvin's *Secunda*, he wrote a treatise against Westphal entitled *An Apologetic Exposition by which the Ministers of the Church of Zürich Demonstrate that They do not Follow a Heretical Doctrine on the Lord's Supper*. Bullinger apparently felt the need to voice additional comments. Other Lutherans also joined the fray. Matthäus Judex (1528–1564) detailed the sacramentarians' arguments with his refutation according to the mind of Luther in his *Defense tou retou* (τόυ ῥητόυ) *of the Words of the Supper: Take, Eat, This is My Body, Published in German by Luther against the Fanatical Spirits of the Sacramentarians, Now Translated for the Benefit of Those Who Do Not Know German* (1556). Erhard Schnepff (1495–1558), a professor at Jena, sought to help his church with his *Confession on the Eucharist* (1556). The superintendent of Hamburg, Paul von Eitzen, supported the cause with his *Defense of the True Doctrine on the Supper of our Lord Jesus Christ* (1557). Tylenda deems these three publications as the most important Lutheran writings to join Westphal in the battle over the Eucharist against the Swiss ("Calvin-Westphal Exchange," 203).

33  Calvin, *Secunda Defensio*, CR 37:60 (emphasis in original).
34  Calvin, *Secunda Defensio Piae et Orthodoxae de Sacramentis Fidei contra Ioachimi Westphali Calumnias* (Geneva: Ioannis Crispini, 1556), CR 37:49.
35  Calvin, *Secunda Defensio*, CR 37:89.
36  In this case, Calvin's reference does not come from any further readings of the ancient writer, Marcion.
37  Calvin, *Secunda Defensio*, CR 37:112.
38  Calvin, *Secunda Defensio*, CR 37:120.
39  Westphal, *Confessio fidei de Eucharistiae Sacramento in qua ministri ecclesiarum Saxoniae solidis Argumentis sacrarum Literarum astruunt corporis et sanguinis Domini nostri Iesu Christi, praesentiam in Coena sancta et de libro Ioannis Calvini ipsis dedicato respondent* (Magdeburg: Ambrosium Kirchner, 1557).
40  Tylenda, "Calvin-Westphal Exchange," 204.
41  Tylenda, "Calvin-Westphal Exchange," 204–5.
42  Westphal, *Confessio fidei*. 10.
43  Westphal and Calvin produced additional documents that were not directly part of the debates but nevertheless dealt with the subject of the Eucharist and included references to the fathers. For example, in 1557 Westphal wrote for the Colloquy of Worms a *Confession on the Lord's Supper* that contained eighteen articles with many patristic quotes. The participants at Worms, however, decided not to treat the sacraments and his contribution was set aside. Nevertheless, Westphal had it published in February 1558.

*Chapter 4*

1  Some German rulers supported the introduction of Reformed doctrine during the Second Reformation, partly because they saw it as a means to enhancing their own princely authority against powerful Lutheran estates at home, and partly because they viewed it as an effective antidote against the Catholic

Counter Reformation abroad. In an age in which religion and politics were
closely interlinked, the spread of the Calvinist-sponsored Second Reformation
was bound to have political repercussions. Where the Reformed gained a foot-
hold in Germany, they not only altered the way people worshipped but also
encouraged a more active pro-Protestant, often anti-Habsburg, foreign policy.
See Nischan, *Lutherans and Calvinists*, xii.

2    John Calvin, *Ultima Admonitio Ioannis Calvini ad Ioachimum Westphalum cui nisi
     obtemperet eo loco posthac habendus erit quo pertinaces haereticos haberi iubet Paulus*
     (Geneva: Ioannis Crispini, 1557), CR 37:137–251. Located on the Elbe River,
     Magdeburg accepted Reformation teaching in 1524 and became one of the
     first cities to publish Luther's writings and other Protestant works such as the
     *Magdeburg Centuries*.

3    Davis, *Clearest Promises of God*, 180.

4    Davis, *Clearest Promises of God*, 170–71.

5    Calvin writes in his *Ultima Admonitio*: "While we are enjoined implicitly to obey
     the words of Christ, we are also permitted to seek the interpretation of them
     . . . The fathers themselves often call the bread the body of the Lord, and the
     wine his blood . . . We are perfectly pleased with this mode of expression; if it
     is clear that they considered the bread as symbolically the body, their authority
     will undoubtedly go to our support" (CR 37:207).

6    Calvin, *Ultima Admonitio*, CR 37:207.

7    Calvin, *Ultima Admonitio*, CR 37:142.

8    Calvin, *Ultima Admonitio*. CR 37:146. See also Calvin's *Selected Works of John
     Calvin: Tracts and Letters*, ed. and trans. Henry Beveridge (Grand Rapids: Baker
     Book House, 1983), 2:352.

9    Calvin, *Ultima Admonitio*, CR 37:149.

10   Calvin, *Ultima Admonitio*, CR 37:151–52.

11   Calvin, *Ultima Admonitio*, CR 37:152.

12   Calvin, *Ultima Admonitio*, CR 37:154.

13   Calvin, *Ultima Admonitio*, CR 37:154 (emphasis added).

14   Calvin, *Ultima Admonitio*, CR 37:159–60.

15   Calvin, *Ultima Admonitio*, CR 37:163.

16   Calvin, *Ultima Admonitio*, CR 37:163.

17   Calvin, *Ultima Admonitio*, CR 37:154–55 (emphasis in original).

18   Calvin, *Ultima Admonitio*, CR 37:156 (= CT 2:365).

19   Calvin, *Ultima Admonitio*, CR 37:156 (= CT 2:365).

20   Calvin, *Ultima Admonitio*, CR 37:157 (= CT 2:366).

21   Calvin, *Ultima Admonitio*, CR 37:157 (= CT 2:366–37).

22   Calvin, *Ultima Admonitio*, CR 37:157–58 (= CT 2:367).

23   Calvin, *Ultima Admonitio*, CR 37:158 (= CT 2:367).

24   Calvin, *Ultima Admonitio*, CR 37:159 (= CT 2:369–70).

25   Calvin, *Ultima Admonitio*, CR 37:164–65 (= CT 2:377).

26   Calvin, *Ultima Admonitio*, CR 37:166 (= CT 2:378) (emphasis in original).

27   Calvin, *Ultima Admonitio*, CT 2:379.

28   Calvin, *Ultima Admonitio*, CR 37:168 (= CT 2:381).

29   Calvin, *Ultima Admonitio*, CR 37:168 (= CT 2:382).

30   Calvin, *Ultima Admonitio*, CR 37:171 (= CT 2:386).

31   Calvin, *Ultima Admonitio, CR* 37:173 (= *CT* 2:389).
32   Calvin, *Ultima Admonitio, CR* 37:192–93 (= *CT* 2:415).
33   Calvin, *Ultima Admonitio, CR* 37:181 (= *CT* 2:399).
34   Calvin, *Ultima Admonitio, CR* 37:189 (= *CT* 2:410–11) (emphasis in original).
35   Calvin, *Ultima Admonitio, CR* 37:207 (= *CT* 2:435).
36   Calvin, *Ultima Admonitio, CR* 37:207 (= *CT* 2:435).
37   Calvin, *Ultima Admonitio, CR* 37:208 (= *CT* 2:435–36).
38   Calvin, *Ultima Admonitio, CR* 37:208 (= *CT* 2:436).
39   Calvin, *Ultima Admonitio, CR* 37:209 (= *CT* 2:437).
40   Calvin, *Ultima Admonitio, CR* 37:209 (= *CT* 2:437).
41   Calvin, *Ultima Admonitio, CR* 37:215 (= *CT* 2:446.)
42   Calvin, *Ultima Admonitio, CR* 37:242 (= *CT* 2:482).
43   Joachim Westphal, *Confutatio aliquot enormium mendaciorum Ioannis Calvini* (Ursellis: Henricus, 1558).
44   Joachim Westphal, *Apologia confessionis de Coena Domini contra corruptelas et calumnias Ioannis Calvini scripta* (Ursellis: Henricus, 1558).
45   Tylenda, "Calvin–Westphal Exchange," 208.
46   Westphal, *Apologia*, 9 (emphasis added).
47   Westphal, *Apologia*, 21.
48   Westphal, *Apologia*, 88.
49   Westphal, *Apologia*, 90.
50   Westphal, *Apologia*, 88.
51   Westphal, *Apologia*, 96.
52   Westphal, *Apologia*, 100.
53   Berengar of Tours (c. 1010–1088) maintained the fact of the real presence but denied that any material change in the elements was needed to explain it. His teaching on the Eucharist forced church leaders to clarify the doctrine of transubstantiation, and he was later branded, somewhat unfairly, as offering a symbolic interpretation. See Gary Macy, *The Theologies of the Eucharist in the Early Scholastic Period: A Study of the Salvific Function of the Sacrament according to the Theologians c. 1080–1220* (Oxford: Clarendon, 1984); and H. Chadwick, "Ego Berengarius," *JTS* 40 (1989): 414–45.
54   Westphal, *Apologia*, 108 (emphasis added).
55   Westphal, *Apologia*, 111.
56   Westphal, *Apologia*, 112.
57   Westphal, *Apologia*, 119.
58   Westphal, *Apologia*, 182.
59   Westphal, *Apologia*, 202–3.
60   Westphal, *Apologia*, 203.
61   Westphal, *Apologia*, 204.
62   Westphal, *Apologia*, 205.
63   Westphal, *Apologia*, 216 (emphasis in original).
64   Westphal, *Apologia*, 220.
65   Westphal, *Apologia*, 224.
66   Westphal, *Apologia*, 232–33.
67   Westphal, *Apologia*, 269 (emphasis added).
68   In chapter 32, Westphal addresses the interpretation of 1 Corinthians 10 with

citations from Ambrose, Chrysostom, Augustine, and Cyril. He writes, "The Apostle [Paul] called manna, spiritual food [and] water from the rock, spiritual drink which were not natural, but because those who believed ate spiritually, Ambrose explains that the elements are prepared, created for a while by God's power and holding in themselves a figure of a future mystery which we now consume in commemoration of Christ" (*Apologia*, 292). Listing Cyril, Ambrose, and Chrysostom, Westphal says that they teach that the manna and the rock are figures but that Christ's body and blood are attained in the Eucharist. He proceeds to cite specific passages from Cyril, Ambrose, and Chrysostom in order to uphold his argument that the Israelites' figurative food differs from the true food of Christ's holy body and blood.

69    Westphal, *Apologia*, 256 (emphasis added).
70    Westphal, *Apologia*, 178.
71    Westphal, *Apologia*, 318.
72    Westphal, *Apologia*, 321.
73    Westphal, *Apologia*, 322.
74    Westphal, *Apologia*, 322.
75    See Lane, *John Calvin*, 3. Lane's second thesis is that Calvin's use of the fathers, especially in the *Institutes* and in the treatises, is primarily a polemical appeal to authorities.
76    Calvin, *Institutes* 4.17.6 (= CO 2:1006).
77    Calvin, *Institutes* 4.17. 21 (= CO 2:1020). Calvin is building on his citation of Augustine in the *1543 Institutes*. See Augustine, *Epistola ad Bonif.* (= *Letters* 98.9, PL 33:364, FC 18:137).
78    Calvin, *Institutes* 4.17. 21 (= CO 2:1020).
79    Calvin, *Institutes* 4.17.21 (= CO 2:1020).
80    Calvin, *Institutes* 4.17.21 (= CO 2:1020-21); Augustine, *Contra Adimantum Manichaeum* 12.3 (= PL 42.144); *Psalms* ad loc. Ps. 3:1 (= PL 36:73; NPNF, First Series 4:5).
81    Calvin, *Institutes* 4.17.23 (= CO 2:1021-22); Epiphanius, *Panarion sive arcula adversus octoginta haereses* lxx.2.4 (= GCS 37:234, PG 42:341); Theodoret, *Ecclesiastical History* IV.10 (= GCS 19.228; NPNF, Second Series 3:114).
82    Calvin, *Institutes* 4.17.24 (= CO 2:1024); Augustine, *Epistola ad Dardanum* (On the Presence of God) *Letters* 187.3.10 (= PL 33:835-36, FC 30:228-29).
83    Calvin, *Institutes* 4.17.25 (= CO 2:1024).
84    Calvin, *Institutes* 4.17.14 (= CO 2:1012).
85    Calvin, *Institutes* 4.17.26 (= CO 2:1025).
86    Calvin, *Institutes* 4.17.26 (= CO 2:1025).
87    Calvin, *Institutes* 4.17.26 (= CO 2:1026).
88    Calvin, *Institutes* 4.17.28 (= CO 2:1027).
89    Calvin, *Institutes* 4.17.34 (= CO 2:1037); Augustine, *Contra Faustum* 13, 16 (= PL 42:291).
90    Calvin, *Institutes* 4.17.34 (= CO 2:1037-38).
91    Calvin, *Institutes* 4.17.34 (= CO 2:1038).
92    Calvin, *Institutes* 4.17.29 (= CO 2:1029).
93    Calvin, *Institutes* 4.17.32 (= CO 2:1033).

94    Theodore Beza, *De Coena Domini plana et perspicua tractatio in qua Ioachimi West-phali calumniae refelluntur*, in *Tractationes theologicae*, 2nd ed. (Geneva: Eustace Vignon, 1576), 1:211–58.

## Chapter 5

1    Various scholars have addressed the subject of confessionalization, from broad overviews about late sixteenth-century efforts toward confessional consolida-tion to local histories of specific towns where different confessions coexisted peacefully.

2    Nischan, *Lutherans and Calvinists*, 142.

3    Nischan, *Lutherans and Calvinists*, 144.

4    John Calvin, *Dilucida explicatio sanae doctrinae de vera participatione carnis et san-guinis Christi in sacra coena, ad discutiendas Heshusii nebulas* (Geneva: Conrad Badius, 1561), CR 37:457–518.

5    John Calvin, *Optima ineundae concordiae ratio, si extra contentionem quaeratur Veri-tas* (Geneva: Conrad Badius, 1561), CR 37:517–24.

6    Tilemann Hesshusen (Heshusius), *Verae et Sanae Confessionis de Praesentia Corpo-ris Christi, in Coena Domini, Pia Defensio aduersus Cauillos & Calumnias, I. Iohannis Caluini. II. Petri Boquini. III.Theodori Bezae. IIII. Wilhelmi Cleinwitzii* (Magdeburg: Ex Officina Typographica Wolfgang Kirchener, 1562). (Hereafter cited as *Pia Defensio*.) The name spelled "Cleinwitzii," or "Kleinwitz," is the derogatory nickname for the actual name "Klebitz."

7    The question of Luther's authority was debated among the Lutherans them-selves in the Crypto-Philippist and Crypto-Calvinist controversies. See Robert Kolb, *Martin Luther as Prophet, Teacher, Hero: Images of the Reformer, 1520–1620* (Grand Rapids: Baker Books, 1999).

8    Nischan, *Lutherans and Calvinists*, 145.

9    Tilemann Hesshusen, *De Praesentia Corporis Christi in Coena Domini, contra Sac-ramentarios* (Jena: Donatus Ritzenhain, 1560), B4, 21 .

10    Hesshusen, *De Praesentia*, C1, 32.

11    Hesshusen, *De Praesentia*, C5, 39.

12    Hesshusen, *De Praesentia*, D3, 52.

13    Steinmetz, *Calvin in Context*, 182–83.

14    Hesshusen, *De Praesentia*, E1, 63.

15    "*Si enim vere Verbum caro factum est, & nos vere verbum carnem cibo dominico sumi-mus, quomodo non naturaliter in nobis manere existimandus est*" (Hesshusen, *De Praesentia*, E1, 63).

16    Hesshusen, *De Praesentia*, E3, 68.

17    Hesshusen, *De Praesentia*, E3, 68.

18    Hesshusen, *De Praesentia*, E5–E6, 72–73.

19    Hesshusen, *De Praesentia*, E5, 72.

20    Hesshusen, *De Praesentia*, E6, 74.

21    Hesshusen, *De Praesentia*, H6, 121–22.

22    Hesshusen, *De Praesentia*, G8,110.

23    Hesshusen, *De Praesentia*, I1, 128.

24    He is most likely following Melanchthon's method of creating a hierarchy of the fathers based on their views of the Lord's Supper.

25    Hesshusen, *De Praesentia*, I5, 135.
26    Hesshusen, *De Praesentia*, K5, 151.
27    Hesshusen, *De Praesentia*, K2, 145.
28    Hesshusen, *De Praesentia*, K2, 145.
29    Hesshusen, *De Praesentia*, K2, 145.
30    Hesshusen, *De Praesentia*, K2, 146 (emphasis added).
31    Hesshusen, *De Praesentia*, K6, 154.
32    Hesshusen, *De Praesentia*, K5, 152–53.
33    "*Attente observet veritatis inquisitor Chrysostomum adserere, corpus Christi ita nobis propositum esse ut comedamus, & intra nos totum recipiamus . . . Quod Zwingliani, quantumvis expresse hoc adseveret, Paulus & omnes orthodoxi patres, pertinacissime negant*" (Hesshusen, *De Praesentia*, 163).
34    Hesshusen, *De Praesentia*, K7, 156.
35    Hesshusen, *De Praesentia*, L4, 166.
36    Hesshusen, *De Praesentia*, L6, 169.
37    Hesshusen, *De Praesentia*, L7, 171–72.
38    Hesshusen, *De Praesentia*, L7, 172.
39    Hesshusen, *De Praesentia*, M4, 181.
40    "*Origenes discipulus Clementis, aliquanto ineptior praeceptore, de quo Epiphanius gravis auctor non sine causa dicit, non resurget nobiscum in vitam . . . imo insulsissimis allegoriis Christi verba corrumpit*" (Hesshusen, *De Praesentia*, P8, 237).
41    Hesshusen, *De Praesentia*, P8, 237–38.
42    Calvin, *Dilucida Explicatio*, CR 37:463; John Calvin, *Theological Treatises*, trans. J. K. S. Reid, Library of Christian Classics (Philadelphia: Westminster, 1964), 22:260. (*Theological Treatises* hereafter abbreviated LCC.)
43    Calvin, *Dilucida Explicatio*, CR 37:469.
44    Calvin, *Dilucida Explicatio*, CR 37:469.
45    Calvin, *Dilucida Explicatio*, CR 37:490.
46    Steinmetz, *Calvin in Context*,181.
47    Calvin, *Dilucida Explicatio*, CR 37:470–71.
48    Calvin, *Dilucida Explicatio*, CR 37:472.
49    Calvin, *Dilucida Explicatio*, CR 37:473.
50    Calvin, *Dilucida Explicatio*, CR 37:477.
51    Calvin, *Dilucida Explicatio*, CR 37:483.
52    Calvin, *Dilucida Explicatio*, CR 37:480.
53    Calvin, *Dilucida Explicatio*, CR 37:480.
54    Calvin, *Dilucida Explicatio*, CR 37:481.
55    Calvin, *Dilucida Explicatio*, CR 37:481.
56    Calvin, *Dilucida Explicatio*, CR 37:490.
57    Calvin, *Dilucida Explicatio*, CR 37:491.
58    Calvin, *Dilucida Explicatio*, CR 37:491.
59    Calvin, *Dilucida Explicatio*, CR 37:492.
60    Calvin, *Dilucida Explicatio*, CR 37:492.
61    Calvin, *Dilucida Explicatio*, CR 37:500.
62    Van Oort, "John Calvin and the Church Fathers," 689.
63    Calvin, *Dilucida Explicatio*, CR 37:500.
64    Calvin, *Dilucida Explicatio*, CR 37:501.

65  Calvin, *Dilucida Explicatio*, CR 37:501.
66  Calvin, *Dilucida Explicatio*, CR 37:500.
67  Calvin, *Dilucida Explicatio*, CR 37:501.
68  Calvin, *Dilucida Explicatio*, CR 37:493.
69  Calvin, *Dilucida Explicatio*, CR 37:494.
70  Calvin, *Dilucida Explicatio*, CR 37:494.
71  Calvin, *Dilucida Explicatio*, CR 37:495 (= LCC 22:297).
72  See Irena Backus, "Martin Bucer and the Patristic Tradition," in *Martin Bucer and Sixteenth-Century Europe*, ed. Christian Krieger and Marc Lienhard (Leiden: Brill, 1993), 1:55–69; and Thompson, *Eucharistic Sacrifice and Patristic Tradition*, 73.
73  Calvin, *Dilucida Explicatio*, CR 37:495–96.
74  Calvin, *Dilucida Explicatio*, CR 37:496. Tertullian says, "[T]he petition for daily bread may be understood spiritually, because Christ is our bread . . . our life . . . the Word of the living God who came down from heaven."
75  Calvin, *Dilucida Explicatio*, CR 37:496–97.
76  Calvin, *Dilucida Explicatio*, CR 37:498–99.
77  Calvin, *Dilucida Explicatio*, CR 37:499 (= LCC 22:302–3).
78  Calvin, *Dilucida Explicatio*, CR 37:499 (= LCC 22:302–3).
79  Calvin, *Dilucida Explicatio*, CR 37:501–2.
80  Calvin, *Dilucida Explicatio*, CR 37:519.
81  Calvin, *Dilucida Explicatio*, CR 37:497.
82  Hesshusen, *Pia Defensio*, A3, 3.
83  Hesshusen, *Pia Defensio*, A4, 5.
84  Hesshusen, *Pia Defensio*, B1, 6.
85  Hesshusen, *Pia Defensio*, B2, 8–9.
86  Hesshusen, *Pia Defensio*, B2, 9.
87  Hesshusen, *Pia Defensio*, B2, 9.
88  Hesshusen, *Pia Defensio*, V1-b1, 151–90.
89  Hesshusen, *Pia Defensio*, V2, 153.
90  Hesshusen, *Pia Defensio*, V3, 154.
91  Hesshusen, *Pia Defensio*, V4, 156.
92  Hesshusen, *Pia Defensio*, V4, 156.
93  Hesshusen, *Pia Defensio*, Y4, 173.
94  Hesshusen, *Pia Defensio*, Y4, 173.
95  Hesshusen, *Pia Defensio*, Z3, 178–79.
96  Hesshusen, *Pia Defensio*, Z1, 174.
97  Hesshusen, *Pia Defensio*, Z3, 178.
98  Van Oort, "John Calvin and the Church Fathers," 680.

*Chapter 6*

1  For more details, see p. 123.
2  Paul-F. Geisendorf, *Théodore de Bèze* (Geneva: Labor et Fides, 1949). The enhanced collection of Beza's letters and other works by the former Director of the Geneva Library made Geisendorf's work possible. A later publication of the same work, edited by Alexandre Jullien and dated 1967, has been cited.

3    Geisendorf, *Théodore de Bèze*.

4    Jill Raitt has written a monograph on the eucharistic theology of Theodore Beza, as well as a chapter serving as an introduction to Beza in an anthology. See Jill Raitt, *The Eucharistic Theology of Theodore Beza: Development of the Reformed Doctrine*, AAR Studies in Religion 4 (Chambersburg, Penn.: American Academy of Religion, 1972); and idem, "Theodore Beza," in *Shapers of Religious Traditions in Germany, Switzerland, and Poland, 1560–1600*, ed. Jill Raitt (New Haven: Yale University Press, 1981), 89–104. Scott Manetsch's work explores Beza's role in the development of the French Reformed Church. See Scott M. Manetsch, *Theodore Beza and the Quest for Peace in France, 1572–1598* (Leiden: Brill, 2000). Jeffrey Mallinson describes the Reformation in the context of determining religious authority as an "appeal to history." See Jeffrey Mallinson, *Faith, Reason and Revelation in Theodore Beza, 1519–1605* (Oxford: Oxford University Press, 2003).

5    Raitt, "Theodore Beza," 104.

6    Raitt, "Theodore Beza," 91.

7    Geisendorf, *Théodore de Bèze*, 156.

8    Raitt, "Theodore Beza," 92–93.

9    Robert Kolb, "Jakob Andreae, 1528–1590," in Raitt, *Shapers of Religious Traditions*, 55.

10   Kolb, "Jakob Andreae," 57.

11   Kolb, "Jakob Andreae," 57.

12   Kolb, "Jakob Andreae," 60.

13   Robert M. Kingdon, "Barriers to Protestant Ecumenism in the Career of Theodore Beza," in *Probing the Reformed Tradition*, ed. Elsie Anne McKee and Brian G. Armstrong (Louisville, Ky.: Westminster John Knox, 1989), 240.

14   Kingdon, "Barriers," 241–42.

15   Kolb, "Jakob Andreae," 60.

16   See Robert Kolb, "Luther, Augsburg and the Concept of Authority in the Late Reformation," in *Controversy and Conciliation: The Reformation and the Palatinate, 1559–1583*, ed. Derk Visser (Allison Park, Penn.: Pickwick, 1986), 37–38. Kolb explains that Andreae and other Lutherans saw the Augsburg Confession (unaltered version) as carrying just as much authority as the early church creeds.

17   Jill Raitt, "The Emperor and the Exiles: The Class of Religion and Politics in the Late Sixteenth Century," *Church History* 52 (1983): 146.

18   In 1541, when Emperor Charles V called for a colloquy between Protestants and Catholics at Regensburg, he sought to unite the empire behind him as he faced the armies of Turks advancing on Vienna. In order to facilitate agreement among the Protestants themselves, Melanchthon altered article X of the Augsburg Confession, the article dealing with the Lord's Supper. Instead of saying that the body of Christ is given and eaten, as does the 1530 version, the 1541 *Variata* says that the body of Christ is offered to communicants. This wording allows for both a literal interpretation for Lutherans and a Reformed interpretation—namely that, while Christ is offered to all, his body is eaten only by the mouth of faith, not by the physical mouth. The political implications of Melanchthon's changes proved enormous, since from 1555 through the rest of

the century, the Lutherans insisted that only the 1530 unaltered form of the Augsburg Confession (the *Invariata*) served as the basis of the Peace of Augsburg and that the Reformed were therefore illegal in the empire. Those persons who were neither Catholic nor able to accept any form of the Augsburg Confession were subject to exile, imprisonment, or even death.

19    Lyle D. Bierma, "Lutheran-Reformed Polemics in the Late Reformation: Olevianus's Conciliatory Proposal," in Visser, *Controversy and Conciliation*, 58.

20    Bierma, "Lutheran-Reformed Polemics," 59. In 1577 Reformed thinkers met in a conference in Frankfurt to promote discussions with Lutherans that might result in a Protestant unity and to convince Lutheran princes that the prospects of a divided Protestantism, and thus a divided Germany, were far more serious in the face of a resurging Catholicism. In the late 1570s the German Reformed thinkers were still on an intensified quest for German Protestant unity, not for the sake of doctrinal agreement but for the sake of tolerance (see Bierma, "Lutheran-Reformed Polemics," 54).

21    Jill Raitt, *The Colloquy of Montbéliard: Religion and Politics in the Sixteenth Century* (New York: Oxford University Press, 1993), 5.

22    Robert Kingdon, foreword to Raitt, *Colloquy of Montbéliard*.

23    While Beza was called in jest but with some seriousness "the pope of the French Reformed churches," Andreae was the self-styled "pope of the Lutheran churches." See Raitt, *Colloquy of Montbéliard*, 5; and Raitt, "Emperor and the Exiles," 153-54.

24    Raitt, *Colloquy of Montbéliard*, 73.

25    Kingdon, "Barriers," 249.

26    Jill Raitt, "The French Reformed Theological Response," in *Discord, Dialogue and Concord: Studies in the Lutheran Reformation's Formula of Concord*, ed. Lewis Spitz and Wenzel Lohff (Philadelphia: Fortress, 1977), 181-82.

27    Raitt, *Eucharistic Theology of Beza*, 28.

28    Dingel, "Streben."

29    "Es steht ausser Zweifel, dass das reformatorische Insistieren auf dem 'sola scriptura' keineswegs ausschloss, dass man zugleich deutlich bestrebt war, gerade in einer solch kontroversen Frage wie dem Verständnis des Abendmahls den eigenen Anknüpfungspunkt in der Kirche der Väter nachzuweisen" (Dingel, "Streben," 182).

30    Dingel, "Streben," 182. According to Dingel, the situation becomes different with the beginning of confessionalization. For the Philippist-Calvinist school of thought, the fathers (in order to be able to support a particular opinion and to claim the continuity of the right understanding of the Eucharist) turned to a meaningful, even decisive argument against the christological teaching of the presence of the humanity of Christ in the bread and wine, as those who saw themselves as followers of Martin Luther had formulated.

31    Although Raitt has explored the development and ramifications of the Colloquy of Montbéliard, this study focuses on the use of the fathers by Beza and Andreae during the process of confessional consolidation. For the sake of clarity, Appendix I summarizes the Württemberg theses and Appendix II outlines Beza's theses.

32   Raitt, *Colloquy of Montbéliard*, 81.
33   Jacob Andreae, *Acta Colloquij. Montis Belligartensis: Quod habitum est, Anno Christi 1586* (Tübingen: Per Georgium Gruppenbachium, 1587), 76.
34   Andreae, *Acta Colloquij*, 85. For example, Cyril supports the divinization of the body when he writes that Christ vivifies others by using his body, touching people, and speaking to them. Thus Christ acts with divine power through his body, since vivification is a divine property. See also Raitt, *The Colloquy of Montbéliard*, 84.
35   Raitt, *Colloquy of Montbéliard*, 85.
36   Andreae, *Acta Colloquij*, 79.
37   Andreae, *Acta Colloquij*, 86.
38   Andreae, *Acta Colloquij*, 86.
39   Andreae, *Acta Colloquij*, 164.
40   Andreae, *Acta Colloquij*, 167.
41   "*Sic in praesenti negocio Coenae Domini, non disputamus de una tantum parte, sed de toto Sacramento, quod Irenaeus testator duabus rebus constare, videlicet terrena & coelesti. Non dicit Irenaeus, Sacramentum constare Una Re, videlicet pane & vino . . . hoc est, habitudine & relatione ad absens corpus Christi coniunctis. Nam panis & vinum non est Sacramentum, corpus, & sanguis Christi quoque non est Sacramentum: sed haec duo simul in Mysterio per verba Testamenti coniuncta, sunt Sacramentum, quod appellatur Eucharistia. Et haec est unanimis sententia omnium Orthodoxorum Patrum, qui simul omnes Sacramentum non una du[m]taxat parte, sed duabus simul definiunt*" (Andreae, *Acta Colloquij*, 168).
42   Andreae, *Acta Colloquij*, 67.
43   Andreae, *Acta Colloquij*, 74.
44   Andreae, *Acta Colloquij*, 168.
45   "*Cum igitur consensus omnium Orthodoxorum Patrum constet, naturam divinam nec exaltari nec exinaniri posse (quod proprium humanae naturae est)*" (Andreae, *Acta Colloquij*, 95).
46   See Dingel, "Streben," 182. This distinctive usage of *consensus orthodoxus* refers to the fathers as proof of the correctness and the accordance with Scripture of a particular teaching as described in an anonymously published pamphlet of 1574 that appeared in Heidelberg. The Nürnberg council and Melanchthon's former student Christoph Herdesianus (1523–1585) mentioned the *Consensus Orthodoxus* as an eloquent example. It was reprinted in revised and extended form three more times in Zürich, so that one can assume it was widely read at least among scholars, although not necessarily accepted as correct. The author of the *Consensus Orthodoxus* claimed the "consensus of the orthodox" as a key phrase for challenging the Lutheran formation. The first chapter provides an exegetical foundation: an "interpretation of the words of the Lord's Supper from John, Luke, and Paul." Its methodological basis is not completely new, but it is prepared in the manner of the first generation of reformers.
47   Andreae, *Acta Colloquij*, 95.
48   Andreae, *Acta Colloquij*, 169.
49   Andreae, *Acta Colloquij*, 172.
50   Andreae, *Acta Colloquij*, 175.
51   Andreae, *Acta Colloquij*, 175.

52  Raitt, "French Response," 183.
53  "*Non video ego, quomodo caro Christi possit esse omnipraesens. Si de fructu consentia-mus, quid opus est de aliis minime necessariis disputare? Patres multos habent errores, quos tamen non propterea abjicimus. Sacramentalem modum manducationis corporis Christi concedimus*" (Andreae, *Acta Colloquij*, 99).
54  Andreae, *Acta Colloquij*, 106.
55  Andreae, *Acta Colloquij*, 112.
56  See Appendix II.
57  Raitt, *Eucharistic Theology of Beza*, 45.
58  Raitt, *Eucharistic Theology of Beza*, 47.
59  While the discussion at Marburg seems to have been isolated to the Eucharist, by the later sixteenth century (as became blatantly apparent at the Colloquy of Montbéliard), a discussion of the person of Christ became a closely related sequel to the debate on the Lord's Supper. Consequently, an array of church fathers is ushered in on the topic of Christ's humanity and divinity.
60  Raitt, *Colloquy of Montbéliard*, 79.
61  Irena Backus, *Historical Method and Confessional Identity in the Era of the Reformation, 1378–1615* (Leiden: Brill, 2003), 173–78.
62  Andreae, *Acta Colloquij*, 76.
63  Raitt, *Colloquy of Montbéliard*, 89.
64  Raitt, *Colloquy of Montbéliard*, 89.
65  Theodore Beza, *Ad Acta Colloquii Montisbelgardensis Tubingae Edita, Theodori Bezae Responsio* (Geneva: Joannes le Preux, 1587), 43. (Hereafter cited as *Responsio*.)
66  Beza, *Responsio*, 42.
67  Beza, *Responsio*, 49.
68  Beza, *Responsio*, 49.
69  Beza, *Responsio*, 68.
70  Beza, *Responsio*, 51.
71  Beza, *Responsio*, 58.
72  Beza, *Responsio*, 58.
73  Raitt, *Colloquy of Montbéliard*, 80.
74  Beza, *Responsio*, 57.
75  Beza, *Responsio*, 59.
76  "*Si nobis non credit D. Andreas, credit Suevico Syntagmati, id est ipsi D. Brentio nondum Ubiquitario, cuius haec verba sunt*" (Beza, *Responsio*, 59).
77  Beza, *Responsio*, 60.
78  Beza, *Responsio*, 64.
79  Beza, *Responsio*, 105.
80  Beza, *Responsio*, 112.
81  Beza, *Responsio*, 168.
82  Beza, *Responsio*, 70.
83  Beza, *Responsio*, 72.
84  See Backus, *Historical Method and Confessional Identity*, 173–79.
85  Beza, *Responsio*, 72.
86  Raitt, *Colloquy of Montbéliard*, 125.
87  Beza, *Responsio*, 94.

88   Beza, *Responsio*, 94.
89   Beza is basically arguing that, just as there must be no separation against Nesto-
     rius, there must also be a distinction against the error of Eutyches and the
     followers of Brenz. Beza summarizes that the common effect of this diversity of
     the two natures—especially in the work of human redemption—is done so that
     the humanity is not a mediator of salvation without the divinity, nor does the
     divinity redeem without the humanity (Beza, *Responsio*, 128).
90   Beza, *Responsio*, 95.
91   Beza, *Responsio*, 177.
92   Beza, *Responsio*, 181.
93   Kolb, "Jakob Andreae," 58.

## Conclusion

1   Davies, *Problem of Authority in the Continental Reformers*, 80-81.

## Appendix I

This appendix is a summary from Raitt, *Colloquy of Montbéliard*, 75-76.

1   Note reformed theology's creative extension of believer's ascension vs. Lutheran
    theology's creative extension of ubiquity.

# Bibliography

## Primary Sources

Andreae, Jacob. *Acta Colloquij Montis Belligartensis: Quod habitum est, Anno Christi 1586.* Tübingen: Per Georgium Gruppenbachium, 1587.

Augustine, Aurelius. *Against the Letter of Parmenianus.* Edited by J. P. Migne. PL 43. Paris: Garnier Frères, 1844–1890.

———. *Contra Adimantum Manichaei discipulum liber unus.* Edited by J. P. Migne. PL 42. Paris: Garnier Frères, 1844–1890.

———. *Contra Faustum Manichaeum.* Edited by J. P. Migne. PL 42. Paris: Garnier Frères, 1844–1890.

———. *De Civitate Dei.* CCSL 47–48. Turnholt: Brepols, 1955.

———. *De Doctrina Christiana.* CCSL 32. Edited by Josef Martin. Turnholt: Brepols, 1962.

———. *Epistola ad Dardanum (Epistola 187).* Translated by Sister Thomas Aquinas Goggin. PL 33 (= FC 30). New York: Fathers of the Church, 1957–1959.

———. *Letter to Boniface.* Translated by Sister Thomas Aquinas Goggin. FC 18. New York: Fathers of the Church, 1957–1959.

———. *Psalms 3.* CCSL 38. Turnholt: Brepols, 1956.

Beza, Theodore. *Ad Acta Colloquii Montisbelgardensis Tubingae Edita, Theodori Bezae Responsio.* Geneva: Joannes le Preux, 1587. (This project uses the second Latin edition of 1588.)

———. *De Coena Domini plana et perspicua tractatio in qua Ioachimi Westphali calumniae refelluntur.* Tractationes theologicae 1. Geneva: Eustace Vignon, 1576.

Brenz, Johannes. *Grundt der heiligen geschrifft, darvon ungeverd in dem gesprech zu*

179

Martburg in des Sakraments sach gehandelt worden (1529). In Frühschriften, vol. 2, edited by Martin Brecht, Gerhard Schäfer, and Frieda Wolf, 424-27. Tübingen: J.C.B. Mohr, 1974.

———. Syngramma Suevicum. In Frühschriften, vol. 1, edited by Martin Brecht, Gerhard Schäfer and Frieda Wolf. Tübingen: J.C.B. Mohr, 1970.

Calvin, John. Calvin's New Testament Commentaries, vol. 8: Romans and Thessalonians. Translated by Oliver and Boyd Ltd. Grand Rapids: Eerdmans, 1995.

———. Christianae Religionis Institutio, 1536. CO 1. Brunswick: Schwetscheke & Sons, 1863.

———. Commentarius in Epistolam Pauli ad Corinthios I. Edited by Wilhelm Baum, Edward Cunitz, and Edward Reuss. CO 49. Brunswick: Schwetschke & Sons, 1863.

———. Commentarius in Evangelium Ioannis. CO 25.

———. Commentarius in Harmoniam Evangelicam. CO 23.

———. Commentary on Ezekiel. 2 vols. In Commentaries on the First Twenty Chapters of the Book of the Prophet Ezekiel. Translated and edited by Thomas Myers. Grand Rapids: Eerdmans, 1948. In John Calvin's Commentaries, The Comprehensive John Calvin Collection, [CD-ROM] Rio, Wis.: AGES Digital Library, 2002.

———. "Dedication to Simon Grynaeus of Basel." In Commentary on the Epistles to the Romans. Grand Rapids: Eerdmans, 1995.

———. Defensio Sanae et Orthodoxae Doctrinae de Sacramentis eorumque natura, vi, fine, usu & fructu: quam pastores & ministri Tigurinae Ecclesiae & Genevensis antehac brevi Consensionis mutu formula complexi sunt: una cum refutatione probrorum quibus eam indocti & clamosi homines infamant. Geneva: Oliva Roberti Stephani, 1555.

———. Dilucida explicatio sanae doctrinae de vera participatione carnis et sanguinis Christi in sacra coena ad discutiendas Heshusii nebulas. CR 37 (= CO 9). Geneva: Conrad Badius, 1561.

———. Institutes of the Christian Religion, 1539. Edited by Richard F. Wevers. Grand Rapids: The Meeter Center for Calvin Studies, 1988. (Previously published as CR 29: Halle: Schwetschke & Sons, 1847).

———. Institutio 1536. OS 1:151-52.

———. Institutio Religionis Christianae, 1539-1554. CO 1-2.

———. John Calvin's Commentaries. The Comprehensive John Calvin Collection. CD-ROM. AGES Digital Library, 2002.

———. Letter to Bullinger. May 3, 1554. CR 43.

———. Optima ineundae concordiae ratio, si extra contentionem quaeratur Veritas. CR 37. Geneva: Conrad Badius, 1561.

———. Preface to the Homilies of Chrysostom. CO 9.

———. Secunda Defensio Piae et Orthodoxae de Sacramentis Fidei contra Ioachimi Westphali Calumnias. Geneva: Ioannis Crispini, 1556.

———. *Selected Works of John Calvin: Tracts and Letters*, vol. 2. Edited and translated by Henry Beveridge. Grand Rapids: Baker Book House, 1983.

———. *Theological Treatises*. Translated by J. K. S. Reid. Library of Christian Classics 22. Philadelphia: Westminster, 1964.

———. *Ultima Admonitio Ioannis Calvini ad Ioachimum Westphalum cui nisi obtemperet eo loco posthac habendus erit quo pertinaces haereticos haberi iubet Paulus.* Geneva: Ioannis Crispini, 1557.

Chrysostom, John. *Consensus Tigurinus.* CO 13.

———. *Homilies on Hebrews*. Edited by J. P. Migne. PG 63. Paris: Garnier Frères, 1844-1890.

———. *Homily 82* [Matthew 26:26-28]. *NPNF* 10.

———. *Homily 27* [1 Corinthians 11:17]. PG 61.

Eck, Johannes. *Enchiridion locorum communium adversus Lutherum et alios hostes ecclesiae* [1525-1543]. Edited by Pierre Fraenkel. Münster: Aschendorff, 1979.

Epiphanius. *Panarion, sive arcula adversus octoginta haereses lxx.2.4.* GCS 3:234 (= PG 42:341). Edited by Karl Holl. Berlin: Akademie-Verlag, 1985.

Hesshusen, Tilemann. *De praesentia corporis Christi in Coena Domini, contra Sacramentarios.* Jena: Donatus Ritzenhain, 1560.

———. *Verae et Sanae Confessionis de Praesentia Corporis Christi, in Coena Domini, Pia Defensio aduersus Cauillos & Calumnias, I. Iohannis Caluini. II. Petri Boquini. III.Theodori Bezae. IIII. Vvilhelmi Cleinvvitzii.* Magdeburg: Ex Officina Typographica Wolfgang Kirchener, 1562.

———. Luther, Martin. *Against the Heavenly Prophets in the Matter of Images and Sacraments.* In *Karlstadt's Battle with Luther: Documents in a Liberal-Radical Debate.* Edited by Ronald J. Sider. Philadelphia: Fortress, 1978.

———. *D. Martin Luthers Briefwechsel*, vol. 3. Edited by G. Bebermeyer. Weimar: Hermann Böhlaus, 1933.

———. *D. Martin Luthers Werke. Kritische Gesamtausgabe.* 62 vols. Edited by Joachim K. F. Knaake, Gustav Kawerau, and E. Thiele. Weimar: Böhlaus, 1883-.

———. *Das Marburger Gespräch und die Marburger Artikel 1529.* WA 30.III:92-171.

———. *Luther's Works.* American edition. 55 vols. General Editor H. T. Lehmann, vols. 31-49, edited by H .J. Grimm. Philadelphia: Fortress, 1955-.

Melanchthon, Philip. *De Ecclesia et Autoritate Verbi Dei [1539].* CR 23:585-642.

———. *Defensio Phil. Melanchthonis contra Joh. Eckium.* In *Melanchthons Werke,* edited by Robert Stupperich, 12-22. Gütersloh: Bertelsmann, 1951.

———. *Epistola de Lipsica disputatione.* In *Melanchthons Werke,* edited by Robert Stupperich, 3-11. Gütersloh: Bertelsmann, 1951.

———. *Loci Communes, 1521.* Translated by Horst Georg Pöhlmann. Gütersloh: Gütersloher Verlagshaus, 1997.

———. *Loci Communes, 1555.* Edited by Clyde Manschreck. New York: Oxford University Press, 1965.

———. *Melanchthon: Selected Writings.* Translated by Charles Leander Hill. Minneapolis: Augsburg, 1962.

———. *Melanchthons Briefwechsel: Kritische und kommentierte Gesamtausgabe,* vol. 1. Edited by Heinz Scheible. Stuttgart: Frommann-Holzboog, 1977.

———. *Philippi Melanchthonis opera quae supersunt omnia.* Edited by C. G. Bretschneider. CR 1.

———. *Sententiae Veterum aliquot scriptorum de coena Domini.* CR 23.

———. *Werke in Auswahl.* Edited by Robert Stupperich. Gütersloh: Bertelsmann, 1955.

*A Select Library of Nicene and Post-Nicene Fathers of the Christian Church.* First Series, vol. 4. Grand Rapids: Eerdmans, 1956.

*A Select Library of Nicene and Post-Nicene Fathers of the Christian Church.* Second Series, vols. 2 and 9. Grand Rapids: Eerdmans, 1956.

Tertullian. *Adversus Marcionem.* Edited by Josef Martin. CCSL 1. Turnholt: Brepols, 1954.

Theodoret. *Ecclesiastical History.* Edited by T. Gaisford. GCS 19. Berlin: Akademie-Verlag, 1971.

Westphal, Joachim. *Adversus cuiusdam sacramentarii falsam criminationem iusta defensio.* Frankfurt: Petrus Brubacchius, 1555.

———. *Apologia confessionis de Coena Domini contra corruptelas et calumnias Ioannis Calvini scripta.* Ursellis: Nicolaus Henricus, 1558.

———. *Collectanea sententiarum D. Aurelii Augustini ep. Hipponensis de Coena Domini. Addita est confutatio vindicans a corruptelis plerosque locos quos pro se ex Augustino falso citant adversarii.* Ratisbon: Ioannis Carbonus, 1555.

———. *Confessio fidei de Eucharistiae Sacramento in qua ministry ecclesiarum Saxoniae solidis Argumentis sacrarum Literarum astruunt corporis et sanguinis Domini nostri Iesu Christi, praesentiam in Coena sancta et de libro Ioannis Calvini ipsis dedicato respondent.* Magdeburg: Ambrosium Kirchner, 1557.

———. *Confutatio aliquot enormium mendaciorum Ioannis Calvini, secuturae Apologiae adversus eius furors.* Ursellis: Nicolaus Henricus, 1558.

———. *Epistola Ioachimi Westphali, qua breviter respondet ad convicia Iohannis Calvini.* Ursellis: Nicolaus Henricus, 1557.

———. *Farrago confusanearum et inter se dissidentium opinionum de Coena Domini, ex Sacramentariorum libris congesta.* Magdeburg: Christian Rödlinger, 1552.

———. *Fides diui Cyrilli episcopi Alexandrini de praesentia corporis & sanguinis Christi in sacrae coenae communione.* Frankfurt: Petrus Brubacchius, 1555.

———. *Recta Fides de Coena Domini ex verbis apostoli Pauli et evangelistarum demonstrata ac communita.* Magdeburg: Lotther, 1553.

Zwingli, Ulrich. *Commentary on True and False Religion.* Edited by Samuel Macauley Jackson and Clarence Nevin Heller. Durham, N.C.: Labyrinth, 1981.

———. *De Vera et Falsa Religione.* Zürich: Froschauer, 1525.

——. *Huldreich Zwinglis sämmtliche Werke*. Briefwechsel, vol. 1 (1510–1522). Edited by Emil Egli, Georg Finsler, and Walther Köhler. Leipzig: M. Heinsius, 1911. CR 94.

## Secondary Sources

Backus, Irena. "Calvin and the Greek Fathers." In *Continuity and Change: The Harvest of Late Medieval and Reformation History. Essays Presented to Heiko A. Oberman on his 70th Birthday*, edited by Robert J. Bast and Andrew C. Gow, 253–76. Leiden: Brill, 2000.

——. *Historical Method and Confessional Identity in the Era of the Reformation (1378–1615)*. Leiden: Brill, 2003.

——. "Martin Bucer and the Patristic Tradition." In *Martin Bucer and Sixteenth-Century Europe*, vol. 1, edited by Christian Krieger and Marc Lienhard, 55–69. Leiden: Brill, 1993.

Bagchi, David V. N. *Luther's Earliest Opponents: Catholic Controversialists, 1518–1525*. Minneapolis: Fortress, 1991.

Battles, Ford Lewis. *Introduction to 1536 Institution*. Atlanta: John Knox, 1975.

Benedict, Philip. *Christ's Churches Purely Reformed: A Social History of Calvinism*. New Haven: Yale University Press, 2002.

Bierma, Lyle D. "Lutheran–Reformed Polemics in the Late Reformation: Olevianus's Conciliatory Proposal." In Visser, *Controversy and Conciliation*, 51–71.

Brecht, Martin. *Martin Luther: Shaping and Defining the Reformation*. Minneapolis: Fortress, 1990.

Burnett, Amy Nelson. "Basel and the Wittenberg Concord." *Archive for Reformation History* 96 (2005): 33–56.

Cameron, Euan. *The European Reformation*. Oxford: Clarendon, 1991.

Chadwick, Henry. "Ego Berengarius." *Journal of Theological Studies* n.s. 40 (1989): 414–45.

Davies, Rupert E. *The Problem of Authority in the Continental Reformers*. London: Epworth, 1946.

Davis, Thomas J. *The Clearest Promises of God: The Development of Calvin's Eucharistic Teaching*. New York: AMS Press, 1995.

Dickens, A. G. *The English Reformation*. New York: Schocken Books, 1964.

Dickens, A. G., and John Tonkin. *The Reformation in Historical Thought*. Cambridge, Mass.: Harvard University Press, 1985.

Dingel, Irene. "Das Streben nach einem 'consensus orthodoxus' mit den Vätern in der Abendmahlsdiskussion des späten 16. Jahrhunderts." In Steinmetz, *Die Patristik in der Bibelexegese des 16. Jahrhunderts*. Edited by David C. Steinmetz, 181–204. Wiesbaden: Harrossowitz, 1999.

Edwards, Mark U., Jr. *Luther and the False Brethren*. Stanford, Calif.: Stanford University Press, 1975.

Evans, Gerald R. *Problems of Authority in the Reformation Debates.* Cambridge: Cambridge University Press, 1992.

Farmer, Craig. "The Johannine Signs in the Exegesis of Wolfgang Musculus." Ph.D. diss., Duke University, 1992.

Fischer, Danielle. "L'histoire de l'Eglise dans la pensée de Calvin." *Archiv für Reformationsgeschichte* 77 (1986): 79–125.

Foxe, John. *Book of Martyrs.* Edited by W. Grinton Berry. Grand Rapids: Baker Book House, 2003.

Fraenkel, Pierre. *Testimonia Patrum: The Function of the Patristic Argument in the Theology of Philip Melanchthon.* Geneva: Droz, 1961.

Ganoczy, Alexandre, and Klaus Müller. *Calvins Handschriftliche Annotationen zu Chrysostomus. Ein Beitrag zur Hermeneutik Calvins.* Wiesbaden: Franz Steiner, 1981.

Geisendorf, Paul-F. *Théodore de Bèze.* Edited by Alexandre Jullien. Geneva: Jullien, 1967.

Gerrish, Brian A. *Grace and Gratitude: The Eucharistic Theology of John Calvin.* Minneapolis: Fortress, 1993.

Grane, Leif, Alfred Schindler, and Markus Wriedt, eds. *Auctoritas Patrum: Contributions on the Reception of the Church Fathers in the 15th and 16th Century.* Mainz: von Zabern, 1993.

———. "Some Remarks on the Church Fathers in the First Years of the Reformation (1516–1520)." In Grane, Schindler, and Wriedt, *Auctoritas Patrum,* 21–32.

Hagen, Kenneth. *Foundations of Theology in the Continental Reformation: Questions of Authority.* Milwaukee, Wis.: Marquette University Press, 1974.

Hanna, Eleanor B. "Biblical Interpretation and Sacramental Practice: John Calvin's Interpretation of John 6:51-58." *Worship* 73, no. 3 (1999): 211–30.

Hazlett, W. Ian P. "Calvin's Latin Preface to His Proposed French Edition of Chrysostom's Homilies: Translation and Commentary." In *Humanism and Reform: The Church in Europe, England and Scotland, 1400–1643: Essays in Honour of James K. Cameron,* edited by James Kirk, 129–50. Oxford: Blackwell, 1991.

Heath, Malcolm. "Invention." In *Handbook of Classical Rhetoric in the Hellenistic Period, 330 B.C.–A.D. 400,* edited by Stanley E. Porter, 89–119. Leiden: Brill, 1997.

Heimbigner, Kent A. "The Evolution of Luther's Reception of the Early Church Fathers in Eucharistic Controversy: A Consideration of Selected Words, 1518–1529." *Logia: A Journal of Lutheran Theology* 7 (1998): 3–11.

Hoffmann, Hermann Gottfried. "Sententiae Patrum: Das Patristische Argument in der Abendmahlskontroverse zwischen Oekolampad, Zwingli, Luther und Melanchthon." Ph.D. diss., Ruprecht-Karls-Universität zu Heidelberg, 1971.

Hsia, Ronnie Po-chia. *Social Discipline in the Reformation: Central Europe 1550–1750.* New York: Routledge, 1989.

Kingdon, Robert M. "Barriers to Protestant Ecumenism in the Career of Theodore Beza." In *Probing the Reformed Tradition,* edited by Elsie Anne McKee and Brian G. Armstrong, 237–51. Louisville, Ky.: Westminster John Knox, 1989.

Köhler, Walther. *Das Marburg Gespräch 1529.* Leipzig: Eger & Gievers, 1929.

——. *Zwingli und Luther: Ihr Streit über das Abendmahl nach seinem politischen und religiösen Beziehungen,* vol. 1: *Die religiöse und politische Entwicklung bis zum Marburger Religionsgepräch 1529.* Leipzig: Eger & Sievers, 1924,

Kolb, Robert. "Jakob Andreae, 1528–1590." In *Shapers of Religious Traditions in Germany, Switzerland and Poland 1560–1600,* edited by Jill Raitt, 53–68. New Haven: Yale University Press, 1981.

——. "Luther, Augsburg and the Concept of Authority in the Late Reformation." In Visser, *Controversy and Conciliation,* 33–49.

——. *Martin Luther as Prophet, Teacher, Hero: Images of the Reformer, 1520–1620.* Grand Rapids: Baker Books, 1999.

Koopmans, Jan. *Das Altkirchliche Dogma in der Reformation.* Munich: Christian Kaiser, 1938.

Kraus, Hans-Joachim. "Calvin's Exegetical Principle." *Interpretation* 31 (1977): 8–18.

Lane, Anthony N. S. *John Calvin, Student of the Church Fathers.* Grand Rapids: Baker Books, 1999.

Lindberg, Carter. *The European Reformations.* Oxford: Blackwell, 1996.

Lohse, Bernhard and Gabriele Borger. *Luther und Athanasius. Evangelium in der Geschichte,* vol. 2: *Studien zur Theologie der Kirchenväter und zu ihrer Rezeption in der Reformation: Aus Anlass des 70. Geburtstags des Autors,* edited by Gabriele Borger. Göttingen: Vandenhoeck & Ruprecht, 1998.

Macy, Gary. *The Banquet's Wisdom.* Mahweh, N.J.: Paulist Press, 1992.

——. *The Theologies of the Eucharist in the Early Scholastic Period: A Study of the Salvific Function of the Sacrament according to the Theologians c. 1080–1220.* Oxford: Clarendon, 1984.

Mallinson, Jeffrey. *Faith, Reason and Revelation in Theodore Beza, 1519–1605.* Oxford: Oxford University Press, 2003.

Manetsch, Scott M. *Theodore Beza and the Quest for Peace in France, 1572–1598.* Leiden: Brill, 2000.

Meijering, E. P. *Melanchthon and Patristic Thought: The Doctrines of Christ and Grace, the Trinity and the Creation.* Leiden: Brill, 1983.

Mooi, R. J. *Het Kerk-en Dogmahistorisch Element in de Werken van Johannes Calvijn.* Wageningen: Veenman, 1965.

Muller, Richard A. "Biblical Interpretation in the Era of the Reformation: View from the Middle Ages." In Muller and Thompson, *Biblical Interpretation in the Era of the Reformation,* 3–22.

Muller, Richard A., and John L. Thompson, eds. *Biblical Interpretation in the Era of the Reformation.* Grand Rapids: Eerdmans, 1996.

Nischan, Bodo. *Lutherans and Calvinists in the Age of Confessionalism.* Aldershot, UK: Ashgate, 1999.

Oberman, Heiko. *Luther: Man between God and the Devil.* New Haven: Yale University Press, 1989.

Old, Hugh Oliphant. *The Patristic Roots of Reformed Worship.* Zürich: Theologischer Verlag, 1975.

Parker, T. H. L. *Calvin's New Testament Commentaries.* Louisville, Ky.: Westminster John Knox, 1993.

Pettegree, Andrew. "The London Exile Community and the Second Sacramentarian Controversy, 1553–1560." *Archiv für Reformationsgeschichte* 78 (1987): 223–52.

Polman, Pontien. *L'élément historique dans la controverse religieuse du XVIe siècle.* Gembloux: Duculot, 1932.

Pruett, Gordon E. "Protestant Doctrine of the Eucharistic Presence." *Calvin Theological Journal* 10 (1975): 142–74.

Quere, Ralph Walter. *Melanchthon's Christum Cognoscere: Christ's Efficacious Presence in the Eucharistic Theology of Melanchthon.* Nieuwkoop: de Graaf, 1977.

Raitt, Jill. *The Colloquy of Montbéliard: Religion and Politics in the Sixteenth Century.* New York: Oxford University Press, 1993.

———. "The Emperor and the Exiles: The Class of Religion and Politics in the Late Sixteenth Century." *Church History* 52 (1983): 145–56.

———. *The Eucharistic Theology of Theodore Beza: Development of the Reformed Doctrine.* AAR Studies in Religion 4. Chambersburg, Penn.: American Academy of Religion, 1972.

———. "The French Reformed Theological Response." In *Discord, Dialogue and Concord: Studies in the Lutheran Reformation's Formula of Concord,* edited by Lewis Spitz and Wenzel Lohff, 178–90. Philadelphia: Fortress, 1977.

———. "Theodore Beza." In *Shapers of Religious Traditions in Germany, Switzerland, and Poland, 1560–1600,* edited by Jill Raitt, 89–104. New Haven: Yale University Press, 1981.

Reinhard, Wolfgang, and Heinz Schilling, eds. *Die katholische Konfessionalisierung: Wissenschaftliches Symposion der Gesellschaft zur Herausgabe des Corpus Catholicorum und des Vereins für Reformationsgeschichte.* Gütersloh: Gütersloher Verlagshaus, 1995.

Rorem, Paul E. *Calvin and Bullinger on the Lord's Supper.* Bramcote, Nottingham: Grove Books, 1989.

———. "The Consensus Tigurinus (1549): Did Calvin Compromise?" In *Calvinus*

*Sacrae Scripturae Professor: Calvin as Confessor of Holy Scripture*, edited by Wilhelm H. Neuser, 72–90. Grand Rapids: Eerdmans, 1994.

Rupp, Gordon. *Patterns of Reformation.* Philadelphia: Fortress, 1969.

Sasse, Hermann. *This is My Body: Luther's Contention for the Real Presence in the Sacrament of the Altar.* Minneapolis: Augsburg, 1959.

Schilling, Heinz. "The Reformation and the Rise of the Early Modern State." In *Luther and the Modern State in Germany*, edited by James Tracy, 21–30. Kirksville, Mo.: Sixteenth Century Journal Publishers, 1986.

Schreiner, Susan. "Calvin and the Exegetical Debates about Certainty." In Muller and Thompson, *Biblical Interpretation in the Era of the Reformation*, 189–215.

Selge, Kurt-Victor. "Kirchenväter auf der Leipziger Disputation." In Grane, Schindler, and Wriedt, *Auctoritas Patrum*, 197–212.

Steinmetz, David C. *Calvin in Context.* New York: Oxford University Press, 1995.

———, ed. *Die Patristik in der Bibelexegese des 16. Jahrhunderts.* Wiesbaden: Harrassowitz, 1999.

———. "The Re-Evaluation of the Patristic Exegetical Tradition in the Sixteenth Century." In *The Bible as Book*, edited by Paul Saenger and Kimberly Van Kampen, 135–42. London: The British Library, 1999.

Steinmetz, David C., and Robert Kolb. Introduction to Steinmetz, *Die Patristik in der Bibelexegese des 16. Jahrhunderts*, 7–18.

Stephens, W. P. "Bullinger's Defense of the Old Faith." *Reformation & Renaissance Review* 6, no. 1 (2004): 35–55.

———. *The Theology of Huldrych Zwingli.* New York: Oxford University Press, 1986.

———. "Zwingli on John 6:63." In Muller and Thompson, *Biblical Interpretation in the Era of the Reformation*, 156–85.

Thompson, Nicholas. *Eucharistic Sacrifice and Patristic Tradition in the Theology of Martin Bucer, 1534–1546.* Leiden: Brill, 2005.

Tylenda, Joseph N. "Calvin and Westphal: Two Eucharistic Theologies in Conflict." In *Calvin's Books: Festschrift dedicated to Peter De Klerk on the Occasion of his Seventieth Birthday*, edited by Wilhelm H. Neuser, Hermann J. Selderhuis and Willem van't Spijker, 9–21. Heerenveen: Groen, 1997.

———. "The Calvin–Westphal Exchange: The Genesis of Calvin's Treatises against Westphal." *Calvin Theological Journal* 9 (1974): 182–209.

Van Oort, Johannes. "John Calvin and the Church Fathers." In *The Reception of the Church Fathers in the West*, edited by Irena Backus, 661–700. Leiden: Brill Academic, 2001.

Van't Spijker, Willem. *Calvin: A Brief Guide to his Life and Thought.* Translated by Lyle D. Bierma. Louisville, Ky.: Westminster John Knox, 2009.

Visser, Derk, ed. *Controversy and Conciliation: The Reformation and the Palatinate, 1559–1583.* Allison Park, Penn.: Pickwick, 1986.

Walchenbach, John. "John Calvin as Biblical Commentator: An Investigation into Calvin's Use of John Chrysostom as an Exegetical Tutor." Ph.D. diss., University of Pittsburgh, 1974.

Wengert, Timothy. *Philip Melanchthon's "Annotationes in Johannem" in Relation to its Predecessors and Contemporaries*. Geneva: Droz, 1987.

Wright, William J. "Philip of Hesse's Vision of Protestant Unity and the Marburg Colloquy." In *Pietas et Societas: New Trends in Reformation Social History*, edited by Kyle C. Sessions and Philip N. Bebb, 163–79. Kirksville, Mo.: Sixteenth Century Essays and Studies, 1985.

# Index